Global Turmoil

Capitalist Crisis - A Socialist Alternative

Resolutions and conclusions of
the 7th World Congress of the Committee for a Workers International
held in November 1998

The Committee for a Workers' International has affiliated parties and
organisations in more than 35 countries on all continents. These include
Argentina, Australia, Austria, Belgium, Brazil, Britain, Canada, Cyprus, CIS,
Czech Republic, France, Germany, Greece, Israel/Palestine, India,
Ireland (South), Ireland (North), Japan, Mexico, Netherlands, Nigeria, Norway,
Pakistan, Poland, Portugal, Scotland, South Africa, Spain, Sri Lanka, Sweden,
and the USA. Details of our other CWI publications and how to contact the CWI
sections are available at the back of this publication.

CWI International Office
PO Box 3688; London; E9 5QX; Britain.
Telephone: + 44 181 533 0201
Fax: + 44 181 985 0757
E-mail: inter@dircon.co.uk
Our website is on: http://www.clubi.ie/dojo/cwi/inde

CWI Publications

Global Turmoil

Global Turmoil
- Capitalist Crisis, A Socialist Alternative
© CWI Publications

First Edition May 1999
British Library Cataloguing in publication data:
Committee for a Workers International
Global Turmoil - Capitalist Crisis, a Socialist Alternative
1. Politics
2. Economics
ISBN 0-906582-56-3

Published by CWI Publications
Typesetting and Layout by Eastway Offset Ltd (TU)
Typeset in Usherwood 9 pt
Printed by Biddles Ltd of Guildford and Kings Lynn
Printed on 100% wood-free paper

Distribution by Socialist Books
3/13 Hepscott Road, London, E9 5HB
Telephone 011 533 3311

front cover photo: South Korean workers' strike, 1997
cover design: D Rudd

Global Turmoil

Preface

For millions of people across the globe, capitalism has brought unrelieved poverty, disease, and mass unemployment, particularly in the semi-developed countries of Africa, Asia and Latin America. In the developed capitalist economies, workers and youth face a previously unseen polarisation in wealth. These conditions will worsen as the contagion brought by the economic crisis, signalled by events in South East Asia in 1998, spreads around the world.

The existence of capitalism on a global scale has always necessitated an international alternative for the workers' movement. Historically, the most conscious socialists saw the need for such an alternative not just to build solidarity between workers in struggle in different countries, but also to act as a political and organisational tool to defeat capitalism and imperialism internationally.

A successful socialist revolution originating in one country can only be consolidated if it fully harnesses the productive forces at its disposal and utilises the most advanced productive techniques available internationally. This can only be done by spreading a revolutionary movement internationally. A socialist revolution would pose a mortal threat to capitalism and imperialism internationally, which would attempt to destroy any new workers' state. For this reason it is necessary to build a mass, revolutionary workers' international.

The First Four Internationals

It was for this reason that the First International was set up in 1864 under the leadership of Marx and Engels. Despite representing an enormous step forward, the First International contained groups with differing ideologies and methods of work. The political effects of a world capitalist boom at that time accentuated internal conflicts between socialist, anarchist, and bourgeois nationalist trends within the International, resulting in paralysis and then dissolution in 1876.

In 1889, the Second International was set up. It soon grew into an international force with a membership of millions in its affiliated parties, many of which formally adhered to Marxism. In its early years, the Second International played an important role in developing widespread support for socialist ideas amongst the working class. It developed in a period of general capitalist upswing. This had an effect on the leadership of the parties of the Second International, increasing pressures for collaboration and accommodation with the capitalist class as well as a parliamentary road to socialism. The disastrous effects of this reformist compromise were shown at the beginning of the first world war, when the vast majority of *the leaderships of the parties of the Second International sided with their own national ruling classes in support of the war.*

Russian Revolution

The Russian revolution in 1917, led by the Bolshevik Party, was the first historical example of where capitalism was successfully overthrown. The setting up of the Third International, the Comintern, reflected the importance with which leaders like Lenin and Trotsky viewed the necessity for a revolutionary International to protect and spread the gains of the Russian revolution on a world-wide basis.

The isolation of the Russian revolution in an economically underdeveloped country, and the weaknesses of the young Communist Parties (especially in Europe), which were unable to take and hold onto power, led to the degeneration of the new Soviet state. This was expressed by the seizure of the Communist Party and the Comintern by the Stalinist bureaucracy who usurped political power from the working class in the Soviet Union. The Third International became a top-down transmission belt for policies designed to protect the interests of the Stalinist clique that led it. The political and organisational foundation of the Fourth International was laid within the Comintern with the formation of the International Left Opposition, under the leadership of Trotsky. The Left Opposition initially struggled to change the Comintern from within.

The role played by its leadership in allowing Hitler, and fascism, to come to power in Germany in 1933 resulted in the International Left Opposition declaring that the Comintern was a bankrupt formation and that a new International had to be built. The founding conference of the Fourth International was set up in 1938 to carry on the traditions of fighting for the building of a mass revolutionary International.

After the war

Stalinism and social democracy emerged strengthened as political forces following the Second World War. As a result of this, the revolutionary movements which swept Europe were diverted and resulted in the strengthening of capitalism. This laid the political foundation for the post-war boom of capitalism. This development had not been foreseen by Trotsky, who was assassinated by Stalinist agents in 1940. This new political situation disorientated the leadership of the Fourth International and led to a number of divisions within its ranks.

Committee for a Workers' International

The forces, which came to make up the Committee for a Workers' International, left the United Secretariat of the Fourth International in 1965 as a result of fundamental political and organisational disagreements. The CWI was actually set up in 1974. We base ourselves on the policies of the first four congresses of the Third International, the founding documents of the Fourth International, and their elaboration in the documents of the CWI since its inception.

At its founding 1974 Congress, four sections were represented: Britain, Germany, Ireland and Sweden. The CWI now organises in 35 countries across the globe. Our aim is to build a mass revolutionary International capable of bringing about revolutionary, socialist change to end the barbarism and chaos of capitalism. While this task is in its preparatory stages, many of the CWI's member sections have become a significant factor in leading important struggles of the working class. A general account of the development of the CWI is given in the pamphlet 'A History of the CWI', produced by the Socialist Party - the British section of the CWI.

The CWI's programme and policies are democratically decided at world congresses, made up of delegates from its national sections. This Congress elects an International Executive Committee (IEC) which decides policies between the congresses. The day-to day work of the CWI is run by the International Secretariat (IS), elected at the IEC and based at the CWI's office, which is currently in London, Britain.

Seventh Congress of the CWI

Nearly all the groups and sections of the CWI were represented at this Congress with delegates and observers from the following countries: Australia (Militant Socialist Organisation), Austria (Sozialistiche Offensive Vorwärts), Belgium (Militant Links), Brazil (Socialismo Revolucionário), Britain (Socialist Party), Canada (Socialist Resistance), CIS (CIS section of the CWI), Cyprus (Omada Marxiston), Chile (Democracia Obrera), Czech Republic (Budoucnost), France (Gauche Révolutionnaire), Germany (Sozialistiche Alternative), Greece (Xekinhma), India (Dudiyora Hora'ata), Ireland (Socialist Party), Japan (CWI Japan), Netherlands (Offensief), Nigeria (Democratic Socialist Movement), Portugal (Luta Socialista), Pakistan (United Socialist Party), Scotland (CWI Scotland), South Africa (Socialist Alternative), Sri Lanka (United Socialist Party), Sweden (Rättvisepartiet Socialisterna), US: (Labor Militant).

The CWI also invited guests to the Congress. These included an activist from Indonesia who outlined some of the difficulties facing the movement in the unfinished Indonesian revolution. He also gave a flavour of the burning desire of the masses to overthrow the old order of the corrupt military elite.

Also attending the Congress were two representatives of the Jammu and Kashmir National Peoples' Party (JKNAP), based in Pakistani Occupied Kashmir. In his contribution to the Congress, Mohammad Anwar Khan, President of JKNAP, said: "Our party is enduring to achieve the goal of national liberation for a united, independent, socialist Kashmir. We are determined to rescue the nation from slavery, economic exploitation and cultural domination".

Another enthusiastically welcomed visitor to the Congress was Joe Higgins, a leading member of the Socialist Party in Ireland, and the TD (Member of Parliament) for Dublin West. Joe Higgins is the CWI's first member to be elected to Parliament standing as an independent CWI candidate. His attendance at the Congress demonstrates the importance the CWI gives to the accountability of its public representatives and of them being an integral part of the political and organisational discussions inside the CWI.

This book contains the main resolutions voted upon at the Seventh World Congress of the Committee for a Workers' International. Also included is a separate section of material produced by the International Secretariat (IS) of the CWI on the world economy. This contains a CWI statement on the World Economy written in February 1998 and an article from "Socialism Today" (November 1998), the theoretical journal of the Socialist Party (British section of the CWI), outlining the main processes in the world economy. The Appendix contains amendments which were either remitted for further discussion or defeated during the Congress discussions.

Introduction

The CWI has produced this book as a contribution towards providing the theoretical, strategic, and tactical basis for the building of a revolutionary Socialist International in the run-up to the year 2000 and beyond. It is also designed for those worker activists and socialists who have a general interest in world political, economic and social developments.

The Seventh World Congress of the CWI, held in November 1998, took place in a period of deep crisis for world capitalism, and slump in some areas of the globe. The World Economic Summit in Davos which brought together the world's leading economists, businessmen and capitalist politicians in January 1999, produced no united approach on how to deal with the economic crisis. The attitude of serious capitalist commentators at this time was marked by foreboding and pessimism of what the future would bring.

Triumphalism

This was in complete contrast to their triumphalist approach at the time of the previous CWI World Congress in 1993. Then, their propaganda was an ideological tirade about the superiority of the market, the death of socialism and the obsolescence of working class struggle to achieve change. As far as capitalist commentators were concerned, international conflicts were to be solved by US imperialism's "New World Order". Even at that time the CWI explained that the post-Stalinist euphoria about the supremacy of the market would not last and the fundamental contradictions in the capitalist system would shatter the propaganda of the ruling class internationally.

The Congress took place against a backcloth of world events which confirmed this analysis. It gave the CWI the opportunity to draw up a political balance sheet of the previous decade and to outline perspectives and tasks for the future. It was clear from the discussions that the effect of the development of economic crisis would lead to further political polarisation and radicalisation with the prospect of the emergence of big defensive battles of the working class. It also gave delegates the opportunity to identify the processes leading to the reconquering of socialist ideas amongst the working class internationally - as an alternative to capitalism.

The main discussions at the Congress were on world relations, Europe and the former traditional workers' parties, and revolution and counter-revolution in the semi-developed world. There was also a discussion on Regroupment, which debated the possibilities of fusions with other socialist forces and organisations formally subscribing to Trotskyist ideas. The other main discussion was on the vitally important issue of building the CWI.

The complex world political situation following the collapse of Stalinism in 1989 has posed a number challenges to Marxists internationally on tactics, strategy, and perspectives. This has led to more debates on the challenges and tasks facing the CWI in its work to build a mass revolutionary International. The debates at the Congress helped to clarify the points under discussion. The post-Stalinist period has meant that all forces on the left have encountered difficulties in maintaining their organisations. The forces of the CWI may be somewhat smaller than previously, but the clarity achieved on political perspectives and tasks at the Congress leaves the CWI membership politically strengthened and prepared for the tasks that lie ahead.

One of the main themes in the discussion on world relations was the forthcoming world economic slump, its character and timing. Recent developments in Brazil indicate the possibility of economic slump spreading to the major western economies sooner rather than later, a prospect outlined at the Congress. In mid-January, there was a speculative attack on the Brazilian currency, the Real, following the debt moratorium announced by the governor of the country's third largest state. The Cardoso government devalued the Real by 50%. Brazil's economic crisis threatens to draw the whole of Latin America into deep recession or even slump. The situation had an immediate effect on the Argentine economy. The crisis in Brazil will have a potentially far more damaging effect on the world economy, and in particular the US economy, than the economic collapse in Russia did in August 1998.

One of the main themes of the Congress was the prospect of bitter defensive workers' struggles as a consequence of the crisis. This was demonstrated in Brazil following the sacking of 2800 workers at Ford's factory in Sao Paulo which led to a tenacious struggle by them to maintain their jobs. In an indication of the nature of the crisis that semi-developed countries will face over the next period, sacked workers have turned up to the production line in the factory and demanded to work as part of the tactics to regain their jobs.

Greek school students

Other movements internationally are a harbinger of future struggles of the working class. The four month long struggle of school students in Greece involved the occupation of over 2000 schools and demonstrations of tens of thousands in Athens and other major cities. This struggle resulted from government "reforms" of education which were designed to exclude large numbers of students from entering university education. The government mobilised the media and the police against the movement - at certain stages there were running battles between the police and school students.

The warning strikes by the 3.4 million strong IG Metall union in Germany in February 1999 are a foretaste of the type of struggles that could rock Germany as a consequence of the development of a European-wide economic slump. The concessions forced from the employers as a result of this strike are an answer to the argument that the industrial working class is a spent force in society.

A feature of the discussion at the Congress was the increased instability in the world political situation and the inability of particularly US imperialism, to solve protracted disputes around the world.

It was highlighted following the Congress, by US and British imperialism's decision to implement their threat to bomb Iraq during 'Operation Desert Fox'. The exact timing of the operation was, in all likelihood, determined by Clinton's attempt to avoid impeachment proceedings. However, the main reasons for it were US imperialism's strategic and economic interests in the region - particularly the glut on the world's oil markets and the challenge to US authority that the continued existence of Saddam Hussein's regime represents.

UNSCOM revelations

Despite this concentrated air strike in mid-December, the limitations of US imperialism's power were still shown. Saddam Hussein was not dislodged from power. As the world relations resolution explained, the US could not commit itself to deploying ground forces because of the consequences in the Arab world which would result. The revelations concerning the use of UNSCOM special weapons investigators as spies for US intelligence agencies has further exposed the role of the UN as a puppet for US strategic interests internationally. As far as US imperialism is concerned it is clearly now no longer a question of compliance with UN resolutions on "weapons of mass destruction" but the removal of Saddam Hussein that lies behind their strategy.

Developments in the misnamed "peace process" in Israel and Palestine also illustrate the inability of US imperialism to provide a solution to one of the most intractable conflicts internationally. The Wye Plantation Agreement signed in October 1998, shortly after the world relations resolution was circulated, granted an extra 17% of the West Bank to the full control of the Palestinian Authority. The Wye Agreement represented another humiliating defeat for Yasser Arafat which he attempted to dress up as a victory.

Despite all concessions from the PLO leadership, Netanyahu froze the implementation of the Wye agreement, publicly on spurious grounds but, in reality, in a desperate attempt to save his right-wing coalition government. This failed and Israel faces a general election in May 1999. The falsely named peace process will be in deep freeze until then.

The instability in the Middle East, outlined in the Congress discussions has been further emphasised by the death of King Hussein of Jordan. The media tributes to him as a "peacemaker extraordinaire" indicate the fears that US imperialism has of the vacuum that his death may leave in the region.

Kosova's insoluble conflict

Another insoluble conflict for imperialism - that of Kosova in the Balkans - has flared up again since the Congress. There was an early break in the cease-fire between the Serbian army and the Kosova Liberation Army (UCK in the Albanian language), with the massacre in the Kosova town of Drenica in January 1999. This brought the prospect of full scale war onto the agenda again and forced the western imperialist powers to act, but only after the massacre had taken place.

The western imperialist powers forced the two sides to the negotiating table with threats of NATO bombing raids if there was no agreement. The limitations of the UCK were clearly shown by the fact that they agreed to negotiations in the first place. Their pro-market and narrow nationalist political positions of this kind rule out the possibility of fulfilling the national aspirations of the Kosova Albanians under present conditions. The partial agreement arising out of the negotiations only lays the basis for conflicts at a later stage, since it solves none of the fundamental aspirations of the Kosava Albanians.

One of the features of the 1990s has been the internationalisation of the world economy. There was an in depth discussion about globalisation, as it is more commonly known, at this World Congress. Some capitalist commentators in the past have suggested that globalisation represents a qualitatively new and higher stage of capitalism, and through its adoption the world economy has overcome its fundamental contradictions and limitations.

In its material and at the Congress, the CWI recognised that globalisation did represent a distinct stage in capitalism's development, but within this new phase contradictions had arisen. The CWI has also explained that the process globalisation took place against a backdrop of economic growth in the so-called advanced capitalist economies. In the Congress discussion it was explained that the dominant trend of globalisation of the world economy would be checked and could even go into partial reverse with the onset of a world-wide economic slump.

Globalisation - a new phase?

These issues formed an important part of the discussion on world relations. Some delegates, for example from Austria, questioned whether globalisation actually represented any real change and argued that its main use was as an ideological weapon against the working class internationally (as their amendment in the appendix shows). The Congress concluded that although it is used as a propaganda weapon against the working class, globalisation did represent a distinct phase in world economic developments. Whilst the CWI has produced a number of articles dealing with different aspects of globalisation, it was agreed that the CWI's International Secretariat should produce a full and updated statement on the question following the Congress.

The Swedish comrades also submitted an amendment to the world relations resolution dealing with China. The position of the IS was that the process of capitalist restoration has not been completed in China. However, the Swedish delegates were of the opinion that this process is completed. It was agreed at the Congress that this debate would be carried out in written form in the period after the Congress.

During the discussion on Europe, there was further debate on the perspectives for the Euro and European Monetary Union, an issue which has been raised in previous international meetings of the CWI. The Swedish delegates explained in an amendment to the resolution on Europe that, although a serious world economic slump could lead to the collapse of the Euro and EMU, this was not the only perspective. They explained that the political and then economic effects of the collapse of the EMU would mitigate against the possibility of its breakdown.

The majority of delegates disagreed with this point of view. The IS's point of view was that under the political and economic conditions of a world slump, EMU would not survive in its planned form. The social consequences of huge national debts and mass unemployment - which would result from all the national economies being locked into one currency with no room for manoeuvre through devaluation of their currencies or resort to inflationary measures - would make it extremely difficult for countries to remain in the EMU.

EMU debate

Under such conditions, clearly the major European powers would do their utmost to maintain a fiction of EMU, probably in the form of a "Deutschmark" zone including the Benelux countries and Germany. However, even this would represent a major defeat for the capitalist powers, and would be qualitatively different from the monetary union they first envisaged.

One related issue which was discussed was whether the Euro would be launched as a currency in January 1999. In the view of the IS, it was not excluded that this could be delayed if there was a rapid descent into economic slump in the world economy. As subsequent events have shown, this did not happen, and the Euro was launched. The "euro-phoria" which gripped the world for the first week after the launch has seeped away. The head of the European Central Bank, Wim Duisenberg explained in early February: "The Euro's recent fall is a matter of puzzlement not concern". However, "concern" will rise as the effects of the world economic slump make itself felt on the value of the Euro on the world's currency markets.

In the Congress discussion on Europe and the former traditional workers' parties, delegates commented on the crisis of confidence in the bourgeois establishment. A common feature was the growing hatred towards the establishment and their political representatives as a result of the spate of corruption scandals which have rocked different countries since the CWI's last World Congress in 1993.

An illustration of the effects of the crisis in bourgeois institutions of rule was the attempt to impeach Clinton which took place after the Congress. The narrow political interests of the reactionary right wing of the Republican Party were the driving force behind it. In the end the impeachment attempt failed as public opinion moved decisively against the process. Sections of the US ruling class undoubtedly exerted pressure on the Republicans to ensure there was no drawn out Senate trial. Their fear was that this could lead to a fundamental collapse of confidence in the whole ruling "Establishment".

Developments in the political arena have illustrated the new period of instability for capitalism internationally that was outlined in the resolutions to the Congress. The attempt to deport General Pinochet from Britain to Spain to stand trial for crimes committed under the military dictatorship shattered the relative calm in Chilean society and brought all the fundamental social and class contradictions to the surface.

In a similar way, the arrest since the CWI Congress of Ocalan, leader of the Kurdish PKK, by Turkish security forces has had a direct impact on Greek society. The implication of the Greek PASOK government in these events led to a major political crisis. Immediately three government ministers were sacked and the underlying anger towards the government was unleashed in a tidal wave against the PASOK administration. It is not clear whether the government will survive these developments and early elections may be called.

"Establishment" crisis

The potential for further collapse in the support for capitalist politicians, particularly with the onset of a world-wide economic crisis, has been illustrated by events in Brazil. In Sao Paulo, 50% of people who previously supported Cardoso, the president, now say that they would not vote for him. This is a direct consequence of the inability of the Brazilian ruling class to avert the collapse of its economy.

In Europe, the election of social democratic governments, mainly as a consequence of a reaction against previous right-wing neo-liberal administrations, has not provided a way out for the ruling class. The new SPD-Green government in Germany has not even enjoyed a honeymoon period where the working class has had significant illusions in them. The government is seen as having no clear strategy to chart a way out of the growing difficulties that the economy is encountering. The process of the further 'bourgeoisification' of the former traditional workers' parties, evidenced by the policies of many European social democratic parties in government, was also raised in the Congress discussions. The outlines of the change in the class basis of many of these parties was already under discussion at the World Congress in 1993. Since then their degeneration has accelerated and raised the need for the building of new workers' organisations and parties. This was also an important part of the Congress discussions.

New workers' parties

The perspective of new parties has been illustrated by events in Israel since the Congress. Following the collapse of the Netanyahu government, delegates from all the workplace committees in Israel met in January 1999 to form a party to represent the working class in the forthcoming elections. Headed by Amir Peretz, the leader of the Histadruth, this is the first time such a party has been set up in Israel.

It is potentially the first step towards a workers' party in that country, although its evolution is not guaranteed. The name of the party - 'One People/ One Nation led by Amir Peretz' - is an indication of the confused consciousness of some of the forces involved. Whatever the outcome, it nevertheless indicates the profound changes that have occurred in the consciousness of the Israeli working class and the loosening of the bonds between it and the Zionist capitalist state.

The CWI has repeatedly emphasised the fact that the post-Stalinist era means that Marxists are faced with a new situation where new tasks are posed. In the period after 1989 this sharp change in the international situation caused a crisis in many left organisations. Internationally many organisations which subscribed to Trotskyist ideas were forced to re-examine their previous perspectives and strategies and see where there were common points of agreement. The CWI took part in the process of opening up discussions between different organisations which we believed could lead to fusion on the basis of principled political agreement. The experience of this process showed that there was not the possibility of fusion in the great majority of cases, although the CWI will continue the process of discussion, debate and joint campaigning initiatives with different left organisations. At the Congress there was a debate on this issue between the IS and the French section. These issues are explained in more detail in the resolution contained in this book on 'Building the International, Regroupment, and France'.

Since the last Congress in 1993, the role of the revolutionary party, its programme and tasks in a changed world situation has been constantly reassessed in discussions in the CWI. The twin dangers of ultra-leftism and opportunism have to be avoided. While attempting to rebuild the workers' movement, the maintenance of the distinct political programme and separate organisational independence of the CWI is of vital importance. Part of the debates at the Congress concerned the move by the Scottish section of the CWI to set up a new Scottish Socialist Party. This decision had been discussed within the CWI in the run-up to the Congress. The overwhelming majority of the delegates at the Congress felt that the Scottish comrades were not defending a genuine revolutionary programme or the organisational independence of the CWI within the new party. Documents relating to this debate are available from the CWI offices in London.

Building the CWI

The final Congress discussion on the building of the International demonstrated the sweep and depth of the work of the CWI. In this discussion comrades reported on the work of their different sections, giving other delegates the opportunity to learn from the shared experience. The discussion showed that CWI sections in Britain, Ireland, Nigeria, Sri Lanka and Sweden have become an important factor in leading struggles even on a national basis.

The developments of the new section in the CIS were a source of inspiration to Congress delegates. Working in some of the most difficult political conditions internationally, the CIS comrades had managed to build their section from handfuls of members in St. Petersburg and Moscow to over 74 members in five countries of the CIS. The paper of the section with a print run of over 2000 regularly sells out and is bought in 30 cities.

Since the Congress, the Democratic Socialist Movement (Nigerian section of the CWI) has played a central role in leading a strike of public sector workers in Lagos, Nigeria which won an important wage increase. As a result of the conditions of economic chaos in Nigeria, the government has refused to implement the pay award it agreed. Chilean CWI members have been involved in a leading capacity in the struggle of the Mapuche Indian minority to drive the army and police from their land in southern Chile. In Sri Lanka, the United Socialist Party has participated as part of the New Left Front in provincial elections and in a subsequent campaign against the rigging of the elections by the Popular Alliance government.

Euromarch 1999

In Europe, members of the CWI sections in Belgium, Britain, Ireland, and Sweden will be standing in the forthcoming elections to the European parliament as part of the process of providing a genuine socialist alternative to the working class. CWI sections will also be involved in the build up to the Euromarch in Cologne to be held at the end of May 1999.

It was clear throughout the discussions that, despite the difficulties experienced in the early nineties, the majority of sections were well equipped to take advantage of the new political situation that will open up in the new millennium.

Although a slump could initially stun sections of the working class in some countries, delegates raised the perspective of tenacious and bitter defensive struggles of the working class. The economic slump would smash the illusions that remain in the market and prepare the way for a re-emergence of the ideas of socialism as a much stronger force amongst a radicalised layer of workers and youth. As a result the Congress agreed that the CWI should strive to achieve a fifty per cent increase in the global membership of the individual sections by the end of 1999.

The Congress also decided to produce a number of documents to help prepare the CWI to intervene in the impending struggles that will arise out of the economic crisis that capitalism faces: a written political platform for all the sections to use - a "Manifesto 2000" as well as a platform for the European elections,.

The political and organisational discussions at the Congress undoubtedly helped to crystallise the understanding amongst those attending that the CWI stands at the edge of a totally new period of developments internationally where the pace of events will be much quicker. The debates helped clarify what the tasks would be in this new period and the experience of the Congress left delegates optimistic and confident of what the sections had to do to take advantage of the situation.

Leon Trotsky explained at the founding of the Fourth International: "Our ambition is not only to have more members, more papers, more money in the treasury, more deputies. All that is necessary but only as a means. Our aim is the full material and spiritual liberation of the toilers and the exploited through the socialist revolution". This idea is the same driving force that lies behind the struggle of the CWI to build a mass revolutionary International.

International Secretariat, CWI.

Rally of Marxist Workers Tendency, CWI Section in Sri Lanka

World Relations

1 -Turning points in the Twentieth Century

In this century there have been three decisive turning points for socialism and Marxism: the Russian Revolution and the establishment of the first planned economy; the situation immediately after the Second World War, with the establishment of deformed workers' states in Eastern Europe and China; and the collapse of Stalinism in the USSR and Eastern Europe from 1989 to 1991. Each period has had a decisive effect upon the class struggle and in shaping world relations. We may add that Trotsky's analysis of the bureaucratic degeneration of the Russian Revolution and of Stalinism, - which was correctly reckoned by him to be a greater contribution to the theoretical arsenal of the workers' movement than even his role as the organiser of the October Revolution and of the Red Army - was indispensable in understanding the post-1945 situation and even the period today. With the exception of the CWI, not one serious trend of opinion, either from the ranks of the bourgeoisie or the ex-social democratic and ex-Stalinist leaders, or even those still claiming to come from a Marxist or Trotskyist tradition, correctly understood either the collapse of Stalinism or its political after-effects. The strategists of capital believed that the liquidation of the planned economies of the USSR and Eastern Europe provided the ideal platform for a new capitalist millennium, which would stretch into the next century. The only remaining world military superpower, the USA, would now be allowed to strut the globe imposing 'order' in a new 'Pax Americana'. The market, having established a new 'paradigm' with economic crises, recessions and slumps conjured away by a new global 'humane' capitalism, would be the vehicle for initiating a new period of peace, prosperity and harmony.

The ex-Social Democrats and Stalinists merely echoed the thinking of the bourgeois, as did the overwhelming majority of trade union leaders. In the majority of cases and in most countries they have attempted to swing the workers' parties away from socialism and the class struggle, and in the process have transformed many of these parties into bourgeois formations. Many Marxists and even Trotskyists, completely losing their bearings, have reacted in a one-sided and therefore erroneous fashion. One section has implicitly accepted that 'the game is up', that the collapse of the Soviet Union and with it the planned economies has postponed to the indefinite future the struggle for socialism and the task of creating mass revolutionary parties.

Another section is in 'denial' and cannot accept reality even when it strikes them on the nose. They stubbornly refute any suggestion that a social counter-revolution, the dismantling of the planned economy and its replacement by capitalism, has taken place in Eastern Europe and the former Soviet Union. The CWI, on the other hand, recognised in 1989-90 that capitalism was being restored and that the process has been largely completed in all the republics of the former USSR and in Eastern Europe.

At the same time, we concluded that while this was a defeat for the world proletariat it was not the same kind of crushing social reverse and the change in world class relations that followed the triumphs of Hitler, Mussolini and Franco. Its effects were primarily ideological in that it allowed the bourgeois to conduct an unbridled triumphalist campaign in favour of the 'free market', of capitalism, without having to look over their shoulder and for comparisons to be drawn with the economic achievements of the planned economies of the USSR, Eastern Europe, China and Cuba. This in turn undoubtedly had an effect on the broad consciousness of the working class. 'Socialism', as an ideal and also as a 'practical possibility' for providing the basics of existence particularly for the starving masses of Africa, Asia and Latin America, dimmed. This undoubtedly strengthened the bourgeoisie not just from an ideological point of view, but in its neo-liberal attacks on the working class world-wide.

Acceptance of the market, coming to terms with 'the reality of globalisation', was a necessary credo for the bourgeois to introduce flexibility, short-time working, lengthening of the working day, etc. This undoubtedly did modify the relationship between the working class and the bourgeois to the advantage of the latter. But this could not be compared to the situation, which confronted the proletariat following the victory of fascism in the 1930s. In the fascist countries the workers' organisations were shattered, the proletariat atomised and incapable of resisting the onslaught of triumphant capital. The basic task was to painfully assemble the elements of new workers' organisations. The outright triumph of fascism in a number of countries set back the whole of the proletariat even in those countries where they did not have dictatorships on their backs. The defeat of the proletariat in Spain in particular was the political precondition for the second world war.

Without in any way minimising the difficulties, the situation which now confronts the working class and Marxism could in no way be compared to this. The political after effects of the collapse of Stalinism and the 1990s as a whole were different. The basic power of the proletariat, although weakened, remained intact with its capacity to struggle largely undiminished. Moreover the bourgeois has been compelled in this period to emphasise the 'free' aspect of its doctrine of 'free-market capitalism'. The Wall Street Journal boasts: "Two decades ago the world had only a few dozen democracies... today well over 100 states can plausibly claim to have elected governments, including most countries in Latin America, many in the post-communist world and a significant number in Asia and Africa." Of course, they fail to add that these 'new democracies' provide a screen behind which the rule, sometimes brutal, of big business and the military continues. The German Marxist Wilhem Liebknecht described the Reichstag (parliament) in Germany as a "fig leaf" to hide the real dictatorial character of the Kaiser's regime. However this regime was relatively mild compared to some of the "new democracies". Elections of a kind are held where the military and police resort to death squads, kidnapping, torture and suppression of human, trade union and democratic rights.

The trend towards "democracy" particularly in the under-developed and semi-developed countries arises from a number of causes. Democracy, even in a mangled truncated form, is necessary to give a certain legitimacy to capitalism and imperialism.

Nevertheless the acceptance of 'democracy' is beneficial also for the proletariat, particularly in those societies in which open or veiled dictatorships recently held sway. We will see when we come to the situation in Africa and Asia that this has opened up a space for the development of the workers' movement, particularly of the trade unions.

Capitalism in objectively worse position

The major contradiction of the 1990s so far is that while capitalism has scored an ideological victory, at the same time it has not solved any of the major problems that confronts it. On the contrary, it is objectively in a worse position. Structural mass unemployment, poverty, hunger and homelessness have been enormously aggravated, even when compared to the decade of the 1980s. This has been the source of mass oppositional movements of the proletariat in Western Europe, together with increased national, ethnic and racial tension in Europe, Africa, Asia and Latin America. In the societies that were promised an undreamed of plenty, if only they would restore capitalism, we have seen an unprecedented collapse of the productive forces. And there is no prospect in the immediate period ahead, even according to the experts of the system itself, that these problems will be overcome. On the contrary the 1990s can be compared to a prelude or an overture of a symphony. All the themes, evident in the 1990s albeit in an undeveloped form, will now unfold in all their full drama in the symphony of 'the new millennium'. The contradictions inherent in world capitalism, which will develop with such explosive force, rather than heralding 'the final triumph' of neo-liberal capitalism, guarantee the re-emergence in a powerful mass form of the ideas of socialism.

The more farsighted strategists of capital ruminate on the fact that in this decade, since the collapse of Stalinism, the triumph of their system has been marked by one serious recession in the earlier part of the decade, and now we stand on the eve of a more devastating recession and perhaps even a major global slump. The unemployed or semi-employed still form one-third of the world labour force. The June 1998 demonstrations at the G8 Summit have highlighted the inexorable growth of mass hunger and poverty in the so-called underdeveloped world. In dealing with the colonial and semi-colonial world we will comment on the 'debt problem' later. But even in the advanced industrial countries, with the single exception of the USA and for special reasons, hardly a dent has been made in structural mass unemployment.

USA - The international policeman?

A revolt of the working class in Europe throughout the 1990s has taken on a mass form: the miners' movement in Britain in 1992, the Belgian public sector general strike in 1993, the mass revolt of the Italian workers in opposition to the rise of the right, particularly the 1994 alliance of Forza Italia and the neo-fascists of Fini, and the 1995 public sector strikes in France followed by the explosive lorry drivers' strike. These are just some of the more prominent examples of the combativity of the proletariat. Britain seems to be the exception, with the number of strikes the lowest for a century. But the movement of rail workers and others in 1998 denotes the explosion that is coming, particularly on the scandal of low pay. All of these factors - economic depression, social protest and resistance by the proletariat - have severely circumscribed the power of the bourgeoisie in seeking to establish President Bush's 'new world order'. It is true that in 1991 the success of Desert Storm in the earlier part of the decade, made possible by special and unique reasons, partially mitigated the political effects of the early 1990s recession. But US imperialism's desire to play the role of an unchallenged world policeman came to grief in Somalia and was dramatically emphasised in the new confrontation with Saddam's Iraqi regime in the early part of 1998. A combination of factors allowed Desert Storm to be mounted: domestic support within the US, at least in the initial bombing phase; the Arab coalition which saw no alternative but to confront Saddam; and above all, the support of Yeltsin and the newly emerging bourgeoisie in Russia. At the time of Desert Storm the latter was too weak to develop its own imperialist appetite, which now brings it into collision with US imperialism.

In Bosnia, the US in concert with the European powers partially managed to play a policeman's role, in reality it held the ring. But this was possible only after years of mutual and bloody slaughter and with the major combatants having exhausted themselves. In Haiti also, in the US's own 'backyard', and with overwhelming military force, the US was able to intervene. But in all other situations it has been shown incapable of imposing its military will, let alone confronting the intractable problems that have accumulated in the 'post-communist' world. In the early 1998 conflict with Saddam, over biological and chemical weapons of war, the Clinton administration found itself hemmed in by a combination of domestic opposition and opposition from its Arab allies. Even 'Stormin' Norman' Schwarzkopf warned that a sustained bombing campaign against the Iraqi regime threatened to "repeat the mistakes of Vietnam". The pounding of Vietnam, particularly of North Vietnam, rather than weakening, actually consolidated the population behind the North Vietnamese regime. Moreover in the US itself the memory of Vietnam was rekindled in the vocal opposition expressed in the 'town' meetings convened by Madeleine Albright, US Secretary of State, as a means of mobilising US public opinion to confront the Iraqi regime. Even more vocal and hostile were the statements of those like Mubarak, Arab bourgeois par excellence and a puppet of US imperialism.

Summing up the fear that air strikes against Iraq would provoke uprisings through-out the Middle East, Mubarak declared in the British Financial Times: "We have to deal with public opinion in the Arab and Islamic world, and we're going to face a helluva problem. This is very dangerous - I cannot stand against the whole weight of popular opinion... This is not 1991, the US has lost credibility in the Middle East... You'll not find one [Arab] leader who will say publicly: 'We support the air strike'."

In the US itself, over 50% in a CNN poll were against the bombing of Iraq. Many at the village meetings declared: 'Why bomb Iraq when Turkey has bombed the Kurds and Saudi Arabia has tortured dissidents.' However, faced with the dilemma of what to do about Saddam, US imperialism was damned if it acted effectively, and damned if it didn't. This was summed up by the British Financial Times: "It is dangerous to attack but more dangerous to do nothing."

Of decisive importance is the social situation in the US, where the memory of Vietnam is an ever-present check on the ability of US imperialism to play the role of world policeman. That is why bourgeois commentators refer to it as 'the super-power reduced to shouting from the sidelines'. When military intervention is sometimes used it is of a purely police-type character: 'go in, stabilise and get out'. Imperialism, moreover, is tending more and more to act by proxy. This explains the rise of 'military companies', that is mercenaries, which are playing, in the words of the British Financial Times, "a growing role [which] has coincided with the collapse of Communism. Western governments have little strategic interest in intervening in other countries' civil wars."

The option of intervening with full-scale military force under the UN banner, US imperialism in disguise, has faded in the wake of the Somalia debacle. Moreover, there is not much "domestic appetite for a country's soldiers to fight in other people's wars". At the same time, the scaling-down of the military capability of most of the advanced industrial countries has led to a surplus of private 'military expertise'. This has come together with the collapse of the USSR, and the virtual disintegration of the Red Army at one stage, and has led to "an abundance of cheap ex-Soviet weaponry". The much-publicised intervention by the mercenary outfit,

Sandline, in Sierra Leone is an example of this. In reality, despite the inflated self-publicity of the 'directors' of Sandline, the overthrow of the 'rebel' regime was largely the work of the Nigerian-led Expeditionary Force (ECOMOG).

The liberal wringing of hands by the bourgeoisie over the existence of mercenary companies cannot disguise the fact that they are playing "an increasingly influential role in areas once the domain of sovereign states". (British Financial Times) The same journal adds, "banning them is neither possible - nor necessarily wise". Only 12 countries have signed the 1989 UN Convention on mercenaries, and although UK legislation banning them dates back to the last century, there has not been a single conviction in more than 100 years. The very fact that bourgeois strategists can openly discuss in the press the merits or otherwise of using mercenaries, shows how brazen and open are the imperialist appetites of the major powers. At the time of the intervention of mercenaries in the Congo in the 1960s and 70s there was an outcry from the labour movement in the advanced industrialised world. Now 'military companies', such as the South African Executive Outcomes, have played a role over the last few decades in assisting imperialist intervention. The US company, Military Professional Resources, headed by more than a dozen former US generals, is training both the Bosnian and Croatian armed forces while another 'military company', associated with James Baker the former US Secretary of State, has trained various parts of the Saudi Arabian forces.

While this sinister development must be opposed by the workers' movement at the same time the limitations of their effectiveness must also be recognised. A handful of 'military experts', no matter how well armed, is incapable of acting against the huge social movements which will develop, particularly in the 'underdeveloped' world. A section of US policy makers have allocated to US imperialist forces the role of 'preventive engagement'. This allegedly can replace "what arms control was in the early 1960s". They recognise they will not be able to prevent "ethnic wars entirely" but selective intervention by the US "before things heat up uncontrollably" could possibly prevent wars or "reduce their intensity and duration". The presence of US troops in Macedonia is intended to play such a role. However, at best, US troops, under the guise in the main of the UN, can only play a temporary delaying and minimalist 'police-type' role.

Ethnic and nationalist conflicts

This is particularly the case against the background of a world torn by intensified ethnic and nationalist conflict. Capitalism confronts an economic crisis and resulting catastrophe for millions, as in Asia, social breakdown in parts of Africa and Latin America on a scale never witnessed before, increased impoverishment, hopelessness and despair in the former deformed workers' states and unmanageable environmental catastrophe. The earlier feelings of optimism and faith in capitalism's ability to solve humankind's problems have largely evaporated and in its place has come pessimism bordering on despair. One commentator in the Wall Street Journal uses Colombia as the model of the future for large parts of Latin America, if not the world: "There can be four or five scandals in a single day. Turf wars between 'paramilitary' groups and guerrillas, either of which may be backed by drug lords, is remindful... of the battles of medieval warlords in Europe."

Chaos, a break down of 'social order', is not just restricted to Colombia. We have seen a similar situation in Algeria with well-nigh 50,000 casualties in a never-ending bloodletting of the most vicious type. Similar situations unfolded in Bosnia, Rwanda, and "you can take your pick of the next African country where a new wave of horrible, mindless violence, will be unleashed". (Wall Street Journal) Events in Albania are perhaps typical of the horror that results from an economic and social catastrophe but without a clear alternative being immediately evident.

We should recall what Marx and Trotsky pointed out, there have been periods in history of stagnation and relapse, when no class has appeared which is capable of taking society forward. Such was the case in the slave-owning economy of Rome. Therefore, it inevitably regressed, a collapse of the productive forces took place. Only on the basis of the new foundations of feudalism, which was a partial reversion to the methods that preceded slave society, did history begin to go forward again.

No confidence in capitalist institutions

We have not reached that situation in the modern world, but the 'Mad Max scenario', typified by Albania, threatens to engulf other parts of the world and not just in Africa, Asia and Latin America. There is also a crisis of confidence in all the institutions of the bourgeoisie. On a world scale, the UN, IMF and World Bank, have all demonstrated their role as agencies of imperialism and, particularly, of US imperialism. The bail-out of Indonesia and Thailand has gone hand-in-hand with vicious 'austerity programmes' and the 'liberalisation' of these economies which directly assists imperialist financial and economic penetration. At the same time, the UN is low on funds with the Republicans continuing to withhold US contributions, partly in order to weaken Clinton's hand and also because of their mad 'free-market' philosophy which would allow all countries to go economically to the wall. The UN, since the collapse of the Cold War, is more openly the creature of US capitalism. Kofi Annan, the UN Secretary General, is a product of the American business school education system. He has declared, as the new philosophy for the UN, "a strong UN is good for big business". Such an approach would have been impossible during the Cold War when, as the British Financial Times correctly declares: "The UN walked a tightrope between capitalism and communism [Stalinism], anxious to avoid offending either superpower." Annan now declares that, "thriving markets and human security go hand in hand". As a mark of the UN's embrace of big business, CNN, the giant media corporation, recently gave $1bn to the UN. Addressing the international gathering of big business at Davos, he declared: "Business has a compelling interest in the success of this workforce. Creating wealth, which is your expertise, and promoting security, the UN's main concern, are mutually reinforcing goals."

However, this open, pro-capitalist stance of the UN will increasingly militate against it being accepted as an 'impartial' agency, above all by the masses in the 'underdeveloped' world in the period of social turbulence and upheaval that we are entering. On the other hand, imperialism needs the appearance of 'impartial' agencies to allow it to dominate the world. It is impossible for a single world superpower to dominate an increasingly 'multi-polar' world. At the same time, despite the high expectations following the end of the Cold War, the American people have seen its forces drawn into more and more world conflict. During the 40 years of the Cold War, the US military executed ten major interventions. Since the Cold War ended it has intervened 27 times, including Somalia, Rwanda and northern Iraq. However these have not been on the same scale as during the Cold War. This has been against the background of a more than halving of US personnel.

And what has been the net upshot of its interventions? Haiti was the most successful intervention. As the Wall Street Journal comments: "The US occupation had three rules: 'take no casualties, spend very, very little cash, and get out fast'. Nearly four years later, Haiti's right-wing thugs have all but disappeared but the suffering and poverty have not, and Haiti's democracy is paralysed (more than 200 US Army personnel remain stationed in Haiti to provide civil assistance)."

For all of these reasons the US still needs the screen of the UN, albeit that the US Congress will still strike blows at the UN, particularly when it threatens to become too independent. On a national scale also, the institutions of the bourgeoisie - parliament, the police, judiciary, established churches, monarchy (in the case of Britain), etc. - are increasingly discredited.

As the workers' parties are converted into bourgeois formations, no real mass alternative is therefore offered and participation in elections tends to drop. In America this tendency is very pronounced with less than 50% voting in the 1996 presidential elections. Now the 'Americanisation' of European politics is well under way, with diminishing participation in elections and a tendency for workers and particularly youth to search for other extra-parliamentary means to express their opposition on key issues. The corruption of politicians is integrated into the consciousness of the mass of the population along with that of the police and judiciary.

The crisis of bourgeois institutions is best typified by events in Belgium. The horrible paedophile murders, perpetrated by Marc Dutroux, brought to the surface the festering hostility to the state, particularly the police, judiciary, and politicians. The fact that the police had searched Dutroux's house three times, even hearing children's voices on one occasion, provoked mass fury. This crisis was compounded when this monster actually escaped for three-and-a-half hours in May 1998. These incidents have fuelled deep-seated suspicion that the police were in league with Dutroux and the paedophile ring operated with police and judicial connivance. This provoked the half-million 'White March' in October 1996. This incident has merged in the minds of the masses with the corruption of politicians, mass unemployment, racism, etc. Undoubtedly, if a mass revolutionary party had existed, then on this issue alone, as with the Dreyfus affair in France, not just the government would have toppled but the fate of capitalism in Belgium would have been at stake. The role of the bourgeois state was laid bare. This is an answer to those, like Lutte Ouvrière in France, who take a purely 'economist' approach to political processes. Not just economic events, provoking strikes, etc., but incidents like this, as well as crimes against the environment, etc., can be the starting point for a revolutionary explosion.

2 - The economy and the productive forces

A t the same time, it is the development of the economy, of the productive forces, that is ultimately decisive in determining the march of events. When the Asian crisis first broke in the middle of 1997, our international organisation, in the teeth of considerable scepticism from the 'experts' of capitalism argued that this was the beginning of a world economic crisis, which at the least, would be a serious recession and could topple over into a slump. In a series of CWI documents, articles in the weekly press of the CWI British section and its journal Socialism Today, we have charted the development of this crisis at every stage. We also have a separate resolution that deals with present trends in the world economy and particularly future perspectives. But in any analysis of world relations, it is necessary to touch on some of the fundamental features of the world economy and their impact on political events.

Despite all the frantic urgings of bourgeois strategists, particularly directed towards Japan, like a Greek tragedy, the world inexorably moves towards a serious economic downturn. All the factors which led to the feeble growth which followed the recession in the early 1990s have now turned into their opposite and like great leaden weights are dragging down the world economy. Globalisation was seen up until recently as one of the factors that guaranteed that capitalism had entered a 'new era', had established a new and permanent equilibrium, a 'paradigm'. In reality, as we argued, it has acted ultimately to undermine capitalism. The globalisation of finance capital, in particular, means that the crisis, the 'Asian flu', has spread at lightning speed, touching every part of the globe, resulting in unparalleled gyrations in the stock markets, and resulting in the spectacular and sudden drop in the real economies of Asia in particular. Globalisation has been used an ideological and political weapon against the working class and as one of the main arguments against the idea of struggle. Rather than trade union leaders taking steps to unify workers' struggles internationally, Globalisation has been used by these privileged layers to hold back and derail struggle by workers, especially those concentrated in the powerful multi-national conglomerates.

The empiricism of most bourgeois 'experts', and the panic which events have introduced in the thinking of the serious strategists of capital, was summed up in an article in the British Financial Times by Robert Wade, a professor of political economy at Brown University. He declared: "Those who thought that the Asian crisis had abated have had a rude shock. Forecasters are again chasing Asian economies downhill. Earlier estimates that in 1998 Korea's output would fall by 5%, Thailand's by 7% and Indonesia's by 2% appear to have been too optimistic. Implied falls in consumption and welfare are even bigger, because the output figures include substantial net exports. Asia is in the grip of a debt deflation akin to the Great Depression of the 1930s."

And as the good professor further comments: "Financial systems are grounding down as private and public debtors stop repayments, tipping more and more companies into insolvency."

The contagion has gone from Asia to Russia, parts of Central Europe and Latin America. Yavlinsky, the Russian bourgeois politician who stands for 'clean capitalism' declares that "this is not Asian flu. This is Russian pneumonia". As the crisis has spread to each area, it has amplified "the downturn in the others and fuelling the US bubble through capital flight".

Asian crisis deepens

The fond hopes that the crisis could be restricted to just five countries in east Asia - Indonesia, Thailand, Korea, Malaysia and the Philippines - have been dashed as Hong Kong and, above all, Japan have been burned and, in turn, have aggravated the crisis in Asia. More importantly, as we have pointed out, Japan, the second-most important economy in the world, threatens to drag the whole of world capitalism down with it in the next period. Hong Kong, a haven for finance capital which was supposed to be immune from the Asian catastrophe, is following in the footsteps of Japan with a colossal asset deflation of 40% in six months and a 50% drop in the stock market. The situation has prompted the European and the American bourgeoisie in particular, to hysterically denounce the Japanese capitalists for allegedly refusing to lead Asia out of the crisis. 'Spend, spend, spend' is the cry of even those monetarists who have demanded financial rectitude from governments in the past. Even the guru of monetarism, Milton Friedman, alongside Paul Krugman of the Massachusetts Institute of Technology, has urged Japan to go in for a "sustained dose of rising inflation". The new vogue for neo-Keynesianism has been adopted in the most unlikely quarters, such as the writers of the British Financial Times. The six failed attempts - amounting to a total injection of $1,000 billion has only acted to aggravate Japan's recession, yet the international bourgeois still urge increased state expenditure. The British Financial Times has gone so far as to demand that a new reflationary programme should amount to as much as 3% of Japan's gross domestic product.

Such proposals for Europe, infringing as they do the Maastricht criteria, would be seen as pure financial heresy if there was an attempt by the any European government to implement them. At the same time, the Japanese government has been urged to deal with the colossal $200bn (estimated) total of 'problem loans' of the banks, which is, by the way, three times higher than previously thought. This huge 'debt overhang' has acted as a colossal incubus on the Japanese economy.

But, as bourgeois economists have pointed out, a write-off of these loans, or a foreclosure on bad loans, would force a huge number of Japanese companies into bankruptcy. This, in turn, would risk tipping the Japanese economy into an even deeper slump with huge company closures and a massive credit squeeze. As one Japanese government official complained: "If we don't act at all, we will get criticised. But if we act too fast, we could worsen the recession. We cannot win."

The liquidation of bad loans and with it of companies, despite the economic and social havoc which it causes, is an intrinsic feature of capitalist crisis. It represents the 'slaughter of capital' which is a feature of overproduction and slump. This, in turn, prepares the ground for the emergence of new capital with a higher rate of profit, which plays a role in the recommencement of the economic cycle, the beginning of an upswing. But we are far from that situation in Japan; in fact, we face a further and further deepening of the recession and possibly a slump.

Despite all the wailing of the bourgeois experts, there is very little that Japan can do to postpone the evil day of economic recession and slump. The underlying and fundamental weakness of the Japanese economy is reflected in the collapse of the yen, which has only temporarily been bailed out by the intervention of the US Federal Reserve, which acted to prop up the yen. This was the first currency market intervention by the US since the summer of 1995 and reflects the fear that, if left uncorrected, the fall of the yen was about to trigger a new series of Asian devaluations led by China. The latter had maintained the rate of the renminbi, the Chinese currency, even though its rivals have devalued, which has seriously affected Chinese exports. For instance, the value of the Indonesian rupiah has fallen by 80% in comparison with the Chinese currency.

With Japan also depreciating its currency, this situation threatened to further undermine Chinese exports. A devaluation was clearly threatened which, in turn, prompted the US to intervene. However, such intervention is only a temporary tool, and without any solution being possible in the short term to the underlying problems of the Japanese economy, the yen will probably continue to fall. Therefore, at a certain stage, China will be compelled to devalue which, like the 1930s in the advanced industrial countries, could trigger a new wave of devaluations across Asia which would have an immediate impact on the neighbouring countries of Australia and New Zealand. It could also spread to Central Europe and Latin America, and would have a big effect on Europe and the US.

Despite a certain flight of capital to the 'safe haven' of the dollar, the underlying position of the US economy, as we have explained previously, is unsound. The US trade deficit rose 9.5% in April of 1998 to a record $8.8bn. Moreover, the tightening of credit in the US, the continuing squeeze on wage rates which, in turn, depresses the 'market', the increased competition from Asian imports, all means that the US itself is coming to the end of its economic cycle. There is now a strong possibility that a repetition of the events of Asia, a financial crisis leading to a slump in the world economy (a repetition of 1929), could take place on a world scale in the period that we are entering.

'Anti-foreigner' and anti-imperialist moods

Our broad analysis of the situation in Asia has been confirmed but the suddenness of the drop in the economy in countries like Indonesia, the Philippines, etc., even we could not have anticipated. What haunts the bourgeoisie is the political and social consequences of such a development. Robert Wade comments in a masterly understatement: "We have seen large-scale social protest in Indonesia. But Indonesia may be a special case. South Korea is the key to the wider regional response. There, unemployment is rising at more than 6,000 people a day and, when the big conglomerates start to fire workers towards the end of June, the number will rise much higher. Hyundai recently announced plans to fire 18% of its employees. Korea has only the most minimal social safety net. But it is also has strong trade unions which can be expected to mount resistance.

"If the worse came to the worst, anti-foreign movements could sweep president Kim Dae Jung from office. A new government might declare a moratorium on its foreign debt, turn real interest rates negative and begin to inflate out of the crisis. This would dramatically change other Asian leaders' surprisingly passive acceptance of the IMF strategy. The odds of this happening may be no more than one in five. But it is clear that the IMF's approach is not working."

Korea shows that the slaughter of capital is not a theoretical idea but takes a material, concrete form. The Korean government is set to close a swathe of Korean businesses, including five chaebol. This could unleash an unprecedented movement of the Korean workers.

While the US and Europe have been concerned to contain the Asian crisis for fear of it affecting their own economies, at the same time they have seized the opportunity to enhance their own position at the expense of Japanese and Asian capitalism in general. The IMF has been the instrument to impose austerity programmes, a vital part of which is to open up these economies through flexibilisation and investment of foreign, particularly US, capital. Thailand, a formerly closed economy, has been compelled to ease the rules governing foreign ownership because of the desperation for foreign cash. Even Japan, famed in the past for refusing to create a more favourable climate for foreign investment, under the impact of the crisis, has caved in and is now prepared to 'give its blessing to foreign take-overs'.

This goes together with indications that Japan has been compelled to undertake a partial financial withdrawal from Asia. 56% of companies with investments in Asia have been damaged by the crisis. As we predicted, one consequence of Asia's crisis, and the intervention of US imperialism through the medium of the IMF, is increased imperialist financial penetration. The arrogance of Clinton and his financial representative, Larry Summers, towards Indonesia, for instance, fuelled opposition to the IMF and 'foreigners'.

In 1998 US acquisitions of Asian businesses have reached a value of $8bn, double that of the previous record year, which the British Financial Times correctly comments is a reflection of the "drive by US corporations to take advantage of Asia's deepening crisis". Little wonder that even in Japan, "resentment is building in Tokyo against perceived US economic imperialism".

At the same time, some of the tenets of the 'free-market' economy have been challenged by sections of the Japanese bourgeoisie themselves. Confronted by a plunge in the economy, estimated at 5% this year, the weakness of the yen and the outflow of investors into non-yen assets, such as US government bonds, sections of the ruling Liberal Democratic Party, the main bourgeois party, have raised the need for "controls on the flow of capital". Even the British Financial Times has flirted with "regulating capital flows, particularly short-term speculative capital".

One thing is clear from these developments in Asia, that not just in the underdeveloped part but even in advanced Japan, deep-seated, 'anti-foreigner' moods can be fanned into flames in the teeth of a serious economic downturn. This, in turn, can lead to action being taken against 'foreign capital'. Already we have seen the effect of the 'nationalisation' of companies in some countries and the threat to do so for ailing companies even in Japan. A pronounced anti-imperialist and more nationalist mood will be one of the consequences in Asia and other parts of the underdeveloped world of this economic crisis. And, as we have pointed out, Asia is already having an effect on Europe and the USA. However, irrespective of this effect, the economic cycle in Europe, and particularly in the US, is drawing to an end.

Unemployment in all sectors of the world

Commenting in an American journal recently, Cait Murphy compares the record of the US in creating jobs to the position in Europe. She points out that there were 4.5 million fewer people working in the countries of the European Union in 1996 than in 1991. We have to remember that this is during a so-called 'economic boom'. Moreover, unemployment in Europe amongst those under 24 and not in school is 20% and, as Murphy points out, "There is no more volatile, or violent, section of human society than a pack of idle young males."

The recent OECD report on unemployment shows just how intractable are the problems of capitalism even during an upswing. It points out that the level of registered unemployment in the industrialised world is expected to stabilise at about 35 million people, or 7% of the workforce. However, this perspective is highly optimistic given the likely developments in the world economy and their impact on Europe and the US. It points out that, although unemployment in the OECD area declined to 7.2% of the workforce in 1997, in Europe it is over 10% and "will remain a serious economic and social problem". Bourgeois experts have tried to argue that structural unemployment does not exist and that what takes place is a 'churning', that is, the entry and leaving of unemployment in rapid succession by the majority of those who are counted as out of work. Yet the OECD points out that there is a "growing number of households without any earners" in the industrialised world. It states that as many as "25% of households in Finland and 24.8% of those in Belgium have nobody who is employed".

The layering of the proletariat is also indicated in the OECD report when it states: "There is some evidence of a polarisation of employment", with the growth both in the proportion of workless households and in households containing two working adults. Over the last ten years only Ireland, the US and the Netherlands have experienced a rise in employment strong enough to lead to a reduction in the incidence of household worklessness. In the UK, Japan and Belgium, the OECD found that the household jobless rate had actually risen since 1985, despite the fall in the individual base rate of unemployment. The largest increase in household worklessness took place in New Zealand. This, of course, has been the country, at least in the advanced industrialised world, where neo-liberal attacks on the working class have perhaps gone furthest.

3 - Europe and the world revolution

Europe remains a key area in world relations and for the future of the world revolution. The European proletariat is the oldest, with the longest traditions and, up to the outbreak of the Asian crisis showed most, clearly the re-emergence of the working class. Strikes and movements of the working class have broken out most noticeably in France, in the near general strike in Denmark, in the ferocious bank workers' strike in Greece, in the chemical workers' strike in Italy, and in most countries in Europe. Economic developments in Europe in the next year or so are a guarantee of an increase in the tempo of resistance of the working class to the European bourgeoisie's neo-liberal policies.

At the moment, Europe appears to be out of economic synchronisation with Asia with estimates of an increase in the growth rate of the Euro-zone, which rose by 3.2% in the first quarter of 1998. Bourgeois economists are hoping that Europe will catch up with the US, with annual growth in the first quarter approaching 4%. Exports and imports have increased substantially and even countries with a low rate of growth, such as Germany, seem to have experienced a certain upswing in 1998. However, the Asian crisis and the ending of the growth cycle in the US will have a dramatic effect on Europe's economic perspectives.

If during the 'boom' there is a preparedness of the proletariat to move to defend their position, it is easy to envisage how ferocious defensive battles will probably take place in the event of big rises in unemployment. A heightened political consciousness by the mass of workers and a preparedness to draw far-reaching socialist and revolutionary conclusions by the more advanced layers, will result from a deep recession or slump. It must be remembered that during the 1990s boom, the gap between rich and poor, the differences between wealth patterns between one part of Europe and another, have increased enormously. Parts of Greece, Spain and Italy receive less than a fifth of the annual income per head of richer regions. In the north German port city of Hamburg, the richest single region in Europe, average income is over $60,000 per head, whereas in areas of the Greek island of Crete, in Calabria in Italy, and Extremadura in Spain, incomes are about one-sixth of that.

A tale of two Europes

The poverty belt of Europe is defined as regions where the GDP per head is less than 75% of the EU average. This would include all of Greece and all of Portugal except Lisbon, rural Spain, southern Italy and the former East Germany. Surprisingly, areas of Austria and the British regions of Merseyside and south Yorkshire are included. Apart from the former East Germany, south Yorkshire and Merseyside are the only two 'poor' regions in northern Europe. As an indication of the grinding poverty, which has followed on the heels of massive deindustrialisation in both areas, each area has a per capita income of about £8,400 against an average of £11,400 for the rest of Britain which, in turn, is one of the lowest in Europe. The EU average income is £12,000 ($19, 680).

The divisions within countries are just as stark. Greater London is the only region that makes the top 12 of Europe's regions, with a GDP per head of 139% of the EU average. This disguises the massive belt of poverty that exists in London. In Germany, Hamburg enjoys almost four times the income per head of former East German provinces. Brussels is more than twice as wealthy as the depressed former mining region of Hainaut, barely 80km down the road, while average income in Paris is more than twice as much as Corsica and Languedoc. Lombardy, Italy's richest region, is nearly three times better off than Calabria.

Overall, the statistical picture of two Europes - a rich north and a poor south - according to the British newspaper, The British Guardian, "endures despite decades of subsidies and financial aid from Brussels". And this aid, which has cushioned some of the poorer areas and countries of Europe, is about to be cut back substantially. The German bourgeoisie was prepared to underwrite the EU with massive subsidies up to now. This was the economic price they were prepared to pay for their domination of the EU in tandem with the French bourgeoisie. But the increasing economic difficulties of German capitalism and the approach of the German general election, against the background of rising opposition in Germany to the EU, forced Kohl to demand a cut of Germany's contribution to the EU budget. This is in advance of a serious recession or slump in Europe in the wake of economic events in Asia and the US

These developments, together with the huge economic divisions in Europe, mean that a common economic and monetary policy, including the euro, cannot be fully implemented. The question of the single currency has become more and more of a prominent issue. The Netherlands finance minister warned that his country will vote against Italy joining EMU without a "tough Italian budget". Italy itself is not sharing in the growth that is taking place in other parts of Europe. Its target of 2.5% growth in 1998 has been called into question by bourgeois economic analysts, particularly as GDP fell by 0.1% in the first quarter of 1998. The state debts of Italy remain intractable and in the German Bundesrat, the upper house of parliament, the regions of Bavaria and Saxony abstained in votes on the EMU because of 'concern' about Italian debt levels.

The EMU project will break down in fact. The timing of this breakdown is dependent on economic developments not just in Europe but in Asia and, above all, in the US. It is not a question of 'if' the euro will break down, but of 'when' and 'how'. With the change in the economic situation, and given the colossal accumulation of social problems even during the boom, the European proletariat will inevitably face a revival of its fighting capacity and the renewal of its organisations, particularly the trade unions.

Ethnic tensions in the Balkans

This will be against the background of increased nationalist and ethnic tension in the Balkans and elsewhere in Europe. In Kosova it is clear that the Serbian regime of Milosevic, basing himself on the narrow layer of the Serbian 10% of the population in Kosova, is carrying through a policy of subjugating the Kosova Albanians. He is expelling them from the frontier areas (to stop the supply of weapons for the KLA/UCK) and has carried out the settlement of Serbs in Kosova to change the ethnic composition. All the major imperialist powers are terrified that Kosova will become the spark of a new Balkan conflagration, which would dwarf the conflict in Bosnia.

While the majority of the population of Kosova are in favour not just of self-determination but of complete independence, this is presently opposed by all the main imperialist spokespersons. One of their concerns is the example this could set in the unravelling of other multinational states. They are urging Milosevic to return to the autonomy status Kosova enjoyed, before this was abrogated in 1989. Failure to do this will only stoke up support for the Kosova Liberation Army (UCK) which at one stage controlled one-third of the territory of Kosova. Independence for Kosova could lead to a full-scale military conflict with Serbia, leading to an even greater expulsion of Albanian Kosovars into Albania itself.

This, in turn, would draw in Macedonia with its huge Albanian population, which then could involve both Greece and Turkey. This is one of the reasons why the Greek regime, despite its hostility to Macedonia (which it insists on calling Skopje), recently made a common declaration with the Macedonian government opposing independence for Kosova and arguing for 'autonomy'. Despite all the efforts of imperialism, including Yeltsin's Russia, which has urged Milosevic to make concessions, it cannot be ruled out that a new conflagration could detonate throughout the Balkans.

The deployment of Serbian military forces against the ethnic Albanians led to "a display of force" and the threat to "go further" by NATO forces in the area. Basing themselves, allegedly, on what happened in Bosnia, bourgeois commentators in Britain have urged an immediate military intervention in Kosova unless Milosevic draws back. However, large-scale military intervention with troops on the ground is ruled out, especially at the beginning of a conflict. Air strikes would be as counter-productive as they would have been in Iraq and, moreover, would earn this time the outright opposition of the Russian Yeltsin regime that acts as a shield for Milosevic. The nationalist and ethnic tensions, which have broken out in the Balkans and remain as intractable as ever, are an indication of the impossibility of solving these issues on the basis of capitalism.

The role of the workers' movement, of taking an independent class position, of urging unity between the working class, and opposition to the nationalist poison of the different bourgeoisies, would assume great importance. The initiatives taken by our comrades in Greece and, above all, in Cyprus could be an important example for what we could do in the event of a new Balkan war.

However, it is not just over Kosova but also in Cyprus that the war clouds have gathered recently. The threat of Clerides, the Greek Cypriot President, to deploy Russian missiles on the Greek side and the visit of four mainland Greek F-16 aircraft and transport aircraft to the new Paphos air base in the southern, Greek-controlled, part of Cyprus, led to a reciprocal deployment of airplanes by Turkey in northern Cyprus. Turkey has now threatened to use the air bases in northern Cyprus, where it has stationed 30,000 troops since its invasion in 1974, particularly if Russian missiles are installed by the Greek Cypriot government. While neither the Greek nor Turkish bourgeoisies wish to go to war at this stage, these clashes are an indication of the underlying tension which continues. Cyprus enjoys one of the highest living standards in Europe if not the world. But the fate of former Yugoslavia, considered as part of "civilised Europe" , is a warning of what can happen if underlying national tensions explode. These developments are also against a background of the failures of plans to reunite Cyprus on some kind of federal basis.

The cost to the environment

Moreover, just as environmental disaster in Asia, particularly in Indonesia, went hand in hand with economic collapse, so the recent mud-slides in Italy indicate the price that the peoples of Europe will play environmentally for a continuation of capitalism. Moreover, they are not unique. The destruction and deaths in the Sarno Valley in southern Italy have come after recent lethal flash floods in eastern Spain. Most environmental experts expect that areas of Portugal, Greece and Turkey will suffer the same fate as they become 'richer' and 'more developed'.

Across southern Europe in particular, but not exclusively, vested capitalist interests have based themselves on a system of eliminating natural methods of cultivation by which excess rainfall can be absorbed harmlessly. There has been a continual clearance of 'green belts' for development, by the methods of forest fire. There have been a huge number of forest fires around the Mediterranean that have been started deliberately by developers to ensure that areas they have targeted lose their natural beauty. One of the side effects is to loosen the underlying soil that can lead to the kind of death and destruction witnessed in southern Italy. Moreover, the absence of planning permission can lead to individuals unsafely adding extensions to their houses, or the erection of houses by unscrupulous builders that can easily collapse under the pressure of sudden rain. According to one estimate, 207,000 houses have been built without permission in Italy. This would cover an area more than ten times the City of London. Many have been constructed without proper drainage or even on river beds that seem empty, until the next once-in-a-century storm. One whole town in Campania, in the Naples area, with 15,000 inhabitants has been created without the slightest official authorisation. Even right-wing papers in Italy have spoken of the "collective suicide" and "the environmental pillage" that is taking place.

These environmental disasters are the logical outcome of the 'free market' which has held sway throughout the 1990s. But the reaction against the catastrophe in southern Italy has led to protests, which will swell into mass movements and merge with those which arise from economic and social factors. The period of the 1990s was a watershed for Europe, which will be followed not by environmental but by social storms in the period that we are going into.

Socialist ideas and new workers' parties

The movement of ex-social democratic leaders to a more and more open bourgeois position will leave a space for the development of socialist and revolutionary ideas. At a later stage, these will lead to mass workers' formations. The process of bourgeoisification has affected not just the right wing of social democracy but those who claim to be on the 'left' as well. Oskar Lafontaine, leader of Germany's SPD, declared it firmly in 1995-96 as a "left-wing party". In the run-up to the German general election, he now declares that the decidedly right-wing economic policies of Clinton is a "model" for an SPD-led government if it comes to power after the September general election. At the same time, Lafontaine wants to maintain the fiction of still standing on the 'left'. Therefore, in an attempt to square the circle, while supporting Clinton he also calls for a "move back towards more social justice, more equality of opportunity, more jobs, more opportunities for people to hold the productive capital of society".

Clinton's US is in marked contrast to this latest stated ideal of Lafontaine. Unbelievably he declares that wages in the US have "been geared to growth and productivity". But Lafontaine knows that the productivity growth in the US has been on the basis of the increased exploitation of the working class and that real wages have, in effect, been standing still for the last two decades. At the same time, he has admitted that "net wages fell last year for the first time in Germany's post-war history. Lafontaine to a limited extent merely fills the role of a decorative 'left' to Schröder. Schröder, like Blair in Britain, is an openly bourgeois figure without the disguise, which has been assumed, for instance, by Jospin in France.

Left's ideological capitulation

Indeed, throughout Europe, the left while retaining a lingering terminological difference with the right wing of social democracy, have in effect capitulated to the ideological campaign of the bourgeoisie for the adoption of neo-liberal policies. Even the Rifondazione Comunista (PRC) which was the most left mass party in Europe in the 1990s, adopted policies which can be broadly described as reformist. While it has zigzagged in its support, at one stage supporting the Prodi bourgeois government and then into opposition, in the last period it has supported the government on crucial votes in the Italian parliament. It has voted for public expenditure cuts, which are the biggest since the second world war.

In Britain the Labour left has been reduced to a shadow of its former self, with Benn clinging to the wreckage of the Labour Party and advocating that workers should stay in to 'fight'. Yet every avenue to swing the Labour Party back towards the left has been systematically blocked by the Blairites. The National Executive Committee has been reduced to a rubber stamp for the government. The national conference has been in effect abolished. The Blairites are now proposing to introduce a system of vetting the parliamentary candidates, which will remove all undesirable 'lefts' from any selection process for them to become MPs. In fact, the process has already started in Scotland with the exclusion of lefts like Dennis Canavan and others (who are already Westminster MPs) from Labour candidates' lists for the Scottish Parliament.

The attacks from the right, however, are unlikely to provoke a major defection of the left from the Labour Party, either in Scotland or in the whole of Britain in the next period. This arises from two factors. On the one side, they have no fundamental differences on policies with the right. This is typified in Britain by the stance of Labour MPs such as Chris Mullin - formerly on the 'extreme left' of the Labour Party and close assistant and confidant of Tony Benn. Mullin now states that it is only possible for 'right of centre' governments of the 'left' to be elected in the changed circumstances which have developed in the 1990s. The other factor that determines the indolence and ineffectiveness of the left is their utter pessimism on the capacity and willingness of the working class to fight back at a certain stage against the neo-liberal offensive.

One of the political repercussions of a new serious recession or slump will be a reactivating of the working class in countries in Europe where they have been relatively dormant, as in Britain. In other countries, where there is a serious level of resistance already, the movement will go to new heights. All of this will have an effect on the development of the left.

The movement of the bourgeoisie towards more 'national' policies (in Europe they could also take the form of regional measures), means the more this will provide a basis for the emergence of new reformist moods amongst the working class and, as a consequence of this, the development of new reformist and left reformist movements. The idea that we can by-pass the stage of reformism, left reformism and centrism, because of the weakness of these formations at this stage, is wrong. We in no way mitigate the importance of seizing the opportunities which exist now for the development of the revolutionary organisations of the CWI at the present time. But, as we have stated on many occasions, we cannot fully occupy the vacuum that exists at the present time. However, we can partially fill this vacuum and in fact build powerful revolutionary poles of attraction, which can be decisive in the development of new mass workers' formations in the future. But reformism, left reformism and centrism are not just the inventions of a few leaders at the top but also represent a confused stage in the developing consciousness of the mass of the working class. However, a balanced assessment of the possibility of left reformist and centrist currents emerging in the future is one thing, but to engage in a kind of Sherlock Holmes-type hunt, with magnifying glass in hand, to discover these currents now, is entirely futile. It is vital that the small forces of Marxism, gathered in the ranks of the CWI, dig roots amongst the youth in particular. We must assemble the best layers of the working class under our banner, thereby developing the base to be able to intervene in the future revolutionary storms.

4 - The semi-developed capitalist countries and Australasia

Revolutionary events will not be restricted to the advanced industrial world. In fact, the already calamitous economic and social situation in Africa, large parts of Asia, and Latin America will be enormously aggravated by a new recession or slump. The Asian crisis has already had an effect on many of the 'undeveloped' countries.

The oil producers, led by OPEC, have already been forced to slash production from "over-supplied world oil markets". This comes just six months after OPEC had approved a 10% production increase. The price of oil has dropped by about a third in the first five months of 1998. In real terms, the oil price is now lower than it was before the first oil crisis of 1973-74. The Independent newspaper in Britain estimates that the real drop in oil prices is even greater than admitted; 'Arab Light' has dropped in price from $19 to $9 a barrel in June 1998. It comments: "If the oil price had doubled, think what a story that would have been." Indeed, when there was a dramatic increase in oil prices in 1974 and then in 1979, the bourgeoisie of the West screamed that the oil producers were "holding them to ransom". Now when the oil price is halved, in the words of the British Independent, "most of us have hardly noticed".

But the collapse in the price of oil is just part of the general drop in commodity prices which is already exercising a big depressionary effect on the majority of the 'undeveloped' world. This is not a new problem. The concentration on commodity production, either through food, fuel, metals, diamonds, etc., automatically meant that the economically dominant countries of the advanced industrial world have been able to impose brutally unequal terms of trade. The 'undeveloped' world supplied cheap commodities and received back dear manufactured goods; in the words of Marx, they got "less labour for more labour". It is true that in the 1950s and 1960s the rise of some commodity prices, noticeably oil, fed through into higher per capita incomes and more money for health, education and infrastructure. The struggle between imperialism, particularly US imperialism, on the one side, and Stalinism on the other, allowed the bourgeoisie and the emerging bourgeoisie of the ex-colonial world to balance between the two camps. This led to a certain increase in incomes, which fed through into the development of the economy and, in the words of the Guardian in Britain, "still left something to be gleaned off into Swiss bank accounts".

However, the 1970s, 1980s and 90s, have seen commodity prices slump sharply so that "they are now lower in real terms than during the Great Depression of 70 years ago". (The British Guardian) Non-fuel prices reached depressionary levels in 1992-93 and have, in fact, halved in price since 1980. Metal and agricultural prices have dropped by a quarter from their 1995 highs while, as mentioned, energy prices have fallen dramatically.

Superimposed on the long-term decline of the drop in commodity prices has now come the Asian crisis. Asia, up until recently, accounted for two-thirds of the increase in world petroleum consumption between 1992-96, raising Asia's share of world petroleum consumption from 12% to 15%. Base metals, rubber, grains, fats and oils showed similar trends. Other factors, such as the relatively warm winters in the northern hemisphere and increased crop production, have acted to depress prices. This, in turn, has had a beneficial effect on cutting inflation in the advanced industrial world, and is one of the factors in the so-called economic 'paradigm' in the US of low inflation, low unemployment, etc.

However, a terrible price has been paid by the peoples and countries of the underdeveloped world who are dependent upon commodities, sometimes on a single commodity. At least 25 countries are dependent on petroleum for a fifth or more of their foreign exchange earnings. These include Russia, Nigeria, and several Latin American countries, as well as the familiar Middle East producers. Income from petroleum is vital for maintaining government spending which, in turn, accounts for the feeding of big sections of already impoverished populations. Moreover, falling copper prices have had a catastrophic effect on Zambia and led to a deterioration in the conditions of Chile and Mongolia.

These blows come against the background of a worsening cycle of deprivation, hunger and poverty in the underdeveloped world. The figures of the United Nations on poverty in the underdeveloped world have become familiar. About a quarter of the world's population - some 1.3 billion people - are living on incomes of less than a dollar a day; nearly a billion are illiterate; some 840 million go hungry or are living from hand to mouth. Moreover, whereas those lucky enough to live in the developed West can expect to live until they are almost 80, nearly one third of the people in the least developed countries are not expected to survive to 40.

The chasm between rich and poor is growing ever wider. The share of the poorest 20% of the world people in global income stands at a paltry 1.1%; down from 1.4% in 1991 and 2.3% in 1960. The income of the top 20% was 30 times higher than the poorest 20% in 1960; by 1991 it was 61 times higher. The UN says the latest figures put it at 78 times as high.

Crushing debt problem

Superimposed on this situation, and further dragging them down, is the crushing weight of the debt burden on these countries. The "gangrene of debt" has once again suddenly leapt back into the headlines of the bourgeois press in the West. All kinds of liberals, in the old sense of the term, have denounced the "new slavery" of Africa, Asia and Latin America. The debts of these areas of the world to the West have soared from $600bn in 1980 to $2.2tr today. This is accounted for not just by increased loans to the underdeveloped world during the 1980s but by the huge increase in interest rates which has massively inflated repayments and acts to suffocate the countries affected. Guyana, a former British colony, typifies the situation. Out of every £1 it earns, it pays 45p to bankers and northern treasuries. In the past, Guyana was considered to be 'unstable' by imperialism. The British bourgeoisie, by a combination of gerrymandering and military intervention, secured the removal of Cheddi Jaegan and his People's Progressive Party, which was threatening the nationalisation of important assets in the 1950s. After the collapse of Stalinism, Guyana is now ruled by Jaegan's widow and the PPP, which is now pro-market and Guyana is a model of financial rectitude. It has carried out the IMF's austerity programme for the last 12 years. The IMF official responsible for Guyana says that the IMF prescription is like when you "take antibiotics. You must follow the whole course. It doesn't help to stop." Yet after 12 years of "antibiotics" Guyana has repaid $1,700m without repaying a single cent of the original capital. This 'success story', that is for the capitalists, has left 45% of the population below the poverty line. Moreover, the IMF man admits,"Guyana will never pay its debt".

The figures of the debt burden, when broken down into individual countries and continents and set against the colossal wealth of the rich in the West, are mind boggling. If African countries did not have to repay their debt, the money released would save the lives of about 21 million children by the year 2000 and provide 90 million girls and women with access to basic education. Rupert Murdoch's wealth, on the other hand, is estimated at $4bn, the same as the debt of Lebanon. The 1,000 richest people in Britain have a combined wealth of $175bn - more than the entire $150bn debt of all south Asia, and almost as much as Brazil's $179bn. The debt burden of the 'developing' countries is 94% of their entire annual economic output! The current IMF 'rescue package' for Indonesia approximates to the estimated wealth of the Suharto family. Moreover, 95% of the country's foreign debt - of some $800bn - is owed by 50 individuals, not the 200 million Indonesians who end up suffering the costs. Invariably, loans from the West have been linked to increased access for western firms, arms procurement programmes, etc. Although it is claimed that world military expenditure has decreased, the elite, some of them in the most underdeveloped and semi-developed countries, have been eager buyers of weapons from the West in order to bolster their positions. Of the ten most indebted countries, eight have suffered civil war or violent conflict since 1990. Of the 25 most indebted countries, 15 are 'conflict countries'.

With the resources of the semi-developed countries being squandered, disease and famine are on the increase. Tuberculosis, for instance, is the single biggest infectious killer of young women worldwide. More than one million women between the ages of 14 and 55 will die of it, and 2.5 million will become ill from the disease this year alone, according to the World Health Organisation. British Guardian reporter, Maggie O'Kane, has written searing reports on 'the Grazer', a disease which attacks the muscles, tissues and bones of those it affects. She wrote of the effect of this disease on children in Niger. The pressure of debt repayments means that the public purse is empty. Salaries have not been paid for three months, the hospitals have no wages to pay their doctors and nurses. Every year eighty thousand children in Niger will die because there is no antiseptic cream and mouthwash to fight the Grazer. Just under half-a-million children are scheduled to die in Niger before the year 2000, according to Oxfam...Given the size of the population, that is the equiva-lent of three million children dying in Britain from curable diseases...Niger owes Britain £8m ($13 m)...The country pays £750,000 a year to Britain. If Britain canceled the debt for the millennium, the money saved would be enough to inoculate 750,000 children against killer diseases. One doctor commented: "In the last five years I have seen the number of children dying from infectious diseases related to malnutrition creeping up from around 30% to 50%. It's getting worse."

Little wonder that 70,000 people protested at the recent G8 summit in Birmingham, England, demanding the lifting of the debt incubus from the backs of the poorest nations on the globe. But their pleas have not softened the stone hearts of the bourgeoisie who dismissed them as "soft in the heart, and soft in the head". They are not opposed to a certain mitigation of 'debt relief', but any idea that the debt should be repudiated, that the indebted countries should simply refuse to pay, is met with threats and predictions that the world would be brought to its knees. Indebted countries must demonstrate a 'sustained performance' before relief is at hand. Tell that to Guyana which has taken the 'medicine' for 12 years and finds itself in a much worse situation. One bourgeois commentator declared: "Unfortunately, having one's heart in the right place says little, or nothing, about the state of one's head. The plight of the world's poorest people cannot be explained by the debt their countries owe. They were desperately poor before the money was borrowed; they remain poor because they wasted the money; and even today they receive far more money than they pay out." The latter is a blatant lie, but the philosophy of international capital is the "poor have always been with us, and always will be".

Increased imperialist exploitation

Indeed, western capitalism, rather than lifting the burdens, is intending to impose new ones on the semi-developed and underdeveloped countries, particularly on those countries that have been brought further to their knees by the economic situation. Even a House of Commons committee in Britain has accused the European Commission of introducing measures, 'Fortress Europe', which will enormously aggravate the problems of the 'Third World'. There are plans to replace the Lomé Convention, which allowed favourable access to European goods for 71 African, Caribbean and Pacific (ACP) countries. Most of these were former colonies of European powers. But this agreement will expire in the year 2000 and any new agreement must fit in with the tougher new rules set up by the World Trade Organisation (WTO), which is - like the World Bank and IMF - a tool of western imperialism.

The WTO frowns upon 'special deals' for particular countries. This has produced the catastrophe for the banana-growing islands of the Caribbean which, by diktat of the WTO, has resulted in them being denied access to Europe's markets. The European Commission is proposing that 'developing countries' should set up regional free-trade areas, which would then enter into an agreement with the EU. But this, in turn, would allow the opening of the markets of these countries to European goods which, according to the Commons committee, would "devastate their fledgling economies". It sums up the situation: "To put the matter crudely, ACP countries will have a choice of either opening up their markets to EU products or suffering an increase in taxes on their exports to the EU. This threat was tantamount to blackmail." At the same time, the Commons committee shows naivety, to say the least, when it argues, "It is immoral for the EU to misuse its economic strength to dictate clearly unfavourable terms [to the developing countries]."

But there is nothing new in this. When it serves its purpose, European capitalists dispense with 'free trade'. For instance, Europe's big farms and the sale of agricultural goods, are protected, and kept artificially high by the maintenance of high tariff walls which protect them from the cheaper agricultural products of developing countries. The proposal to replace the Lomé Agreement with the WTO measures, have been compared to a "battering ram for free trade, forcing the infant industries of the developing countries into unfair competition with the industrial economies of Europe". In other words, the pattern of the past imperialist domination is set to continue.

If anything, what these facts represent is a new imperialist penetration, which has developed on a massive scale in the aftermath of the collapse of Stalinism. The constraints on imperialism, in competition with the Russian Stalinists in particular, have been shredded. The UN set targets of a miserly 0.7% of GDP to be channelled to 'developing nations' as a lever for transforming their situation. Only about five countries actually meet the 0.7% target on aid. Clinton on his visit to Africa, bluntly stated that "trade must replace aid". And yet, as we have seen, the unequal terms of trade mean that the underdeveloped countries will be further punished by the economic giants of the West. Under GATT (the General Agreement on Tariffs and Trade), the WTO, and all the battery of imperialist restrictions, increased barriers to trade are actually put in the way of the underdeveloped countries competing on a level playing field with the monopolies in the West.

And the bourgeoisie in the former colonial and semi-colonial world have collaborated in forging new chains for Africa, Asia and Latin America. The bourgeoisie in these countries have been incapable of carrying through to a completion tasks of the bourgeois democratic revolution. (We do not include here the newly-industrialised countries, which cannot be fully included in the underdeveloped world. However, many of these countries are 'semi-colonial' because of the crushing economic weight of the advanced industrial countries, which limits, restricts and stultifies the development of their national economies.) A thoroughgoing land reform, the solution of the national problem and the genuine unification of many of these countries have not been carried through - nor is this possible on a bourgeois basis.

The role of the working class

The CWI needs to reaffirm the central role of the working class in the revolutionary storms which loom in the underdeveloped world. The collective consciousness and capacity to struggle as a class allows it to play the leading role in the revolutionary process and lays the basis for the building of socialism.

The composition of the working class internationally has changed in geographic and gender terms as a result of the industrialisation of the "developing countries". In these countries women make up 31% of the labour force. In many of the industrialised countries there will be as many women working as men by the year 2000. The global capital of the 80s and 90s has sought out a cheap female workforce. 80%

of those employed in the export processing zones in South East Asia are women. The capitalists have reverted to a pre-industrial mode of production: home working. 90% of those who produce goods in the homes are women. The recruitment of women into the workforce does not automatically mean better rights. In Europe figures show that most new jobs go to women, but what kind of jobs are they? Women only make up one third of the full-time jobs in Europe - the rest are part time, casual etc. But the entrance of women into the production process gives them collective strength.

The 'urban poor', which often constitute an important layer within the cities, despite often being able to play an important part in the mass struggle, are not able to assume the leading role of the organised working class.

In Asia, Africa and Latin America a massive crisis has developed in agriculture that has already provoked big movements amongst the peasantry and rural workers. The massive movement of the MST in Brazil illustrates this process. It is important to realise that in many areas of the world the peasantry of today does not resemble the totally isolated and inward looking sector that it did in the past. There is far more contact and interchange with the cities. This has partially broken down the isolation of rural sectors of society and linked them more with the working class. If armed with a revolutionary socialist programme this process will make it easier for the proletariat to win the support of the poor and middle layers of peasantry and rural workers.

Guerrillaism, which is in general the traditional method of the radicalised peasantry, can also come back onto the agenda. The 1990s has witnessed the demise in Latin America of guerrilla movements, with the exception of a few countries, like Colombia, Mexico, etc. In Africa, given the weakness of the proletariat, guerrillaism can develop as a manifestation of mass discontent with dictatorial, unstable regimes, as the Congo demonstrates.

In the competition between Stalinism and imperialism in the post-1945 situation, reinforced by the world economic upswing of 1950-75, the bourgeoisies of these countries were able to play a relatively independent role. But the collapse of Stalinism led to the bourgeoisie of the underdeveloped world going over completely to the market. Lavish promises were made that Latin America and Asia, in particular, would escape from their cycle of economic weakness, poverty, mass unemployment, and degradation. That promise, however, has turned to ashes, particularly in the wake of the Asian meltdown.

The bourgeoisie of the former colonial and semi-colonial countries in the course of the 1990s has, in effect, become a broker for imperialism. It is mainly a transmission mechanism for the programme, policies and ideology of imperialism. Countries like Ghana, led by Jerry Rawlings, once 'Africa's Castro', have moved from 'socialistic' measures to firmly 'market orientated' regimes. The prospect was held out that Ghana would become the Tiger of West Africa, while Uganda would become the Tiger of East Africa. While not as seriously affected as other parts of Africa, Ghana has, nevertheless, not managed to escape from the economic domination of imperialism. Its problems are those of all African countries to one degree or another.

The turn towards the market has been shown to be a failure. The new imperialist penetration, the buying up of already weakened domestic industry on the cheap, as a consequence of the worsening of the economic situation, will lead to a revolt from below. The growth of an anti-imperialist mood, sometimes initially taking the form, in countries like Indonesia and even Japan, of "an anti-foreigner" attitude will compel a change of tactics on the part of the national bourgeoisie in many of the countries in the underdeveloped world. The demand for action to be taken against foreign capital, alongside the intervention of the state in the form of the nationalisation of failing industries, can grow enormously. Above all, the demand for the cancellation and repudiation of the debt can develop into hurricane proportions. This accounts for the concern expressed in the media in the West.

At the same time, learned articles have appeared showing how 'impractical' are proposals to cancel the debt. Yet radical figures, like Noam Chomsky, have pointed out that Britain, France and Italy defaulted on US debts in the 1930s: "Washington 'forgave (or forgot)', as the Wall Street Journal reported." Moreover, Hitler, when he came to power in 1933, repudiated Germany's foreign debts. More recently, Mexico in 1982 repudiated its debt, which compelled US imperialism to step in and bailout the Mexican economy. Any other course could have triggered a worldwide economic financial crisis and, above all, the Mexican economy would have plunged, resulting in millions of Mexicans pouring over the border into the USA itself, with the social and political instability that would have meant for the US.

Fearful that there is now a real possibility of the debts being repudiated not just by one but a series of countries, the West has developed a new line of argument. They now argue that it will not be the bankers or financiers in New York, Tokyo, London and Frankfurt who will pay for any cancellation of the debt but the workers and middle class of the advanced industrial world. It is true that it is the workers and the middle class, through the imposition of increased state taxes, who pay for the 'mistakes' of the banks and finance houses in the advanced world. But this should not dissuade either the workers and peasants in the underdeveloped world or the masses in the advanced industrial countries from demanding that the 'pound of flesh', in the form of debt, extracted from the underdeveloped world should be immediately cancelled.

But the workers of the world should go further than this and demand that it should be the financiers and big business who should pay the price for their blunders, and not the workers themselves. Our slogan in the underdeveloped world has got to be the immediate cancellation of the debt. In the advanced industrial countries it should be, 'no increased taxes to pay for debt cancellations', 'for the nationalisation of the banks'.

The suffering of Africa

No continent has suffered more than Africa from the unequal relationship between the advanced and the underdeveloped world. The debt trap and the incapacity of capitalism to develop the colossal natural potential of the continent are the key issues. Measured in dollars, the output of Africa south of the Sahara is less than that of Switzerland! In the words of the Wall Street Journal: "Who cares if Africa has fallen off the edge of the global marketplace? With the end of the Cold War it has lost its strategic significance... it is too poor to matter... Africans do not have the money to buy Coca-Cola. They lack the education and the use of Windows. The continent cannot pay its debts... Save for the beacon at its southern tip, it is a place best left to mercenaries and missionaries."

The statistics are horrifying and are getting worse. Annual income per head stands at less than $500. In the advanced industrial rich countries of Europe, US and Japan, the average is nearly $26,000. Mortality rate for children under five is 147 per 1,000. In the advanced industrial countries the comparable figure is 7. Of the 32 low income countries officially classified as severely indebted, 25 lie in sub-Saharan Africa. Outstanding debt of these countries is $140bn, representing more than three-quarters of their annual income. They spend more than four times as much on debt servicing than health. It is in Africa that diseases like tuberculosis, yaws and yellow fever are widespread, mainly as a result of the poverty that exists.

Despite the acres of newsprint bewailing the 'inadequacies' of Africa to 'help itself' it is imperialism and the weak native bourgeoisie of Africa who are responsible for the growing disease, the great army of the poor, and the terrible wars which have ravaged the continent. Seven countries are still experiencing war or 'destabilisation': Angola, Rwanda, Burundi, Uganda, Sudan, Eritrea and Ethiopia. The almost million who died in Rwanda's genocide dwarfs the numbers who were massacred in the ethnic conflict in Bosnia. It was imperialism that invaded, plundered the continent, carved out spheres of influence, and eventually countries, which cut across the living bodies of tribes and peoples. They therefore left a legacy, a time-bomb for future tribal and ethnic conflict which, with the worsening of the economic situation, has now exploded throughout the continent.

Even bourgeois commentators note that the mind-numbing poverty in Sierra Leone has been almost incidental while the 'ethical foreign policy' of the Blair government has been subject to endless discussion in the British media. Yet in Sierra Leone, which is a former British colony, economic and social chaos has been endemic for a long time. At $200, its per capita income is now less than half the shameful average for sub-Saharan Africa as a whole. Life expectancy is less than 40 years. But it is not just imperialism but the African bourgeoisie who have completely failed the 700 million people throughout the continent. The plight of Zambia demonstrates this clearly. It was one of the more favourably situated countries in southern Africa. It was a very 'prosperous' (for the whites) colony of British imperialism. Its wealth was founded on the mining and sale of 'red gold', copper. The development of a black proletariat led, in turn, to the foundation and consolidation of a relatively strong trade union movement. After winning independence from Britain in 1964, and ruled by Kaunda, the Zambian bourgeoisie failed to completely break the stranglehold of imperialism. On the contrary, it became even more dependent on copper which, since the late 1970s, fell in price. In the 1990s it has hit catastrophic levels because of the growing use of fibre optic cables, and other factors, where copper is not needed.

The general drop in commodity prices, dealt with earlier, has also had a decisive effect. Now, freshly mined copper is being illegally traded within Zambia at prices lower than European rag-and-bone men get for scrap metal. This illegal trading is "arguably now the most dynamic economic sector in this nation of ten million people" (The Guardian, Britain, 14 May 1998). With the plunge in the price of copper have gone the jobs and living standards of the masses. This has been enormously aggravated by the coming to power of the government of Frederick Chiluba, who once headed the Zambian trade union movement.

Under the whip of international capital, Chiluba has enthusiastically embraced the 'market' in place of Kaunda's 'socialism'. Kaunda, like many of the bourgeois regimes in the underdeveloped world, under the pressure of the situation nationalised sections of industry, such as copper, but maintained the general framework of capitalism. Chiluba, under the whip of international capital, has engaged in a huge privatisation programme since he came to power in 1991. In fact, the World Bank made the sale of Zambian Consolidated Copper Mines (ZCCM) a precondition for loans. Privatisation is synonymous with redundancy. As workers lose their jobs, poverty is increased. Now 98% of the population live on less than $2 a day. Moreover, Zambia is crippled by its debt burden - now $7bn - and by the 'structural adjustment targets' of the World Bank. Chiluba's programme involves selling off state enterprises to the highest imperialist bidders; it represents a return back to the open imperialist control of the past. In the process, Chiluba and his coterie of ministers are skimming off the best privatisations for themselves. Even workers with jobs will lose the free schools and hospitals that have existed up to now. Kaunda's 'state capitalism' was a failure, but the return to the market has been an absolute disaster. The idea of socialism, which in general has been off the agenda through the recent travails of the workers and peasants of Africa, typified by Zambia, will come back in the next period.

Africa's feeble ruling classes

The weak African bourgeoisie has failed and is more dependent on imperialism than ever. Between 1985 and 1995 the public external debt climbed from $90bn to more than $200bn. Yet the myth of an African renaissance through the market and under the benediction of imperialism has been built up by the recent visits of Clinton and French President Chirac to Africa. These visits have been conditioned by a growing realisation by the international strategists of capital that the complete neglect of Africa could have 'unforeseen consequences' for them in the future.

The stark contrast between sub-Saharan Africa and East Asia has been highlighted in the past period. Average per capita income in Africa halved, in relative terms, from 14% of the industrial countries' level in 1966 to 7% in 1995. On the other hand, before the recent crisis, Asia's newly industrialised economies increased per capita income from 18% to 66% of industrial countries' level. Even if the miserly 1% growth per year in per capita incomes in sub-Saharan Africa continued they would be no higher in 2006 than in 1982, and 5% lower than in 1974. Even in the most favourable circumstances of growth, the coming decade would see Africa only recover the ground lost over the last 20 years. Moreover, in recent years sub-Saharan Africa's share of global foreign direct investment has been very small and declining - down to 3.3% of all developing country inflows in the mid-1990s from 6% in the latter half of the 1980s. At the same time, the lion's share of investment goes to a tiny number of African countries: Angola, Nigeria, Ghana and South Africa. This is largely for the exploitation of Africa's natural resources, principally in mining and oil. Mass revolt, which is inevitable on the basis of these conditions, will mean a rejection of capitalism and a searching for the alternative, socialism.

Clinton's visit was a 'wake-up call' to the world bourgeoisie. At the same time, its purpose was to open up Africa even more to the insatiable search for profits and markets of the imperialist firms of the West. Clinton took with him the largest entourage of US businessmen to have ever visited Africa. He noted that US trade with the region was already 20% bigger than with the countries of the former Soviet Union and declared, "I hope they're listening back home. The average annual return on investment in Africa is 30%. That's a good deal, folks." We would clearly condemn such super exploitation of the masses of the underdeveloped world and the imposition of neo-liberal policies as a precondition for investment

Remorseless pressure is being exerted on all the countries of Africa to dismantle state industries and to open up 'markets'. This usually means the dismantling of the very limited protective measures these countries have had. Even South Africa, the strongest economy in Africa, has been subjected to relentless pressure to dismantle 'inefficient restrictions' and sell off state industries. The collapse of the rand and the flight of capital from South Africa, which are problems that other 'emerging markets' have experienced, have been used to step up the pressure of the South

African and world bourgeoisie for further privatisations. The head of the Anglo-American conglomerate put the position bluntly: "There is no other choice in today's internationalising and deregulating world but to commit to the bold implementation of this policy." The spokesperson denounced the "slow pace of privatisation" and also "the government's proposed labour legislation".

Pressure of the masses - South Africa, Zimbabwe...

However, against a background of an official 30% unemployment (in reality, much higher than this), the pro-capitalist ANC government's programme has completely failed. It has envisaged that the real output growth would be 6%, yet last year it reached only 1.7%. With the population expanding at 2% a year, per capita income is falling. The ANC government has replaced its reformist Reconstruction and Development Programme (which was supposed to provide the masses with housing, jobs and education) with the neo-liberal GEAR (Growth, Employment And Redistribution) strategy. The ANC government has relied on the tripartite Alliance of itself, the SACP (South African Communist Party), and COSATU (Congress of South African Trades Unions) to hold back the working class from struggling for better conditions. Amongst the best worker activists there is uniform opposition to GEAR, which they see as being responsible for privatisation, retrenchments, and falling living standards. In reality the leadership of the SACP and COSATU have no alternative to the policies of their pro-capitalist ANC partners. However, because of pressure from below they have to express verbal opposition to GEAR. They have even organised some national action against GEAR and intend to organise a national day of action on September 23, 1998. But this is not part of a serious strategy to defeat GEAR, merely an attempt to allow workers to 'let off steam."

The scene is set for the break up of the Alliance. At a recent SACP conference Mandela informed its members: "Stay in the Alliance and toe the line or get out and campaign as a separate party with all that implies." Thabo Mbeki, South African President-in-waiting, followed this by questioning whether the Alliance should continue at all. Paradoxically, it is the COSATU and SACP leaders who are desperate for the Alliance to continue, for fear of being cast into the wilderness, as they see it. Under the hammer blows of events, particularly the worsening economic situation of South Africa, the trade unions will be compelled to come out under their own banner and separate from the government. This may happen prior to the next general election, scheduled for 1999, but the pressure of the masses on COSATU will either compel it to become much more radical or new forces will move to take its place. In any event, the question of an independent workers' party will re-emerge in South Africa in the next period.

The same is also true in other countries, such as Zimbabwe. The 18-year regime of Mugabe has been rocked with massive demonstrations of students followed by two days of rioting in January 1998, with the chaos and violence that followed. The main opposition comes from the trade unions. There has been outrage at the Mugabe government's increases in taxes to fund those connected with the ruling ZANU (PF) party. The trade unions staged a one-day general strike in December 1997 and then a two-day strike in March. The trade union leaders are considering more extended general strike activity which incensed Mugabe and led to a gang of his thugs beating up the Secretary General of the Zimbabwe Congress of Trade Unions (ZCTU).

The workers and peasants of Zimbabwe were encouraged in their opposition by the movement against the Indonesian dictatorship. Their banners read: 'After Suharto, it's one down, two to go.' They were referring to Mugabe and Malaysia's Mahathir Mohamed. The former 'Marxist', Mugabe, has enjoyed (along with his wife) a lifestyle that rivals any other African dictator. Two weeks after the January food riots, Mugabe put forward a proposal for free cars, air travel, entertainment, and bodyguards and staff for life for himself, his family and his two vice-presidents. This is against a background where the wholesale price of a sack of mealie-meal, the staple diet of the mass of Zimbabweans, is $147.

Loss of jobs, evictions from homes, lack of opportunities for the youth, is a powerful cocktail which is preparing the ground for the removal of Mugabe. Attempting to mollify the anger of the masses, Mugabe promised to take some of the land away from the 80,000 whites who still own the best farming lands. One thousand five hundred white farms have been scheduled to be handed over to blacks, most of them former fighters for ZANU(PF) in the guerrilla war almost two decades ago. However, these measures are unlikely to still the opposition of the masses whose placards have read: 'Mugabe, you're now irrelevant, go and rest, old man.'

The attempt to carve out new spheres of influence is not the preserve of Clinton and US imperialism. The US has increasingly stepped into the vacuum vacated by France in West Africa. France has been compelled to abandon its role as the mini-policeman of Africa and has devalued the CFA - the common currency - in the region. Irked by the role of the US in West Africa, Chirac has turned to the economically weightier region of southern Africa. The British Financial Times commented: "Commercial and economic interests appear to dominate the switch in policy but France also wants to respond to increasing US influence in Africa."

Dropping a policy of propping up the dictators in the Congo, Rwanda and elsewhere, Chirac lauds 'democracy' and declares that "France wants to open itself and create new partnerships with southern Africa".

However, these fine words must be set against the continued sanctions and restrictions placed on the entry of African exports to the markets in the West. The trade bill being discussed in the US Congress has as its stated purpose to open US markets to African exports. But there are heavy preconditions that the US has set for such privileged treatment. The US pharmaceutical companies are objecting to South

Africa's practice of allowing cheap medicines to patients because this allegedly undermines their 'patent rights'.

Bending the knee to imperialism

Yet despite some clashes between the African bourgeois regimes and imperialism, the trend is clearly towards a further bending of the knee to capital, and an incapacity to solve either the problems of each country or the continent as a whole. This applies as much to the so-called 'new leadership' which has emerged and has pushed the old guard into retirement. This is as true of Museveni in Uganda, hailed until recently as the leader of the new 'African tiger' as it is to the increasingly discredited Mugabe and the late Mobutu. Museveni, in particular, has played a key role with the blessing of Washington in Rwanda and also in the triumph of Kabila in Zaire, now the Congo. These 'new leaders' have "ditched Marxism in favour of structural adjustment", have told imperialist institutions in the West that they would dictate the pace of development. However, Uganda has seen its growth rate fall from 7% to 5% as the infrastructural limitations of the economy and increased corruption have taken their toll.

Moreover, Museveni's attempt to play a dominant regional role has begun to excite the opposition of the West. His troops intervened in Rwanda in 1994, helped Kabila to oust Mobutu and is now considering intervention, if only by proxy, to topple the Islamic government in Sudan. However, the consequences of action in Sudan, opens up a very risky situation which could spill over into the whole region of East Africa, in particular.

The aroused expectations following the victory of Kabila in the Congo have been dashed. Faced with the complete collapse of the infrastructure, a virtual absence of roads, and what passes for basic 'civilisation', Kabila's regime is powerless in the face of absolutely horrendous and intractable problems. Instead of a return to 'democracy' Kabila has begun to imitate many of the features of the Mobutu dictatorship. Corruption is rife and Kabila is seen as autocratic. The jails are overflowing with 'trouble makers' who are dealt with by military tribunals and there is a ban on party politics which will only be lifted when elections are held, if they are ever held in the foreseeable period. The plight of the Congo on a bourgeois basis is summed up by the fact that the IMF has even threatened to suspend the Congo should it refuse to honour, by 29 June, the loans built up by the Mobutu regime. Kabila is maintained in power with the military assistance of outside forces and by a government made up of a number of competing factions held together for the time being in an uneasy alliance. Five ministers were recently dismissed because of corruption, which is inevitable and endemic on a bourgeois basis.

Nigeria - a greater disaster

But there is one country, Nigeria, which seemed in the past to be the most favourably placed to succeed on the basis of capitalism. Genuine Marxists long refuted this claim. Now, Nigeria is a by-word for the failure of the 'African experiment'. Second only to South Africa in the sub-Saharan region of Africa, Nigeria's rulers used to refer to it as the "giant of Africa". Its rulers even talked about having a seat in the UN Security Council at a certain stage. But, as the British Financial Times comments: "Burdened by debt, debilitated by corruption and victimised by decades of military mismanagement, Nigeria has long been the symbol of continental failure. Now, under yet another khaki-clad president, it faces the possibility of something much worse: not merely drift but disaster."

Its decline has been spectacular; from an income per head of $1000 in the early 1980s to $230 today. A large part of a total of $300bn of oil revenue has been squandered on grandiose projects or salted abroad into private accounts by a succession of military regimes. It has debts of $35bn and, as bourgeois commentators fear, could slip towards the fate of the former Zaire, the collapse of civil and physical infrastructure and of minimum basics of life. The most favourable perspective held out by bourgeois commentators is that Nigeria could drift on as a 'pariah state' with an impoverished hinterland increasingly detached from an enclave, and still functioning, oil economy.

Once held up as an irrefutable proof of the success of British imperialism's nation building ingenuity, Nigeria, made up of several heterogeneous nationalities and ethnic groups, presently faces the danger of disintegration. Probably for this reason the northern based Hausa-Fulani section of the ruling class, which since independence largely controls the political power and the army, is stoutly opposed to the clamour, mainly from the south, for the convocation of a democratically elected Sovereign National Conference. Such a conference is viewed by its advocates as an assembly to "restructure" the country's foundations. But the northern elite fear that this may be used to break up the country and thus cut it off from the oil, found in the south, which accounts for 80% of government revenues and 90% of foreign exchange earnings. One possibility arising from this scenario is a perspective of the northern section of the ruling class and imperialism seeking to "Keep Nigeria One" at all costs. This can be glimpsed from General Abubakar's "transition programme" rules, which insist that only associations that have "national spread" shall be allowed to operate as political parties. At the same time there is the possibility of a rise in Islamic fundamentalism in the Muslim dominated core north, whose masses are in several respects worse off compared with their southern counterparts, which could have an effect on neighbouring states.

All this has to be set against the optimistic perspectives which opened up for Nigeria at the time of independence. It was expected that the country would become the economic motor force of the continent's growth. However, after a turbulent initial period of civilian rule, the very weak Nigerian bourgeoisie took refuge from the anger of the masses in one military regime after another. It once boasted thriving political parties and "the freest press in black Africa". However, tied overwhelmingly to one commodity - oil - Nigeria's future hinged on an optimistic projection of oil continuing at $40 a barrel. However, the price of oil up until recently was half of this and in the wake of the Asian crisis has collapsed to half again. Therefore, the price of oil is about one quarter of the optimistic projection of Nigeria and other oil producers in the past.

In the wake of this has come economic collapse and increased social tensions, which could not be contained within the framework of 'democracy'. In consequence, Nigeria was saddled with military dictators, the latest of which is General Abubukar, the eighth 'khaki-clad president'. There has been much speculation that Abacha, who died in mysterious circumstances, was in fact murdered. There are the same suspicions over the death of Abiola. One thing is clear, before the death of Abacha the international bourgeoisie was urging concessions from the top in order to prevent a mass explosion from below. Abacha gave no indication that he was prepared to mollify the mass pressure for the return of democratic rights.

The same dilemma, however, confronts Abubukar: to screw down the lid on social protests could ignite an even greater explosion later which, in turn, could spin out of control, leading to the long-predicted break-up of the country. But he also faced the internal dilemma of every military dictatorship, that concessions will open the floodgate on mass protest and that this time it will be impossible to contain. Abubukar was clearly discussing with the jailed Abiola, the victor in the 1993 elections. He obviously promised to release Abiola on condition that he would not claim the presidency but allow 'controlled elections' to go ahead without his participation.

Nigeria is a tinderbox, but one thing is clear: the genie is out of the bottle. A new period has opened up with the masses moving onto the political arena. At the same time, the death of Abiola has resulted in a massive reinforcement of ethnic and nationalist tensions. Nigeria is nearer to a complete fracture than at any time since it secured independence from Britain. Unless the military steps back soon a mass explosion is inevitable, accompanied by separatist movements, which could tear Nigeria apart. It would be difficult, if not impossible, to go back to the same repressive military measures in the immediate period ahead. Therefore, Nigeria is probably in the most favourable position for the development of a mass movement, in which Marxists and the supporters of the CWI will be capable of playing a key role.

Conflicts in the Horn of Africa

On the other hand, events in the Horn of Africa show the utter incapacity of the bourgeoisie in general, or the native bourgeoisie of Africa, to solve even the smallest border disputes. Their power, prestige and strategic interests take precedence over the interests of the peoples in the region.

On the one side, the clash between Ethiopia and Eritrea over a tiny stretch of border could result in war between two of Africa's poorest countries. On the other hand, behind what appears to be a meaningless conflict are serious issues touching on the interests of both countries and particularly those of the ruling classes. The roots of the conflict lie in Ethiopian history but particularly in recent history. Ethiopia was a Christian empire, dominated by rival highland peoples, the Tigreans and Amaras. Throughout the 19th century it expanded to include other ethnic groups - some Christian, some Muslim, some neither - but the Amaras came out on top.

However, the core of the present government is Tigrean. This was the group which dominated the movement which overthrew the Dergue. The Dergue was the government, led by Mengistu, which came out of the overthrow of the Emperor Haile Selaisse. It looked towards the Soviet Union with an element of a "planned economy" but on the basis of extreme underdevelopment. It was a one-party totalitarian regime and was incapable of uniting Ethiopia and the different national groups. The famines of the 1980s also undermined the regime, with imperialism consciously using these as a lever to crush the regimes of the Dergue. A struggle unfolded in which the Eritreans, under the leadership of the Eritrean Peoples Liberation Front (EPLF), fought for national independence. They collaborated with the Tigre Peoples Liberation Front (TPLF), the moving force behind Ethiopia's current ruling party. The tanks of the combined force of the EPLF and TPLF rolled into Addis Ababa in 1991. However, the seeds of future conflict existed then. The aspirations of the elite on either side inevitably came to the fore as the basis of a new capitalist class began to take shape.

In 1993 Eritrea was granted independence, albeit reluctantly, by the Ethiopian ruling elite. This meant that Ethiopia was landlocked; its only previous route to the Red Sea being through what is now Eritrea. Within Ethiopia itself there is a conflict between the Amaras, the traditional ruling group of Ethiopia, and the Tigreans who led the struggle to overthrow the Mengistu regime through the TPLF. One bourgeois commentator has drawn the comparison with the overthrow of 'communism' in the former Soviet Union: "Imagine a Soviet Union where communism had been overthrown, not by Russians but by Ukrainians, and where Ukrainians had all the top jobs. That's how Amaras feel about Tigreans."

Therefore, a future conflict between both groups and other ethnic sub-divisions is possible within Ethiopia. However, at the moment the clash with Eritrea seems to have united the peoples of Ethiopia behind the government of Meles Jenawi. The

Amaras were implacably opposed to independence for Eritrea and therefore see the present conflict as a means of striking back. The threat of a war over 150 square miles of territory is absurd but comes after a worsening of relations between the two regimes.

The hopes of building a free trade zone between the two countries has been dashed. Ethiopia was to have duty-free access to the ports of Assab and Massawa. There was even talk of integrating the economies of both poverty stricken countries as a step towards a 'Horn of Africa common market'. Ethiopian traders complained about crippling levels of duty slapped on their goods. The Eritreans hit back accusing Ethiopia of waging 'economic war' on their smaller country. This has fuelled the suspicion that the small economic squabbles were part of a broader political agenda with Addis Ababa, the Ethiopian capital, carrying through an economic blockade: "The Ethiopians want to punish us for daring to go it alone." The smaller Eritrea is much more vulnerable than Ethiopia: 66% of its foreign trade goes to Ethiopia, while only 10% of Ethiopian exports go to Eritrea. And in all of this it is the poverty stricken peoples of the region who suffer.

It is possible that a temporary agreement can be arrived at, but the underlying conflict along with many others in the region will remain. The Eritreans have not just been in conflict with the larger Ethiopia, but with neighbouring Yemen in a dispute over four barren islands in the Red Sea. The suspicion has been fuelled that the Eritreans are being secretly supported by the Israelis who wish to keep the Babal Mandab Straits out of hostile hands. Whether this is true or not, it underlines the absolute incapacity of the bourgeoisie, limited and weak as it is, to overcome the economic, social and national problems which have been inherited from imperialist domination in the past.

The logical solution is for unity, a socialist federation of the region, and beyond this a socialist confederation of the continent of Africa. Only the working class, as small as it is in this region, is capable of advancing such a programme and fighting for its implementation. Therefore, the conclusion that we draw from the situation in Africa is that its great potential, its abundance of natural riches, will not be exploited for the benefit of the 700 million people in the continent. Africa is a living example of the incapacity of capitalist private ownership and the nation state (which is probably more unviable here than in any other part of the world), together with imperialist domination, of developing industry and society for the benefit of the majority of the peoples.

The Middle East

Another region which shows the failure of the world and regional bourgeoisie to solve accumulated historical problems, is the Middle East. Following the Oslo Accords of 1993 and 1995, a new period of peace and prosperity was promised for the region. Yet, if anything, the divide between the Israelis and the Arabs has become even wider. The CWI's perspective that the Oslo agreement represented a betrayal of the national aspirations of the Palestinian people has been completely borne out. Moreover, again as we predicted, the expected beneficial effects from 'huge investments' from outside, particularly from the Arab sheikhdoms, have not materialised. In fact, as they face the effects of their own worsening economic situation, in turn a product of the Asian and the world economic situation, the conditions of the Palestinian people have worsened since Arafat accepted the so-called 'step-by-step' approach towards the establishment of a Palestinian state.

Israel itself has experienced a certain growth but is torn apart by religious divisions which could not only topple the Netanyahu government but produce the greatest divisions since the state was established 50 years ago. Israel has been transformed from a largely agricultural state, with a weak industrial base, into the 'Silicon Valley of the Middle East'. As with other countries, the development of an arms industry has become the handmaiden for the growth of high technology industries. Ironically, it was the arms embargo, particularly applied by the French following the 1967 Six-day War, that forced Israel to develop its arms industry. This was, and remains, an enormous burden on the Israeli economy, swallowing at one stage one-sixth of the national wealth. It produced an unsustainable budget deficit, which culminated in hyper inflation under Mehachem Begin after the 1973 Yom Kippur war. But now this arms industry, 20 years later, has played a key role in the development of a sizeable industrial sector in Israel.

Of course, none of this would have been possible without the annual $1.8bn military subvention from US imperialism and the $500m of private funding from the Jewish population in the US. The early 1990s have seen a quite spectacular growth in production. Between 1990-96, the average growth rate was 5.9% annually. However, this has come to an abrupt halt as the state has been forced to pursue a tighter fiscal and monetary policy. The bombings of Tel Aviv and Jerusalem has meant that tourism - a main source of income - has begun to dry up. Nevertheless, exports from the high technology sector still increased by 35%,, and now represents 64% of total exports. At the time of the foundation of the state in 1948, 99% of exports consisted of oranges.

A decisive factor in the recent development of the economy was the arrival of 750,000 Jewish immigrants from the former Soviet Union in the 1990s. They have been attacked as parasites, with images of doctors sweeping roads and the 'Jewish mafia' buying Jaguar cars "with suitcases of cash". However, the paradox of the situation is that Israel, a client state in the Middle East of the major capitalist and imperialist powers, has benefited enormously from the past human investments made possible on the basis of the planned economy in the Soviet Union. Many of the 'Soviet arrivals' had a very high level of pure science and engineering skills, vital for high-tech industries. As one bourgeois commentator wrote, without their input, a properly trained high-tech workforce "might otherwise have taken a generation to train". What has been Israel's gain has been a loss to the former Soviet Union. It is another example of the crimes of Stalinism which was incapable not only of harnessing the full potential of the plan, but managed to completely alienate the Jewish population and drive them into the hands of the Jewish capitalists.

Crisis of Zionism

At the same time, the original aims of the Zionist pioneers of Israel are disintegrating. Zionism objectively played the role of furthering the aims of imperialism to divide Jew and Arab in the region. It was a movement of colonial conquest, which uprooted and drove a whole people from its traditional homeland. At the same time, it covered its aims with 'socialist' ideology and a 'collectivist approach'. This was harnessed in the Kibbutz movement. However, this was always subject to the laws of capitalism. The tendency towards disintegration of the Kibbutz would, therefore, inevitably be manifested at a certain stage. Last year the Kibbutz movement had to be bailed out of its debts to the tune of $2.05bn. Against the background of a burgeoning capitalist economy, the communal lifestyle is no longer practical and effective and is being abandoned by the new generation.

This went hand-in-hand, as elsewhere, with the bourgeoisie going over to a particularly brutal form of the 'free market'. The Histraduth, a peculiar Zionist relic, which combined the trade unions with some ownership of industry, has been broken up. A massive privatisation programme was introduced and is being pursued with Thatcherite zeal. For instance, the workforce in telecommunications has been cut by 12% and as the Israeli government threatens further privatisations, big redundancies loom. This will inevitably lead to greater class polarisation, which has been an increasing feature of Israeli society in the 1990s. Indeed in 1997 there were important workers' struggles, including a general strike, which mark an historic step forward in developing class struggle.

It is paralleled by the growing opposition to the ultra-orthodox Jews' attempt to transform Israel into a theocratic state. The Netanyahu government only has a majority in the Israeli Knesset because of the 23 seats held by the religious parties. Their ministers in the government have introduced policies that discriminate in favour of ultra-orthodox Jews in housing, for instance, leaving young secular Jews and Israeli Arabs at the bottom of the housing list. Some of the orthodox Jewish groups are a mirror image of the Islamic fundamentalists. Many judges who are secular Jews have received death threats for allegedly being 'too liberal'. There is the rise of mad ultra-nationalist Zionists, one of whose members assassinated Israeli prime minister, Rabin, in 1995. The growing ultra-orthodox political party, Shas, campaigns for the replacement of civil judges and courts by religious judges and rabbinical courts. Young secular Jews are incensed that, while they are compelled to serve in the army, 30,000 orthodox students based in the religious schools can defer military conscription while they are 'studying', which can last for decades! At the same time, decisive sections of the Jewish bourgeoisie who are looking - in the post-Oslo period - hungrily to the new markets they believe they would dominate in the surrounding Arab states, are increasingly opposed to the concessions which the Netanyahu government makes to the religious parties. These help to block off any agreement both with the Palestinians and with neighbouring Arab states.

The divisions amongst the Israelis are mirrored by those that exist amongst the Palestinians and amongst the Arabs in general. Arafat's gamble in accepting the Oslo Accords has failed. He rules a tiny enclave entirely dependent on Israel. Netanyahu has gone back on the promises made by the murdered Rabin and has declared: "Palestinians should have those areas they live on but without a state." His government is prepared to offer half of the West Bank but only 8-10% of 'historic Palestine' to the Palestinians. This is totally unacceptable to even the compromised Arafat, never mind to the mass of the Palestinians and Arab people.

"Peace Process" dead

US capitalism, in collaboration with the EU, attempted at the London conference in May to force Netanyahu to accept a plan under which Israel would cede complete control of 18.2% of the West Bank to the Palestinians over 12 weeks. At the moment, Palestinian forces currently control only 3%. Even if Netanyahu is prepared to move he will not accept the US's proposals, and any concessions by him would probably mean the downfall of his government and either its replacement by a Labour government or, what seems more likely, a coalition between Netanyahu's Likud and Labour. It would go hand-in-hand with the establishment of an American, Palestinian and Israeli committee to discuss "combating terrorism" - a demand Israel has made since it has faced Islamic fundamentalist suicide bombers aimed against Israeli targets. In addition, Arafat must publish a presidential decree forbidding incitement against Israelis. The Palestinians are also required to approve a law banning the possession of private firearms and to give the Israelis a list of Palestinian policemen, a measure aimed at reducing their number.

But at the moment rather than concessions, Netanyahu has moved in the opposite direction, ratifying new Israeli settlements in the West Bank, the extension of settlements in Jerusalem, etc. The leverage which US imperialism has over the Israeli government is weakened by the domestic position of Clinton and the pressure exerted by the six million Jews in the US in the run-up to the mid-term Congressional elections. In addition to this, there is growing opposition to Arafat, and not just on the failure of the Oslo Accords (Netanyahu has already declared the peace process "dead"). There is also vocal criticism from within Arafat's own Fatah movement - which controls 60 of the 88 seats in the Palestinian Legislative Council - against the growing corruption and repression of his regime.

Without any further concessions, the Palestinian and Arab masses will explode. "The second intifada is coming and it will be bigger than the first. This time it will be with guns," declared a Palestinian youth to a bourgeois reporter. But a new conflict will not be just between the Palestinians and the Israelis. Already within Israel, one million Bedouin Arabs - one-sixth of the population and, up to now, relatively docile - have threatened massive strike action over the demolition of their houses and traditional grazing areas by the Israelis. There has been no halt to the expansion of Jewish settlements, no end to confiscation of land or resident identity cards in Jerusalem, no end to the demolition of Palestinian homes and no Israeli troop redeployment from the West Bank.

Little wonder then that the fundamentalists have grown, with Hamas enjoying an estimated 40% support amongst the Palestinian population. Even George Habas, leader of the Popular Front for the Liberation of Palestine (PFLP), has linked up with Hamas in a new 'Palestinian Front'. Promises have been made to "confront Israel with all possible means". Clashes have developed between Arafat supporters and Hamas where the latter's leaders have declared: "We don't want to fight the PA [the Palestinian Authority]... if we fight it could lead to a civil war. This is what Israel wants." But the incipient civil war amongst Palestinians could break out into the open if the situation continues without any concession to Palestinian fears in the next period.

It is highly unlikely that the Netanyahu government will be able to hold onto power. If it falls, it could either be replaced by a Labour government or by a new national government, including the Israeli Labour Party. In fundamentals, the Labour Party does not disagree with most of Netanyahu's approach to the Palestinians. Its leader, Ehud Barak, has declared that it would establish 'red lines'. This means Jerusalem would remain under Israeli control; there would be no return to pre-1967 borders; no modern armed forces west of the Jordan river; and "most of the Jewish settle-ments in few big blocks, but not necessarily all the isolated settlements, would stay under Israeli 'sovereignty'." He generously declared that while he would not "care if they [the Palestinians] established their own state", the provision would be "it had no modern air force or surface-to-air missiles".

War and economic crisis

There are other military strategists within Israel, who speculate that a new war leading to a partial defeat of Israel is the precondition for a 'realistic' mood to develop in Israel. Above all, they calculate, the influence of the religious parties must be broken. It is not excluded, however, that Arafat, who is the main prop for imperialism, and Israel, could be toppled. Even a Palestinian businessman declared to the British Guardian reporter: "I would give it a year... people will wait to see if a Palestinian state will be declared. If there is no state, then maybe there will be no Palestinian Authority and Hamas will take over." Any attempt to resort to repression of Hamas would result in it going underground and in all probability a 'dual struggle' being conducted both against the Israeli military and the troops of the Palestinian Authority.

Any new conflict between Palestine and Israel would be against the background of a more volatile situation throughout the Middle East. Even the seemingly unshakeable Saudi Arabia has been seriously affected by the drop in the price of oil and the Asian crisis. The latest price for Arab Light, at $9 a barrel, has had a drastic effect. It sells oil now at only $3.42 per barrel, the lowest since 1973. Over the past ten years the annual per capita income of Saudi Arabia has fallen below the level of Latvia. The full magnitude of Saudi Arabia's position is not yet fully felt by its population. The full extent of the Asian crisis has also not yet hit home. A deepening of the recession in Japan will be an even bigger blow to the Saudis than the financial meltdown in South-east Asia. Japan is a major market for Saudi Arabian oil and, therefore, will have a crucial effect on the development of the Saudi economy. The attempt to switch greater exports to the most important oil market in the world, the USA, will come up against fierce competition that already exists there, particularly from oil exports from Venezuela and Mexico. In addition to this, the re-entry of Iraq onto the oil markets is bound to further undermine Saudi Arabia's position.

This will find a reflection in the social situation within Saudi Arabia and the outmoded grip that is exercised by the feudal sheikhdoms. The growing opposition of the Shia population in Saudi Arabia and throughout the Gulf states, combined with the worsening of the economic position of these regimes could result in their overthrow in the next period. This, of course, would threaten the strategic and economic interests of US imperialism who would not hesitate to intervene militarily once more to prevent the coming to power, in particular, of a fundamentalist regime.

Profound changes in Iran

The attraction of fundamentalism has lessened, particularly of radical fundamentalism, in the light of the important developments in Iran. However this does not mean that support for fundamentalism will just evaporate. The worsening of the conditions of the great majority of the population in the Muslim world and the growing hatred of the capitalists of the advanced industrial world, combined with the absence of an alternative from Marxism and the organised labour movement, means the ideas of fundamentalism can retain a grip on the minds of significant sections of the masses. But radical fundamentalism associated with the Iranian revolution has waned.

The US State Department's annual report still declares that Iran "remained the most active state sponsor of terrorism in 1997". It says that it "continued to fund and train known terrorist groups", and that it had conducted at least 13 assassinations abroad. However, Iranian society has undergone profound changes, which, in turn, have weakened the position of the hard-line fundamentalists. The previous president, Rafsanjani, had attempted in two presidential terms from 1989 to shift the country towards a more 'modern' and 'liberal' stance. However, he was continually frustrated by the mullahs who, since the 1979 revolution, have considerable material as well as spiritual interests to defend. In theory, the state still controls 80% of the economy, producing some 5,000 goods and services. But this 'state control' hides the fact that the mullahs and their business supporters run these industries and cream off the benefits for themselves. At the same time, the mood amongst the youth and women has undergone a profound change. The majority of the population is under 25 and the students, in particular, have been to the forefront in the struggle against fundamentalism.

Divisions in ruling Iranian theocracy

The opposition to the mullahs and fundamentalism was reflected in the victory of Khatami in 1997. This represented a huge blow to the ruling theocracy. In previous elections the hardliners had, in effect, been able to fix the vote. But now more than 20 million voters turned out, and with the votes of the youth and women, in particular, elected the 55-year-old cleric. He had previously been ousted from office in 1992 "for permissiveness". On the first anniversary of his election, thousands of university students thronged into Tehran University where Khatami was only able to speak after a 15-minute ovation. In a clear warning to the mullahs he declared: "If religion comes into conflict with freedom, then it will be religion that suffers."

Khatami represents that wing of the theocracy that wishes to bend before the growing mass opposition. Failure to do so is a guarantee that the mullahs will suffer the same fate as the Shah in 1979. On every occasion the masses have chosen the slightest concessions to pour out onto the streets and challenge the regime. During the World Cup, especially following the 2-1 victory of Iran over the 'Great Satan' of the USA, millions poured out into the streets with youth and noticeably young women wearing chadors to the fore. This was not just a demonstration on football, but was a blow against the hardliners. The latter had refused to sanction large screens in the centre of Tehran to broadcast the football because they feared any mass gathering. What an irony of history that a regime that was brought to power by one of the greatest mass movements ever witnessed now fears these very masses.

Khatami reflects the yearning of the majority to throw off the dead hand of the mullahs. He also represents the liberal wing of the Iranian bourgeoisie which realises that the old methods, particularly of fundamentalism, are now outmoded. However, the hardliners will not give up without a struggle. They have looked on, in horror, as Khatami has accepted the establishment of nearly 200 new newspapers and magazines, increasing Iranian dailies by a third. His attempt to lean on the youth has been met with threats to repress mass demonstrations.

The hardliners, with a majority in the Majlis (parliament) seeking to stem the tide, have tried to strike a blow against Khatami by putting one of his supporters, the mayor of Tehran, Karbaschi, on trial, which resulted in a five-year jail sentence. The charge against him was one of corruption. But the trial has blown up in their faces. It has been televised live and has vied with the World Cup in capturing the attention of the masses. Moreover Karbaschi is rumoured to have incriminating files on at least two senior Ayatollahs amongst the hardliners who are, allegedly, up to their necks in corruption. Karbaschi is relatively popular because of the more liberal regime he has employed in Tehran, the protection of dissident rallies, his justification of cinemas screening controversial films. All of this has enhanced the popularity of Khatami and Karbaschi. The ground is clearly being prepared for explosive change in Iran.

Détente with Iran

Internationally, the bourgeoisie has reassessed its approach towards Iran, notwithstanding the US State Department's report quoted earlier. Clinton is reported to want to "make Iran his China", emulating Nixon's historic détente with Beijing. Under pressure from the European Union, Congress has waived sanctions against European companies investing in Iranian oil and gas. The Iranian regime is now firmly orientated towards the bourgeoisie. The Iranian revolution, at one stage, looked as though it might develop in the direction of the complete expropriation of the bourgeoisie and the establishment of a peculiar theocratic 'deformed workers' state'. But that process was halted in the 1980s and went completely into reverse following the collapse of Stalinism. It is only a matter of time before some of the 80% of the economy which theoretically remains in the hands of the state, is privatised. This would certainly happen if the forces behind Khatami completely triumph over the Islamic hardliners.

The attraction of radical Islamic fundamentalism has, therefore, dimmed in the light of these developments. Even Hizbollah, in the Bekar Valley in Lebanon, has sought to adopt a more attractive image, even employing 'spin doctors'. The process will go even further under the pressure of internal events in Iran and the pressure exerted from outside. American companies are frantically urging a change in US policy towards 'constructive engagement', a policy of 'rewards and incentives' to Tehran.

Tehran occupies a key strategic position between a number of major areas. It not only adjoins Iraq and the Persian Gulf, but also the Caspian Sea. And, as the Wall Street Journal has commented, the Caspian region contains potential oil reserves of up to $200bn. Licking its lips, it declared: "The demise of the Soviet Union has opened this pot of gold to the outside world." Therefore, opposition to Iran must be jettisoned in favour of the vital economic and strategic interests of US monopoly imperialism. They have pressed Clinton to by-pass the Iran/Libyan Sanctions Act, which compels the president to impose economic sanctions on foreign companies that invest in Iran's energy sector. Recognising the clear interests of the different camps in Iran, the Wall Street Journal declared that: "Iran has embarked on a historic struggle between those open to the West and those openly hostile to the West". As a sign of its coming rapprochement with the Iranian regime, the US has outlawed the opposition group, the Mujaheddin Al-Kalk (MKO).

An additional reason for drawing closer to Iran is because of the ferocious regional arms race and the threat of increased nuclear proliferation. The US has battled in the past period, probably unsuccessfully, to prevent nuclear material reaching Iran from Yeltsin's Russia. One of the main features of the period ahead will be the developments of economic, political and even military conflicts within the main regional blocks as the various powers struggle to defend their own interests.

While the developments in the Middle East give a picture of increased ethnic and national tension, particularly between Israelis and the Arab masses, it is not the full story. The proletariat is beginning to emerge increasingly under its own banner. This is shown in the first instance in the struggle for independent trade unions, both in the Palestinian areas and amongst the Israeli working class. The bread riots in Jordan in 1997, which shook the Hashimite dictatorship, is also an indication of the growing opposition of the Arab masses to the dictatorial Arab regimes.

The struggle for democracy, jobs and bread is inextricably bound up with the overthrow of capitalism in the Middle East and the establishment of a socialist federation throughout the region. On this basis there could be a blossoming and development of the productive forces to the benefit of the great majority of the ordinary workers and peasants. This would also allow full scope for the establishment of a viable independent Palestinian state, if the Palestinian masses so desired, alongside a state for the Israelis.

On the basis of capitalism, a continuation of war, conflict, and even the threat of the use of nuclear weapons, looms. This danger has become more real in the wake of the nuclear tests of India and Pakistan. Alongside a 'Hindu bomb' and a 'Muslim bomb', there has been a clamour throughout the region in favour of an 'Arab bomb'. Israel already possesses the potential to quickly develop nuclear weapons (if it does not already have them) and the Iranian regime is probably a long way towards emulating them.

'Rogue states' and the bomb

The nuclear tests and rivalry between India and Pakistan, which sent a frisson of horror throughout the world, could set off a mad scramble to acquire a nuclear potential amongst 'rogue' states in completely volatile and unstable areas of the world. These tests have served to highlight a new situation, which the world bourgeoisie is frantically attempting to come to terms with. They highlight the explosive conflict between India and Pakistan on the one side, but above all, between India and China for domination of south Asia. The mad spiral of tit-for-tat tests from unstable regimes, could get completely out of hand and produce unforeseen horrors. The past military doctrine, 'Mutually Assured Destruction' (MAD), did sum up in an insane fashion the balance of power between the major nuclear powers, particularly between US imperialism and Stalinist Russia.

We consistently argued against those who predicted a nuclear holocaust whenever the major powers came into conflict. Given the scale of nuclear weapons on both sides - enough to destroy the world a number of times over - there was no likelihood that one of the major powers would initiate a nuclear attack because this would mean complete destruction for themselves. The capitalists don't go to war for the sake of it, but to acquire markets, materials and prestige. A worldwide nuclear conflict would destroy the productive forces and, above all, the most important productive force, the working class.

We did not rule out the possibility of 'accidental' nuclear explosions or an attack by a minor state on another. In this case, the major powers would even consider a limited retaliation as a quid pro quo. However, even in the case of a 'small' nuclear exchange, the social and political fall-out would be incalculable. Therefore, the five nuclear 'haves' (America, Russia, China, Britain and France, who had each tested a nuclear weapon before 1 January 1967) introduced the Nuclear Proliferation Treaty (NPT) in 1970, which was extended indefinitely in 1995. One hundred and eighty-six states signed the Treaty. They promised to work towards nuclear disarmament, as part of an effort towards general and complete disarmament and the 'have nots' promised not to acquire nuclear weapons on their own, in return for help with their civilian nuclear industry. However, India, Pakistan, Israel, Brazil and Cuba remained outside the NPT.

At the same time, the US and Russia moved very slowly to dismantle their nuclear stockpiles. They will each have 3,500 warheads, "finely targeted on the other's cities in 2003" and they are expected to have 2,500 each in 2008. This is not certain however given the likely acquisition of a nuclear capability by more and more states. The US, as the major military superpower, is dragging its feet over the process of disarmament. The five adherents to the NPT are really like a bunch of notorious drunkards inviting everyone else to sign the pledge. They have the sole right to remain as nuclear powers and no one else is to become one.

Blair, Brown and the whole cabal of New Labour, are particularly vulnerable to the charges of hypocrisy. Bourgeois commentators in Britain have pointed out that New Labour was built on nuclear weapons. Opposition to CND and opposition to "giving up Britain's bomb", was the Ark of the Covenant as far as Blairite New Labour is concerned. Now they denounce India and Pakistan for setting down the road that they have already trod.

Asia

Notwithstanding this, the tests have starkly shown that a nuclear conflict between minor antagonistic powers is possible. It is not a question of 'logic' or what is sane. Put together the explosive cocktail of dire poverty, extremely volatile politics, a bitter clash over Kashmir, and add to this nuclear weapons and it is not difficult then to imagine a train of events which could completely spiral out of control and result in the horror of a nuclear exchange. In 1990, India and Pakistan "came so close to a nuclear 'exchange' over Kashmir that the American officials who became involved still cannot recall it without shaking". Seymour Hearsh, a well-known US commentator, has written up the secret history of the crisis in which he comments that it was "much more frightening than Cuba".

The US in the past acquiesced to Pakistan's acquisition of nuclear weapons because it was its 'client' state in the region. This changed with the end of the Afghanistan conflict and the loosening the ties of India with Russia, upon whom it leaned in the past. This has led, in the words of the Brookings Institute in Washington, to a situation where "Pakistan is a profoundly insecure state. It is a state that feels itself surrounded by enemies, beginning with Iran. Afghanistan has turned out to be a terrible disaster for them. The Indians are as troublesome as ever. Their friends are not really friends. The US has moved out of the region and the Chinese have cooled. Add to that their domestic troubles."

In the wake of the tests there has been speculation that the CIA was taken off guard by the first Indian tests. However, the BJP, the communalist victors in the Indian general election, had long signalled that if they won, nuclear tests would begin. Moreover, Indian defence minister, the 'socialist' George Fernandez, gave an interview a week before the tests in which he said India would 'go nuclear'. India probably brought this forward in the light of the successful testing of a rocket in Pakistan which could reach as far as Madras in the southern part of India. Lahore, the capital of Pakistan, is five minutes 'missile time' away from Indian territory. Nawaz Sharif had written urgently and personally to Clinton on 3 April, over a month before the first Indian tests took place, warning in detail about the impending explosions and their implications.

The threat of war, a permanent feature held over the heads of the peoples of the sub-continent, has existed since the formation of the states of Pakistan and India 50 years ago. They have been involved in three wars and India was humiliated in the border war with China in 1962. India's tests were aimed at Pakistan and China also. China is believed to have supplied Pakistan with some of the missile intelligence to allow it to develop its missile capability. Prior to the election, the BJP 'theoreticians' highlighted the "potential strategic threat from China" that lay behind India's desire to prove its nuclear status. One commented to the British Financial Times, "Who is competing with India for investment and for markets? China. Where is the ideological competition? China. And we are face to face on a difficult border, with outstanding territorial disputes."

But it is the mass of the peoples of India and Pakistan who pay a terrible price for the mad arms race between the ruling class of both countries. India has 1.1 million men under arms, compared to 600,000 for Pakistan. However, Pakistan pays a much greater price with at least a quarter of government spending going towards the military. India spends $9.94bn, 2.8% of its GNP, whereas Pakistan spends $2.9bn or 5.2% of its GNP. Given the catastrophic economic situation of Pakistan, a new arms race will be ruinous. The country has a GNP of just $483 per head, and in 1996 had a foreign debt of about $13.12bn. In the wake of the tests and as part of the worldwide financial turmoil, the Pakistan stock exchange has plunged. Pakistan is having difficulty repaying its debt and there was even a threat made by prime minister Nawaz Sharif that it could default on these debts. The popular euphoria that followed the tests could evaporate.

India, on the other hand, which believed it could ride out the threats of sanctions from the West, has also paid an economic price. The stock market lost a quarter of its value. Its foreign investors deserted India in the wake of the tests. It has lost its 'safe haven' status and Moody's, the international financial analysts, have downgraded the country's sovereign credit ratings from "investment to speculative grade". This drop in stocks is partly a reflection of the international financial crisis, but also of the disastrous economic and social policies of the BJP-led government.

Both in Pakistan and in India there are unstable governments, which could rapidly collapse. On the other hand, the desperate economic and social situation coupled with nationalist governments could, 'accidentally', step over the nuclear threshold. It is this nightmare that has prompted the introduction of sanctions against both countries. Although generally ineffective, they can have an effect in this situation, particularly on an already weakened and beleaguered Pakistan. In the wake of the tests, the Indian government has offered to negotiate a 'no first use' agreement. It is possible that under the pressure of international capitalism, both sides will temporarily back away. However, the tests have underlined the terrible danger that confronts the peoples of this region and other parts of the world.

Again the limitations of US imperialism's power have been underlined. After the first Indian tests and before Pakistan had responded, Clinton phoned Nawaz Sharif in order to try to prevent the imminent explosion of five nuclear devices. According to the New York Times, Clinton had "all but begged" Mr Sharif to hold off. Clinton declared: "If you do this, Nawaz, I have to do this [impose sanctions], and it will hurt you a lot more than it will hurt India."

Nuclear horror 'hot spots'

The Indian sub-continent joins the Middle East as a 'hot spot' where nuclear horror, although of a limited character, is possible. But it is not the only one. The very instability and chaos of North Korea, a state possessing nuclear weapons, could result in the unleashing of a nuclear weapon on the South. Iran is attempting to acquire from Russia and from Pakistan a nuclear capability and a rocket delivery system which could hit Tel Aviv. This can speed up the nuclear capability of Israel. Add to this the possibility of Libya acquiring such weapons, of Saddam Hussein or any other unstable dictatorship going down the same road and the horror of a nuclear exchange is not just a Dr Strangelove fantasy.

There is also the spread of fiendish chemical and biological weapons, which can wipe out millions. It is only now being revealed that in the latter stages of the Iran/Iraq War, gas was used by Iraq on a mass scale for the first time since the second world war. This capability was supplied to Iraq by Western imperialist firms. Iraq was at that stage an 'ally' of the West. The horror suffered by Iranian troops has only now been fully revealed.

If a nuclear 'exchange' does take place then it will have massive political repercussions not just in the region concerned, but worldwide. In fact, it could trigger off revolutionary explosions in the form of mass demonstrations and general strikes throughout the world. Undoubtedly, in the wake of events in the Indian sub-continent, the demand for 'disarmament', particularly of nuclear weapons, can grow. We support the genuine sympathy of the masses for disarmament. We have to give critical support to all the peace movements but, at the same time, pointing out that it will not solve the threat of war and particularly of nuclear war, which hangs over the heads of humankind.

It is even possible, not certain, that the bourgeoisie internationally can begin to dismantle their nuclear capability. The stockpile of weapons between the US and Russia could be dismantled fairly rapidly. It is even possible that some kind of programme to destroy chemical and biological weapons could be set in motion. However, this would not remove the threat.

A capability to produce weapons, including nuclear, chemical and biological weapons, can remain even if those weapons are destroyed. Nazi Germany, through its rapid rearmament programme, assisted by Britain and other imperialist powers, because it had the technology and industry, was able to rapidly rebuild its forces. Therefore the threat of a nuclear 'exchange', with millions and millions of victims, the long-term threat which still hangs over humankind of nuclear annihilation, can only be eliminated by removing the source of conflict, that is the system that is based upon private ownership of the means of production and of the nation state. The choice which Karl Marx put before society, of socialism or barbarism means, in the modern era, socialism or nuclear annihilation.

China - a major player

An important by-product of the crisis over the nuclear tests between India and Pakistan is that it illuminated the role of China as a major geo-political player on the Asian and world stages. This was further underlined by the role of the Chinese government in not immediately devaluing its currency, in response to the falling yen. Devaluation of the renminbi could boost Chinese exports but seriously undermine foreign investment under current conditions. Clinton's visit to China, despite noisy opposition from the Republicans in the USA, cemented the growing alliance between the US and China, particularly with regard to events in Asia.

The region does not fall under the hegemony of one power. The USA, Japan and now China rub up against one another for economic and strategic domination of the area. Japan is unable to "punch its military weight", because of the legacy of the second world war. This triangular relationship which has undergone many shifts, is destined to play a key role.

The clash between the Chinese Stalinists and US imperialism as the military super-power that controlled Asia, was the dominant feature throughout the 'Cold War'. However, in 1970, the then Chinese prime minister, Zhou En-lai, declared that China and the US had "identical global interests". Both were in opposition to Russian Stalinism, the only other military super-power at that stage. The collapse of the USSR introduced important changes, a post-Cold War shift in 'geo-political tectonic plates'. The Soviet Union was removed as a threat to China as much as it was to the US. However, China drew closer to Russia because of the enhanced superpower status of the US, which was reinforced in the post-Tiananmen Square massacre period. A period of flux followed in relations between China and the US, which reflected the domestic and international position of both powers. The growing ties between the US and China in the 1990s, occasionally punctuated by sharp clashes, over Taiwan for instance, led to the visit of Clinton to China in June/July 1998.

The role of China, both in Asia and the world, is linked to both the character of the regime today and economic processes which are now unfolding domestically. Statistics are not entirely reliable but at 'market prices', China's gross national product was $966bn in 1998. This would put it seventh in the world after the US, Japan, Germany, France, the UK and Italy. It was, however, the world's 9th largest merchandise exporter in 1997 and the 11th largest importer. China has also become the world's 2nd largest holder of foreign exchange reserves after Japan. Exchange controls, which the openly capitalist economies of Asia have abandoned, allowed China to play a 'stabilising role' in the region's recent financial crisis. China is a peculiar hybrid with an almost pure capitalist sector in Guangdong and the coastal provinces, together with a huge but disintegrating remnant of the 'planned economy' in the hinterland.

The class character of China: Is it capitalist or does it still remain a Stalinist regime?

[note: The question of the current class character of China is an issue that is still being discussed in the CWI. The issue will be featured in discussion bulletins that will be published during 1999. There is agreement on the processes that are taking place and perspectives for China. Some comrades are of the opinion that capitalist restoration has been completed rather than the hybrid described in the paragraph that was presented to the World Congress by the International Secretariat]

Marxists, as Trotsky commented, do not think in 'fixed categories'. It is for us a question of understanding the processes, economically, socially and politically and, in particular, the direction in which society is moving. Of course, it is not sufficient merely to describe processes. The dialectic teaches that quantity becomes quality and therefore the class character of a regime is thereby changed. It is clear that China has a large capitalist sector and, as a whole, is moving irrevocably in a capitalist direction. Yet latest analyses show that the number of people employed in state-owned enterprises actually grew from 72 million in 1977 (79% of the urban labour force) to 112 million in 1996 (still around 65% of the urban labour force). Even in 1996, the share of investment and fixed assets within state-owned and other collective enterprises was 69%. The number of urban companies under state ownership is presently around 80% but is planned to fall to "well under 50%" by the year 2002. On the other hand, a writer in The Guardian newspaper in Britain correctly pointed out: "China's version of capitalism - market Stalinism - is a contradictory mishmash of elements."

The state sector is concentrated largely on central and provincial state-owned enterprises of steel, chemicals, heavy engineering, shipbuilding, textiles, banking and trading. It still makes the largest contribution to non-agricultural gross domestic product. The military, through the Peoples Liberation Army, is an "arena of economic power in its own right involved in manufacturing and exporting, hotels and technology requisition". The Chinese Red Army has also been implicated in illegal gun running and in the organisation of prostitution rings.

In addition to this, China has a large local state sector consisting of township and village enterprises, which are a "form of rural collectivism" but are also a major source of subcontracted manufacturing operations linked to firms in Hong Kong and Taiwan and via these to companies in the US and China. There is also a significant joint venture sector in which foreign and domestic interests have collaborated in manufacturing and services. There has also been a big rise in domestically-owned private companies. Agriculture, on the other hand, still continues as the primary basis of livelihood for about 60% of China's population. These few details, which can be considerably added to in a more thorough analysis, show how contra-dictory is the picture of China today.

However, it is quite clear that the 'planned economy', understood in a Marxist sense and which to some extent existed in China in the past, is rapidly disintegrating. Moreover, there is no significant sector of the Chinese 'bureaucracy' that still adheres to the plan. There are divisions amongst this privileged layer with some in the state sector wishing to maintain it, as a source of privileges and plunder. There is also a fear that the process of privatisation and sell-off of state assets, unless matched by a corresponding growth in industry, will see a massive increase in unemployment with much greater social and political consequences for China than we have hitherto seen in the former USSR and Eastern Europe. But the process of the restoration of capitalism is quite clear.

There has been a long series of 'reform' measures in China since 1979. But the policy of faster reform of state enterprises, ratified at the 15th Communist Party Congress in September 1997, has introduced the most comprehensive privatisation of state assets since the process began. This was summed up by the Chinese prime minister, Zhu Rongji, who visited the British bourgeoisie's 'holy of holies' in the City of London - London's Guildhall. He invited the financial werewolves, gathered to hear him, to intervene in China: "You are welcome to acquire state enterprises." He added the proviso: "But with one condition - that you don't lay off a single worker." This sums up the dilemma of the Chinese regime. A desire to move rapidly to the market but a fear of the social and also the political consequences.

However, the injunction not to sack workers is not being followed by the Chinese cousins of the City of London financial sharks. The process is quite clear in the City of Shenyang. This is located in the former Manchuria and was once known as 'China's Ruhr'. Now there is a massive sale of state enterprises, which on completion would mean that out of 230 large industrial plants, only 16 would remain under the control of the state. Wishing to maintain a state capitalist sector, the plan is to coalesce these firms into five groups modelled on Korea's now discredited chaebol. Some of these companies, according to the British Financial Times, were offered for sale at "just one yuan [about 7p] each". Little wonder that the Wall Street Journal described what is happening in China today as: "The sale of the century."

Emerging Chinese capitalists have been brutal in their treatment of the existing workforce. Their 'shock therapy' includes the immediate removal of the 'iron rice bowl' of 'socialist era benefits'. One worker, after being reprimanded for sitting on a seat 'reserved for dignitaries', smashed the chair in frustration. He was threatened with the sack if he did not donate a new chair by the following Monday. The new boss boasted to the British Financial Times: "He bought the chair but we fired him anyway." The emerging capitalists found that the Communist Party's 'structures', the trade unions and the local party cells, had been 'very useful' in 'settling disputes' largely in favour of the capitalists.

Brutal 'shock therapy'

The result of all this, a brutal sink-or-swim philosophy for former state enterprises, is a massive and deepening divide between the prosperous coastal parts of China, where most businesses are already private, and the inland and northern parts, where the concentration of ailing state industry is highest. These latter industries are scheduled to be rapidly privatised. The 1997 September reforms, introduced by the 'Communist' Party, will result in a huge slashing of jobs in the civil service, together with the restructuring of state-owned enterprises, and also the recapitalisation of the banking structure.

Massive, increased unemployment could only be avoided if China could continue to generate big economic growth. But this has begun to slow down. A predicted growth rate at the start of 1997 of between 9.5-10% has resulted in an actual growth of 8.8% and it is expected to slow down even more in 1998 to under 8%. China, already showing some of the deflationary tendencies of other Asian countries, could see a dramatic worsening in its position by a combination of the reform package and the effects of the Asian crisis. There has been a 40% cut in 1998 in promised Japanese foreign direct investment (FDI) and the contraction in Asia has affected Chinese overseas sales.

But even without the effects of the Asian crisis, the contradictions and imbalance in the Chinese economy were leading to a slowdown. In some senses China's financial crisis is just as bad as that of any other Asian country except, in the words of a writer in the British Financial Times, "foreigners are not involved" because of state control on capital movements. As in Japan, the government has closed down some financial institutions, noticeably the Hainan Development Bank. This bank was unable to pay its debts. In fact, the commercial banks in China have 'problem loans' worth roughly $180bn or 20% of total assets. Private-sector economists believe the situation is even worse, suggesting that most of China's banks are technically insolvent. The Hainan Development Bank is located in the country's largest special economic zone, which is a purely capitalist sector. The state banks are also heavily indebted. The commercial banks are under pressure from the government to hand out financial support to loss-making state enterprises because of the fear of rising mass unemployment. There are estimates that unemployment could rise to almost 400 million from the 200 million presently unemployed. In some industrial cities in the north-east, real unemployment is probably up to 50%. In the countryside, the situation is equally daunting. By the year 2000 the 'surplus labour force' in rural areas will top 370 million. If China is to avoid massive unemployment in the next immediate period ahead, which will inevitably lead to widespread social protests, strikes and upheavals, it can only do so by maintaining its growth or by resorting to another devaluation.

Continued 'record growth', which some economists now say has been exaggerated at least in gross terms, will not be possible in the changed economic situation of Asia and the world. Therefore, despite the collaboration between China and Clinton over the Japanese yen, another devaluation of the Chinese currency is inevitable although the US bourgeoisie and the Japanese capitalists hope that this can be done in a 'controlled' way that will not trigger off a new wave of devaluations.

But strikes and demonstrations will inevitably be a growing feature in China. Already demonstrations of pensioners and workers have taken place in cities in south-western China over the non-payment of pensions and 'unpaid salaries'. According to The Independent in Britain, "In the past two years there have been cases where thousands took to the streets to protest". It is possible that these protests will be much wider and more explosive than even the demonstrations and protests of the Russian workers for non-payment of wages in the past period. The development of independent trade unions and even of workers' independent parties, will inevitably be posed in China in the future and open up the prospect for the development of genuine Marxist forces.

A Chinese capitalism

Various scenarios have been advanced for the development of China in the next period. The regime is clearly set on transforming China to capitalism, but without the 'mistakes' of introducing limited democracy, as in the former USSR and Eastern Europe. Its model is South Korea between the early 1960s and the mid-1980s. However, it seems to forget that these dictatorial regimes, such as South Korea, became completely unviable with the rise of the proletariat, a consequence of rapid industrialisation.

The development of capitalism in China will have the same consequences and will make impossible the rigid control exercised from the centre by the Beijing regime. In reality, processes are developing which can tear the central state apart. In the past, China was rendered apart by local warlords. There are elements of this at the present time in the tremendous regionalisation which has developed through the 'two-speed' China.

On top of this, there are national conflicts. In the north-west, Muslims in the region of Xinjiang have been executed for daring to raise the question of independence. There is the problem of Tibet for China. But even the growth of regionalism could turn, at a certain stage, particularly on an increasingly capitalist background with the growth of huge disparities between different regions, into demands for separation. This would clash with the Great China philosophy of the central Beijing regime which clearly looks toward becoming a superpower alongside US imperialism.

The fate of China is decisive for developments in Asia and the world. In the immediate period, it faces serious economic difficulties. A US expert has commented: "I would not wish [the Chinese government's] assignment on a close friend." It is against this background that Clinton's visit to China took place. This was for a mixture of economic and strategic reasons. The value of direct US investment in China has multiplied six times in six years, bringing overall actual investment to just over $18bn. At the same time, Chinese goods to America have grown in value from just under $9bn in 1992 to more than $32bn today. Given the crisis in Asia, China therefore assumes importance for US big business. Already major US monopolies, such as Boeing, General Electric and others, have lucrative contracts with China.

At the same time, there is growing concern in the US that the trade surplus of China's trade with the US, put at just over $10bn, could spiral to $50bn this year. The relationship is skewed in China's favour at the present time with China's exports to the US rising by 18% in one year while imports from the US into China have grown by only 2.6%. The purpose of Clinton's visit was to enhance US capitalism's prospects in China. China is the US's fifth biggest trading partner and exports to China (including Hong Kong) have doubled since 1990.

With the increase of privatisation of industry and agriculture, US capitalism looks greedily towards a new market at a time when Asia as a whole is declining. However, China is not capable of providing a lifeline either for US or world capitalism. Moody's investor services has warned that China's banking system is "critically weak" and has also stated that poor statistics and low levels of disclosure and a degree of corruption, mask the underlying position of the state banking system.

Powers' struggle in Asia

At the same time, the struggle for domination in Asia between the three giants, the US, China and Japan continues despite the soothing phrases about 'constructive engagement' and a 'tripartite' agreement for 'stability' in Asia. China has come a long way from the time when Mao Zedong advocated a proliferation of nuclear weapons by states throughout the world to break the 'hegemony' of Russian Stalinism and US imperialism. Now Washington and Beijing have come to a tentative agreement that their nuclear warheads will "not be pointed at one another" as a sign of 'peaceful cooperation in Sino-US relations". Up to recently, 13 of China's 18 nuclear intercontinental ballistic missiles were targeted at US cities. The fact that China is considering a bilateral detargeting deal represents an important shift in the Chinese leadership's attitude. Beijing had indicated previously that it would only detarget on condition that the US made a nuclear 'no first use'.

The clear aim of China is to court Washington, thereby undermining Japan and furthering the aim of China to become the major player in the area. At the same time, Beijing continues to push its goal of a 'Greater China' by exerting pressure on the US over Taiwan. As recently as March 1996, China fired missiles towards Taiwan and the riposte of the US was to send warships into the Taiwan Straits, warning of 'grave consequences' if Taiwan was hit. This was a factor, it seems, in forcing Washington and Beijing to avoid the potential dangers of a head-on collision and to build a 'more stable' relationship. However, China is pressing the US for an agreement on the 'three Nos': no 'one China, one Taiwan'; no Taiwan under independence; and no Taiwan membership of the UN. Beijing is attempting to lean on the UN to establish its long-held proposal to bring Taiwan, as with Hong Kong, back into the 'Chinese family'.

Taiwan big business has already built up considerable and lucrative contacts with China: they have invested between $30bn and $60bn on the mainland. But the growth in support of Taiwan's opposition Democratic Progressive Party, which stands for independence, shows the difficulty in securing Beijing's hope of 'one China'. This will remain the case so long as democratic rights are refused by the Beijing regime. Other important factors will have a decisive impact on the prospects for 'one China', such as economic and political developments within Taiwan, between Taiwan and China, and the fact that separation between the two countries has existed for decades. The US switched diplomatic recognition from Taiwan to Beijing in 1979, but it has remained committed to defend Taiwan in the event of an attack. But Washington has leaned on Taipei (the capital of Taiwan) for greater contact with China. It has warned the Taiwanese that while Washington would "protect Taiwan's way of life" its reaction "would not be the same" if there was a move towards independence. This shows that the so-called 'inviolable rights' of small nations, invoked by US imperialism in the past to justify military intervention, is so much small change. They will drop former 'loyal allies' when this conflicts with their wider strategic, economic and political interests.

The courtship between Beijing and Washington has inevitably excited the resentment of the Japanese capitalists, battered as they are by Asia's economic storms. One bourgeois expert correctly characterises the situation: "There is now an undercurrent of frustration against both China and the US." Japan's star is dimmed as that of China rises. A former Japanese ambassador to the US complained: "Five years ago, the US was more interested in its relationship with Japan. Now, the US may be equally or even more interested in its relationship with China."

One of the aims of Chinese foreign policy is to try to keep Japan firmly 'on the back foot', according to one diplomat. No opportunity is lost to remind Japan of its former crimes in China. The popularity of a film, The Fatal Moment, which seemingly lauds the second world war prime minister, Tojo, who masterminded the attack on Pearl

Harbour, was the subject of a complaint by China. The latter also fears the latent nationalism in Japan and the future rearming of Japanese imperialism. It also resents the 'nuclear umbrella' of US imperialism over Japan, which it sees as a threat to itself.

There will be a shift in relationships between the three powers, alongside India, who vie for influence and power in Asia. The other minor powers in Asia view increased Chinese intervention in the region with mixed feelings. There is relief that China collaborated with the US to prop up the yen and to help finance the IMF loan which bailed out Indonesia. But at the same time, they fear the increased role and appetite of Beijing. This has led to a reaffirmation of and a greater leaning on the support of US imperialism.

Ever since US forces were ejected from the Subic Bay Base in the Philippines in 1992, the intervention of the US military in the region appeared to be diminished. Now, however, Singapore has agreed to allow US aircraft carriers and other warships to dock at a new port from the year 2000. In the past, they were only allowed to anchor offshore.

The sands will continue to shift in the complicated relationships between China, Japan and the USA. But this relationship will not be the tranquil and peaceful one envisaged by bourgeois commentators. Big clashes are rooted in the present and, particularly, the future situation in the region. The open aim of China, to become a superpower in the 21st century does not sit easily either with Japan or US imperialism. Conflicts and even outright clashes are possible. Apart from Taiwan there are a series of territorial disputes in the South China Sea.

Indonesia - The beginning of a revolution

Asia, which up to 1997 was seen as the one bright spot for world capitalism, is the region of the world where the contradictions of capitalism are most glaring, the failures of the system are most obvious, and the force that represents the greatest danger to it, the proletariat, is rising from its knees. Economically, socially and politically, Asia, of course, is in turmoil. We correctly predicted the certain downfall of the Suharto dictatorship, which has now opened the floodgates of revolution. We have a special document on Indonesia but it is still necessary to draw out some general points and see how they relate to the general situation in Asia as a whole and throughout the world.

The downfall of Suharto represented the beginning of the revolution in Indonesia. A feature of revolution is the conscious intervention of the masses in shaping their own fate. This is clearly seen in the elemental movement from below of the Indonesian workers and peasants. Hardly had Suharto vacated office on May 21, when the announcement of the creation of a myriad of parties and organisations began. The British Guardian reports: "A new party appears almost every day." There has even been the creation of a party based upon the Indonesian Chinese, the Reform Party, in the wake of the attacks on the ethnic Chinese. They are pledged to "defend our rights and create true harmony amongst Indonesian citizens". Ethnic Chinese make up less than 5% of the 202 million population but control more than 70% of the economy and have been singled out as a focus of the masses' discontent with the Suharto regime because of the wealth of a small layer of top Chinese millionaires and billionaires.

The ruling Golkar Party, which sustains Suharto and now props up his puppet Habibie, is breaking up with affiliates separating themselves and membership collapsing. Civil servants are now no longer obliged to support this party and, therefore, its 'mass base' is rapidly disappearing. Habibie was put in as a stopgap by Suharto, the army and the ruling class as a whole. He and Rais are clearly intended as the figureheads to derail the revolution. Habibie is the Indonesian 'Berenguer', who opened the floodgates of revolution in Spain in 1931. Habibie and Rais are the 'gatemen' of the revolution in Indonesia.

An important feature of revolution is a split amongst the ruling class. This is clearly evident in the split among the Indonesian elite, and particularly the army, on how to control the mass movement. They are also divided over what to do about East Timor, where a mass movement has reactivated in the aftermath of the overthrow of the Suharto dictatorship. The dilemma of the ruling class is summed up in the attitude of the army towards demonstrations of workers and strikes in June 1998. A demonstration and strike by the Indonesian Prosperity Union was met with army repression. Bus drivers, factory workers and unemployed labourers carrying banners and placards, demanded Habibie's resignation, the release of detainees and lower prices. However, the strikers backed away, complaining afterwards: "The army has said they will kill us if we try and march on the House of Representatives." The army's leading spokesman expressed the intentions of the army tops by declaring to a British Financial Times reporter: "We warned the people, the society, that it is dangerous if the reforms are uncontrolled; reforms should be conducted step by step. That is not necessarily slow." At the same time, another section of the military has warned that there cannot be a return to 'the old regime'.

The masses are paying a heavy price for Indonesia's economic crisis. Unemployment will probably reach 15.4 million in 1998, about 17% of Indonesia's workforce of 90 million. Gross domestic product contracted 6.21% in the first quarter compared with the same period last year, and is likely to contract by more than 10% (some say 20%) which vastly exceeds forecasts of a drop of 4% this year. Added to this must be an increased rate of inflation to about 52%.

East Timor
At the same time, the national question, particularly in relation to East Timor, has

roared back onto the agenda. Some 200,000 Timorese paid with their lives in the struggle against Indonesian imperialism, a higher proportion of the population than died even under Pol Pot in Cambodia. Habibie has responded by suggesting 'special status' for the former Portuguese colony but only on condition that Portugal and the United Nations recognise it as an "integral part of Indonesia". Political prisoners have been released, but Gusmao, the leader of the guerrillas, has not been released and 'political autonomy' is completely ruled out by the regime. This position, however, is not fixed in stone for two main reasons. Firstly, although the bourgeois trends among the representatives of East Timor outside the country, namely the Nobel Prize winner Ramos Horta, are trying to get the idea of 'autonomy' accepted, there is an active struggle inside the country for self-determination and total independence. It is being conducted by the military resistance of FALANTIL and by the underground organisations in the factories, schools, etc along with the East Timorese in Indonesia and workers and youth in the present movement. Secondly, under the whip of the revolution, as the Financial Times commented, the government is "obliged to make new concessions to an angry public almost every day". It should also be remembered that before the annexation of East Timor, the Timorese Liberation Front (Fretilin), which stood for independence, had majority support amongst the population. The international bourgeoisie, recognising the long-term incapacity of the regime to hold East Timor, has urged the release of all political prisoners, the opening of negotiations with Gusmao and the guerrillas, and free elections.

Undoubtedly, the revolution would have developed even quicker than the pell-mell speed at which it unfolded but for the absence of a mass revolutionary party capable of going the whole way. The bourgeois opposition of Megawati Sukarnoputri (daughter of former president Sukarno), and Amians Rais (leader of the Muslim Front), has tried to apply the brake: "They have been careful not to rock the boat." (British Financial Times)

The fear of the masses' 'uncontrolled' movement is summed up in the comment of one bourgeois: "Decent people will become anarchists. They will have to, because they need to eat." Indonesia is in for a long economic agony but with massive upheaval that will go beyond Asia and affect the world.

Diktats of the IMF

It is not the only country to have been affected. Thailand, according to conservative estimates, is likely to contract economically by 4.1%, and even Malaysia, if it grows at all, will be by a miserly 0.2%. The latter was supposed to have stood on the verge of becoming a new tiger only two years ago. Malaysia's prime minister, Mahathir Mohamed, has attempted to stand up to international capital and has blamed the crisis on 'foreigners'. He has also warned of a 'guerrilla war' by Asians "if foreigners use the crisis to take over regional economies". Thailand, gripped by economic desolation, has been forced to step in to 'nationalise' banks for fear of a complete collapse of the finance sector. This represents, in effect, a 'nationalisation of the debt', which the government will attempt to pass on to the workers and peasants in the country. The Malaysian regime is split from top to bottom, with Mahathir at odds with his deputy prime minister, Anwar Ibrahim. Despite the threats made by Mahathir to international capital, the regime remains firmly within the framework of world capitalism and Mahathir has conceded that he may have to eventually bend the knee and accept the 'diktats of the IMF'.

In South Korea, again as we have predicted, the price being demanded of the proletariat has provoked a huge wave of strikes, which could see the downfall of the government. Korea faces a summer of massive discontent by the proletariat, which will pit the Korean Confederation of Trade Unions against the chaebol and government. The effects of the movement in Korea could spill over to the rest of Asia.

At the same time, North Korea faces mass hunger and, possibly, imminent collapse. This is not seen as a lifeline for capitalism, as initially was the case with the swallowing up of East Germany by West German capitalism. South Korea in 1998 is not Germany 1989-90. Neither Japan nor the US would be happy to step in and underwrite economic Korean reunification, although a sudden collapse would mean that they would have no alternative. The regime of Kim Dae Jung is attempting to open up a 'dialogue' with the North Korean regime, to push for "greater economic integration" and a gradual weaning away of North Korea from the brutal Stalinists who still cling to power. But it is the mood of the proletariat that will be decisive. Korea is likely to undergo a series of waves of struggle, presenting an opportunity for the genuine forces of Marxism to intervene, on the basis of our programme and, in particular, the idea of an independent mass workers' party.

Even in the Philippines, the election of Estrada disguises the underlying explosive economic and social situation. Estrada was surrounded before, during and after the election by former business cronies of the Marcos regime. The spectre of a return of Marcos's 'crony capitalism' is provided by the victory of Estrada. But he struck a populist note and with the absence of a mass alternative, was seen by the poor as something of a champion. He has even declared that "business will not be allowed to dictate under an Estrada presidency". However, in practice, as with the previous Ramos government, Estrada will carry out pro-capitalist policies, including further privatisations. The strike of Philippines Airlines employees against attacks on union representatives is a symptom of what is coming.

Even Singapore and Hong Kong, bastions of Asian capitalism and seen as virtually ring-fenced against the threat of economic crisis, have been touched by the Asian storms. Indeed, it has been a very bad year for Asia's rich. According to the latest 'rich list' in Foyles magazine, the number of billionaires in the region is down from

119 in 1996 to 44 in 1998. Two years ago, the same magazine, on the reading list of anybody with wealth, declared that "it's Asia's turn". Now, as The British Guardian laments: "There is no more talk of the Asian century." Thailand, for example, has seen its billionaires wiped out. Hong Kong and Singapore, havens for the rich, although not as affected as other parts of Asia, have seen their economic performance undermined. Singapore, a city state, has seen its growth rate for this year drop from 7.8% last year to a projected growth of 0.5-1.5%. The value of the stock market has dropped by 40%. There is a financial, economic and wealth meltdown in Hong Kong where the stock market has dropped by 40% and land prices by 50%. Many of the rich British and other expatriates, victims of the crisis, are flooding onto aircraft and other transport out of the former British colony.

The effects of the crisis will, of course, not just be positive for the labour movement and the working class. Migrant labourers, conservatively estimated to be at least 6.5 million, are the major victims of the crisis as they are hounded from one country to another. Malaysia and Thailand, in particular, have evicted Chinese Indonesians and others in the most brutal fashion.

Unstable India

India, which only a matter of months ago was held up as a 'safe haven' from Asia's hurricane, has been plunged into crisis in the aftermath of the nuclear explosions. The BJP-dominated coalition is on the point of collapse. India Today summed up the achievements of the government: "A hundred days of just being there. Even the aides of the Indian prime minister, Atal Behari Vajpayee, have urged him to go. One aide declared: 'We've been saying to him, if it goes on like this, is it really worthwhile continuing'."

It is not just the nuclear tests but the disastrous June budget of the BJP and the splits, both within the government and within the BJP, that have undermined the Coalition. This budget indicated a 'tax and spend' policy and the threat of 'Indian self-reliance', that is, of protectionism for Indian industry. The debate between the reformers and advocates of Swadeshi, or 'self-reliance', has raged within the government and within the BJP. This threat of protectionism completely undermines the evolution of Indian capitalism towards the world market. Naturally, there was a prompt response by the speculators with equity prices marked down by a fifth and, as we have reported earlier, Moody's (the US credit-rating agency) downgrading Indian debt and leaving it with a 'junk bond rating'.

It is quite clear that the present government is more shaky and chaotic even than the United Front coalition government of 14 parties, which it replaced in the March general election. The economic shambles produced by the BJP-dominated government is amplified by the threat of building a temple at the previous site of a Muslim shrine at Ayodhya. This could trigger massive communal upheavals in India, which, even a section of the BJP are worried about.

At the same time, there is no viable parliamentary alternative to the BJP. The Congress Party and their allies are not able to muster a majority to topple the government. The role of the Communist Parties in propping up different bourgeois formations has had a calamitous effect on the prospects of the workers' movement in India. Nevertheless, the growth of opposition within both the CPI(M) and the CPI, combined with the small but nevertheless steady growth of the genuine forces of Marxism in India, is a portent of the possibilities which exist in the next period.

Japan and Australisia

In relation to Asia's crisis, Lee Kuan Yew, head of Singapore, has declared that the Asian region "will not fully recover until Japan recovers". He added the caveat: "Nobody, at present, can say with confidence when that will be." We have dealt earlier with the crisis in Japan from an economic standpoint. The social and political repercussions of this are, however, vital. We said at the beginning of this decade that the most important changes that would be registered politically would be the emergence of the German and Japanese proletariat alongside that of the USA.

This economic crisis has had an unprecedented effect socially. Job security is vanishing, spending is down dramatically, the jobless rate is rising by 300,000 a month; more than in Britain during the worst of the 1992 recession. The ruling party of Japan, the Liberal Democratic Party, suffered dramatically in the earlier part of this decade in the aftermath of the collapse of Stalinism and the beginning of the recession in Japan. However, the move to the right of the former workers' parties has meant that they have failed to offer a real alternative and, therefore, the LDP has not suffered the fate, for instance, of the former Christian Democrats in Italy. In elections there has been an increased vote for the Communist Party where the masses have registered their opposition to the LDP. Now faced with a serious recession and slump, the LDP suffered serious reverses in elections to the upper house in July.

The spectacular losses suffered by the LDP in elections to the Upper House in July, is a dramatic reflection in the political sphere of the economic crisis of Japanese capitalism. An important feature of this election was the performance of the Japanese Communist Party (JCP) which massively increased its vote from 3.5 million to over 8 million.

Instead of giving voice to the desire for change represented by its increased vote, the JCP leadership has called for a coalition with the Democratic Party. This party is composed of renegades from the LDP and the former right-wing pro-business wing of the Social Democratic Party. The leader of the Democratic Party has called for a Japanese version of the 'Olive Tree' to replace the present LDP government. It cannot be ruled out that an 'Olive Tree' type government could take power. There is massive discontent with the LDP and big support for new elections. If such a government comes to power with the CP involved, an unprecedented period of upheaval within the party will develop.

Japan has entered a stormy economic and political period. The depth of the crisis is indicated by an article in the British Sunday Telegraph: "Japan has a savings mountain - but much of it has been moved overseas. Japanese households are obsessed by the collapse in the value of, and income from, their retirement savings. A dollar millionaire in Japan eight years ago now faces retirement on an annual income of barely $2,000 - the result of the slump in equity values and low yields on domestic bonds. Returns on capital are derisory: the long-term interest rate is 1.5 per cent, the yield on the Nikkei is 0.9 per cent. In a scramble to secure higher yields, Japanese households have pushed a colossal $685bn offshore - much of it into US Treasury bonds."

The consciousness of the masses is very confused. It is clear that the self-employed, other sections of the petty bourgeoisie and, probably, some workers in the first instance blame the financial crisis on the 'bad management' of the Japanese government. One taxi driver complained to The (British) Guardian: "The ministry of finance is responsible. They should get rid of the bad loans at the banks." However, this will soon change as the recession bites and the masses begin to see the brutal side of Japanese capitalism.

Even Vietnam is on the eve of convulsions. An unprecedented struggle has broken out in the ruling party over which direction the country should take. A clear pro-capitalist trend exists in the majority of the bureaucracy but is being resisted by a section which wants to see the party 'democratise', but at the same time declares that, "the market economy was incompatible with a socialist orientation". Given the processes in China and elsewhere, it is unlikely that Vietnam will be able to hold out from the process of a return back to capitalism and the liquidation of the planned economy.

Asia expresses in a very vivid form the Marxist law of 'combined and uneven development'. We have countries in the grip of extreme underdevelopment in which the tasks of bourgeois democratic revolution have not been carried through. We have, on the other hand, newly industrialised countries, like South Korea, in which most of the tasks of the bourgeois democratic revolution were carried through under the aegis of US imperialism.

Australasian crisis

But at the same time, the fate of Australasia - Australia and New Zealand - is intrinsically linked to developments in Asia. These countries in the post-1945 period, enjoyed some of the highest living standards in the world. Australia is the 'lucky country'. However, this has not always been so; Australia had one of the highest unemployment rates in the world in the 1930s, being badly affected by the world economic crisis and depression. Now history seems to have turned full circle with both countries witnessing the immediate effects of the crisis.

The collapse in commodity prices has had an effect on Australia with its exports set to fall in 1998 for the first time in 20 years. Once reliant on the British market, the Australian capitalists successfully switched to Asia, particularly to Japan, which is its largest trading partner and takes nearly a third of its exports. Exports grew by 7.2% last year but are due to drop dramatically this year. Commodity exports account for nearly two-thirds of Australia's total exports, which, in turn, represent about 22% of gross domestic product. Compounding Australia's problems, the Japanese capitalists have begun to cash in their investments in Australia's capital markets. The current account deficit is likely to swell to 6.5% of gross domestic product as its exports drop and its currency collapses.

This, in turn, together with the collapse in Japan, has undermined New Zealand and particularly its currency, the dollar. The economy in New Zealand actually contracted by 0.9% in the first quarter with economists warning that the country was "halfway down the road to recession". Asia takes 37% of New Zealand's exports. Consequently, the right-wing New Zealand government, led by Jenny Shipley, has promised a further savage cut in government spending. This comes months after promising to keep spending up, and increase it somewhat, as the condition for keeping the minority party, New Zealand First, within the government. New Zealand has the highest number of homeless people of any of the 'advanced industrial countries'.

Even before the Asian crisis began to bite, the employers and the government in Australia began to unload responsibility for the crisis on the shoulders of the working class. The attempt to break the power of the wharfies - the Australian dockers - was part of this. The workers won a marvellous victory, which was sold out by the trade union leadership. Inevitably the employers and government are already extracting revenge.

Into this already heated situation has come the crisis for the Australian bourgeoisie and government provoked by the relative success of Pauline Hanson's 'One Nation' party in Queensland. She has fed on the joblessness and insecurity of the rural and regional population as well as the fear that, under a new law, Aboriginal people will be able to take back some land and farms stolen from them by the colonial plunder of the past. The ruling Liberal National government was prepared to sup with the devil and lean on Hanson in order to undermine its political opponents. However, Hanson's heady brew of racism, protectionism and virtual autarchy is very risky for Australian capitalism.

The spectre of a flood of 'Asian immigrants' drowning Australia's 'Anglo-Saxon majority' endangers Australian capitalism's relations with Asia itself. In the

Queensland election in June "business, which knows how important Asia is to the state, prefers a Labor government". This compelled Howard to distance himself from Hanson but not before the Labor Party had won the election in Queensland.It is the small but significant forces of the CWI who have played a key role in highlighting the policies of One Nation and given a real lead to the labour movement.

4 - The Americas

L atin America, despite the claims of bourgeois commentators to the contrary ("Latin America looks fit enough to fend off crisis", British Financial Times), has been affected by Asia's crisis, as is the case with all the 'emerging markets'. It is estimated by the World Bank that this will result in a drop of 1.5% of Latin America's growth for 1998. Low commodity prices still have a severe effect on most of the countries of Latin America dependent as they are on exports of primary produce.

Venezuela has been severely affected by the drop in oil prices, notwithstanding the ceiling on production that has been introduced by OPEC on oil production in 1998. In 1997, oil generated four-fifths of Venezuela's exports and represented 72.2% of its gross domestic product. Venezuela's budget projections are based on the price of $13 a barrel, compared to $8.73 for the 'basket' of its 'crudes' and an average price, last year, of $11.27. Clearly the country faces a period of austerity which the Venezuelan bourgeoisie fears would boost the electoral prospects of Hugo Chávez, a 'radical populist' who led an unsuccessful military coup in 1992 and has been ahead in recent opinion polls.

Mexico and Venezuela stand to lose $920m and $843m respectively for every dollar that the price of oil falls. It will also have a significant spin-off effect in Colombia, Ecuador and many other countries in Latin America. The drop in the price of copper has severely hit the Chilean and Peruvian economies. It is true that many Latin American companies are still making historically high rates of profit, but this cannot last, particularly when the crisis bites in the USA itself. Even Argentina has had to cut back spending plans and severe poverty exists among big sections of the Argentinian masses.

In Brazil, the financial and economic crisis has had serious repercussions. There is intense polarisation in the country. This has exploded in the north-east of Brazil, which contains some of the poorest sections of the Brazilian population. There is widespread hunger. This has triggered a social explosion of the kind that took place at the end of the 1970s and 1980s. Organised groups of the disabled and the hungry have raided supermarkets and distributed food. Convoys of lorries carrying food have been stopped on the highways and food taken from them and given to the hungry. Eighty percent of the movements have been spontaneous but also the landless labourers' organisation, MST, has organised some of them. At the same time, the government is carrying through a neo-liberal policy, which meets with increased resistance from the masses. Sixty-one of the 62 large universities were on strike in June and the movement involved both teachers and students. The government was forced to pay the salaries of strikers.

The coming election in Brazil is one of the most important for the country and the rest of Latin America. Opinion polls put Lula, the PT's candidate, level with the candidates of the governing party. The PT has moved to the right and Lula is linking up with the PDT of Brizola for the elections. In fact, Brizola has taken a position to the left of Lula on some issues and has called for the reversal of all privatisations. Big opportunities are opening up for the forces of Marxism in Latin America both in the mass movements and on the left of the PT as well as the PSTU.

If the major countries have been affected by the crisis, it has meant a catastrophe for the already poverty-stricken countries and regions of Latin America. The crisis in Mexico continues with the simmering opposition in Chiapas. Although a rural movement of this character cannot succeed by itself (and the Zapatistas have downplayed their original socialist phraseology), nevertheless, we cannot underestimate the effects that the struggle has had on the formerly conservative native population of Chiapas. The British Guardian reported in January that, "On the ground... there is a new confidence amongst the Indian people. Indian men and women used to walk with heads bowed; now they look you in the eye and discuss world politics. 'Sometimes you go to bed with a sore head from thinking so much,' one villager said after a lengthy discussion on the Irish peace process." The state governor of Chiapas and the PRI will undoubtedly move to crush the movement at a certain stage but will find it difficult against the background of an increased radicalisation in the urban areas.

In Colombia, the election of Pastrana, a former newscaster and son of a former conservative president, opens up a new situation. There was a big turnout in the election and Pastrana achieved the greatest number of votes of any candidate in the country's history. Pastrana has vowed to talk to the guerrillas in an attempt to end a 35-year conflict. Nevertheless, he is clearly seen as a candidate of business and takes power against the background of a catastrophic economic situation with official unemployment of 14.5% of the workforce and more than 20% inflation.

The United States of America

The US is "the anvil upon which the fate of humankind will be forged". It is the world's major capitalist power. It is the only real military superpower today. It is the economic engine of world capitalism, and the US proletariat will be decisive in the struggle for world socialism.

In terms of consciousness, the US working class lags behind its counterparts in most of the world, particularly the European proletariat. In the past class relations softened in those periods when US capitalism was able 'to deliver the goods' in terms of rising living standards at least for the majority of the population.

The class gulf widened, however, and became more generalised on an all-US scale when economic progress slowed or broke down. Then the class struggle developed with 'American speed' and ferocity. The period prior to the First World War showed some of these features in the epic industrial battles at this time, and was expressed politically in the one million votes for the Socialist Party US presidential candidate in 1912, Eugene Debs (this is the equivalent of about five million votes today).

Similar developments took place after the First World War with a colossal radicalisation of the most advanced workers under the influence of the Russian revolution. Following the 1929-33 Wall Street crash, the US workers poured into the new unions, engaged in some of the most inspiring industrial battles, in which the Trotskyists played a key role, for instance, in Minneapolis. Hundreds were killed and wounded in the 1930s and the question of US labour breaking from the Democrats and forming its own party, the Labor Party, was posed.

The knot of history, however, was broken by the Second World War, which saw US capitalism emerge enormously strengthened as the major capitalist power on the globe. Notwithstanding this, a huge strike wave convulsed the US in the post-1945 period, exceeding at one stage even the mighty revolutionary strike wave of the 1930s. However, the colossal development of the productive forces allowed the US ruling class to grant significant concessions to the majority of the US working class. This did not mean that the accumulated historical contradictions within US society were overcome. Searing racism and the effects of the movement for colonial liberation led to mass movements of the black population in the 1950s and 60s. Also, US imperialism's role as world policeman built into its foundations the explosive material of world capitalism, as was shown in the Vietnam war, which still exercises a powerful effect on the consciousness of the US's people.

Reality of the US economic 'paradigm'.

In the past, the economic largesse of US capitalism has guaranteed it a relative social stability; that is about to come to an end. The seven-year boom of the 1990s has hidden all the underlying weaknesses, which will be dramatically highlighted in the coming recession or slump. The US's so-called economic 'paradigm', of low inflation and unemployment officially at its lowest level for 24 years, has hidden (or more accurately, been ignored by the US's ruling class's strategists) the serious economic decline and the continued erosion in the living standards of the working class. In the fourth quarter of 1993, for the first time in nearly a century, the outflow of financial returns paid to foreign investors on the assets they held in the US exceeded all of the profits, dividends and interest payments that US firms and investors collected from their investments abroad. In the following year, 1994, the annual outflow was negative for the first time since 1914. William Greider in his book, One World Ready Or Not, comments: "The outflow of these so-called factor incomes reflected the nation's true balance sheet in the global economy. They were the net sum of earnings on assets going both ways - the profits and interest payments foreigners got from what they had lent or bought in the United States minus what Americans got from their assets overseas."

As recently as 1980 the US had enjoyed a net surplus in 'factor incomes' every year of $35bn or so, equal then to 1.5% of the national income. The income of the US had exceeded the outflows by nearly two to one. This was the product of the massive foreign investments (and exploitation of workers) throughout the world by US imperialism. Now, comments Greider, "It was like a bill for interest due on previous borrowings. The negative flow was certain to continue and increase because it was based on the underlying debts and obligations that had been accumulating for 20 years, primarily from the US's annual trade deficit with other nations. Cumulatively, since 1980, the US has brought $1.5trillion more than it sold in its merchandise trade with foreign nations. The trade deficit started modestly in 1975, exploded during the 1980s and, despite ebbs and surges, set a dollar volume record of $180bn in 1995."

This enormous gap was filled either by borrowing money from abroad in the form of government bonds and private borrowings, or foreign capitalists came to the US and bought up assets in Los Angeles, New York, etc. This added up to an "epochal shift of wealth, probably unmatched in human history in its size and speed, as the richest nation on earth swiftly redistributed wealth to others".

The British economist, Wynne Godley, has pointed out that the US went from holding a net surplus of foreign assets equal to 30% of its own annual economic output in 1970 to a debtor position by 1994 of -8.5%. And the situation, unless "corrected, is going to get much worse". Each year, the American economy is taking on new balance of payments deficits equal to 2-2.5% of its total economic output. This is covered by capital inflows and borrowing to make up the shortfall. It also means that the US's foreign debt obligations were growing at a much faster pace than the underlying economy would have to pay for them. Wynne Godley has estimated that the US's debt position in net foreign assets - now around 9% of GDP - would roughly double in five to six years, reaching 20% of the US GDP by the year 2000. Then, by 2005, it would reach 30% and, five years later, more than 40%. Long before this situation was reached, a seriously deflationary programme would have to be implemented.

The economy's problems have undoubtedly been compounded by the majority of the US bourgeois falling prey to the same disease as their British counterparts. The maintenance of a manufacturing base is now perceived as not important; 'services' are the new engine of capitalism. Such ideas have contributed to the calamitous de-industrialisation of British capitalism. The Clinton administration has also embraced the false notion that the US service sector - banking, insurance, etc - which is producing a growing surplus in global trade, would eventually offset the nation's deteriorating position in manufactured goods. Service exports were in surplus and growing, but they were no replacement for the production of real goods. The service sector would have to quadruple its annual trade volume immediately in order to reverse the trade deficit in real goods. Greider comments: "This was not just unlikely, it was impossible." A symptom of the de-industrialisation of US capitalism is that the employment agency, Manpower, is now the biggest employer of labour. There are also one million lawyers!

The problems with the US economy are undoubtedly compounded by the fact that it is the 'buyer of last resort' for world capitalism. The US absorbed "a generous share of the [world's] excess production every year". In 1980 the US absorbed 27% of world vehicle exports, more than 41% in 1989 and then fell back to 23% by 1993. Germany, by contrast, absorbed only 8% and Japan, of course, a trivial share. The US took 15% of world exports in office and telecommunications equipment in 1980 and 23% in 1993. It absorbed 10% of all steel exports, 18% of heavy machinery, 9% of chemicals. One bourgeois economist wailed: "You got excess capacity and you can't sell it any place? Sell it to the Americans. We're also the market that props up development. If you're China or Indonesia, Thailand or Korea, you achieve rapid economic growth by supplying the Americans. You run a trade surplus with the US and that's how you can earn the capital to finance the rapid growth."

Notwithstanding Clinton and US imperialism's enthusiasm for globalisation and its attendant policies of deregulation, the serious underlying economic position of US capitalism and, at a certain stage, growing unemployment, will lead to a clamour for measures to limit the import of foreign goods. Measures to extend 'free trade' have rebounded on the US.

Unemployment and job insecurity

NAFTA, originally proposed by the Republicans and continued by Clinton, put the US, Canada and Mexico in a 'common market'. Clinton claimed that this would create 200,000 good new jobs for US workers by boosting US exports to the Mexican economy. However, two years later, Mexico was gripped by an economic depression. It was also used by US and foreign multinationals as a convenient low-wage export platform into the rich US market. The US deficit with Mexico soared and contributed to the growing US trade debt. Instead of benefiting the US, NAFTA's effect was an estimated negative job loss of 200,000.

This seems to be contradicted by the drop in unemployment. But highly-paid jobs in manufacturing were being replaced by low-paid jobs (with many workers compelled to do two or three jobs). Many of these jobs were part time and 'contingent', that is, not permanent or secure. US workers who lost their jobs in the recessionary years of 1990-92, suffered a 23% drop in wages, on average, when they found full-time work again. 80% of male workers in the US have seen their wages stagnate or decline. The pay of workers on the median wage in the US has shrunk in real terms by 1% a year, every year from 1989-94. Indeed, over a longer period there has been a stagnation and decline of the real wages of US workers, for something like 20 years. Even Clinton has been compelled to admit, "Most people are still working harder for lower pay than they were making the day I was sworn in as President."

This goes together with insecurity. The number of managers, let alone workers, who feel confident about their job security has plummeted from 79% to 55% from 1982 to today. At the same time, there has been a fabulous piling up of wealth by the rich, Al Gore, in the 1994 presidential elections, stated that the richest 1% owned as much as the lowest 90%. Profitability has increased to "levels last seen in the 1960s". (British Financial Times)

At around 20%, the return on capital earned by companies in the S&P 500 index is well ahead of other industrialised countries where profits have also risen in this boom, but by an average of 10-15%. Now, however, profits have begun to slow down as the cycle begins to come to an end. On the other hand, it is now claimed that the wages of US workers have begun to improve, with a 2.6% annual rise since 1996. This is because of 'tight labour markets', low unemployment, low inflation, and an increase in the minimum wage. It is not uncommon that in the very last stages of an economic upswing, the working class manages to capture a greater share of the wealth it creates. However, the Economic Policy Institute in Washington, which produced this report (The State of Working America 1997-98), admits that: "American families are working harder to stay in the same place and have seen little of the gains in the overall economy."

It also reports: "Amidst positive overall growth, significant economic disparities persist as trends in wages, income and inequality in the 1990s continue to follow patterns set in the 1980s." Most workers, the report says, have grown less secure, and the jobs created are less likely to offer health and pension benefits. Moreover, "Middle class wealth (the value of tangible assets such as houses and cars, plus financial assets, minus debt) has also fallen."

Significantly, it also points out the main reason for current income trends is a continuing wage deterioration among middle and low wage earners and white collar and some college educated workers. The growing discontent of US workers is not yet fully reflected in strike statistics.

Trade union strength

The crude figures on strikes and union membership show that US labour, under the leadership of predominantly right-wing trade union leaders (and tied to the coat-tails of the Democratic Party), has stagnated and, in some senses, has declined. The Wall Street Journal jeeringly declared early in 1998: "Union membership continues to drop in the US."

In the past, a boom or growth in production generally meant an increase in union membership. In the 1950s and 60s, when union membership peaked, growth in the economy created jobs and with it union membership. However, this was largely because of the growth of jobs in already unionised shops. In the seven years of one of the US's 'greatest economic expansions', according to the Wall Street Journal, union membership "continues to fall, both in absolute numbers and as a percentage of the workforce". The AFL-CIO, the trade union federation of US workers, points out that its affiliated unions recruited 400,000 workers in 1997 but this was still not enough to produce a net gain. In the same year, an estimated 2.8 million jobs were created in the US and yet the number of workers represented by unions fell by 159,000 to about 16.1 million. The unions' share of the workforce has dropped to 14.1% last year from 14.5% in 1996.

The labour leaders say membership numbers are not as bleak as capitalist spokes-men point out. Many of the AFL-CIO's biggest unions have reported significant recruitment in the last year. The Teamsters, with 1.4 million members, claim they recruited more than 30,000 workers, while the Service Employees International Union, with 1.1 million members, picked up 58,000 workers. The drop in union membership is exaggerated, they claim, because many of the new workers recruit-ed in 1997 have not yet shown up in the US Labor Department's data. In general, workers are not counted as union members until they have a contract and are paying dues.

This stagnation or decline is in the teeth of significant attempts to increase union membership. John Sweeney, President of the AFL-CIO, pointed out on Labor Day to the increased resources thrown by the unions into recruitment drives. Of the nation's 580 Central Labor Councils, 56 now have programmes that have trained 792 organisers. The Steelworkers' Union has tripled its organising budget, the Carpenters' Union is devoting half of its resources to new campaigns.

There are a number of factors that account for the present position of US unions, which similarly affect the union movements in other advanced industrial countries. The decline of manufacturing and heavy industry, where union density is at its greatest, is one reason. Another, and more important one, is the shift to the right, to a more openly bourgeois position (acceptance of the market, etc) of the union leaders. This acts to undermine and sometimes cancel out attempts at union organi-sation, even where they are successful at first. Militant methods and leaders have, in general, been the most successful. Those who are politically opposed to the capitalist system are the best union organisers. The swing of the trade union leaders to a pro-capitalist position carries with it the ideas of class compromise, 'partnership', and a reliance on so-called pro-labour laws and the bourgeois parties, which enact them rather than on militant class struggle and fighting policies.

In the past in the US, the ideas of 'business unionism' held sway in the summits of the trade union movement. Such ideas, however, clash with the new realities of the world of work in the US and the crisis facing the trade unions. What point is there in workers joining unions unless these new recruits see a palpable benefit in increased wages and changed conditions? Experience has shown that a union leadership, which is tied to class collaboration and is completely out of touch with the wages and conditions of those they purport to represent, is incapable of mobilising effective action against the employers. Therefore, new recruits in this period have tended to drop away as the right-wing trade union leaders show they are incapable of standing up to the bosses' offensives.

This is particularly the case in the US where the class struggle (more than in Britain for instance) has always contained an element of civil war when industrial battles take place. Nowhere is the resistance to the unions more brutal, open and unbridled as in the US. 32% of US companies contesting recognition go on to sack union activists, in violation of the law, and then pay the penalties (which they view as a kind of anti-union licence) for violating the law. The US National Labor Relations Board charged corporations with committing 'unfair labour practices' in no fewer than 12,000 cases last year.

The case of a female worker in Landers Plastics gives a little glimpse of the lengths to which the vicious US bosses will go to prevent union organisation. She signed up a majority of her co-workers into the United Steelworkers Union and petitioned for a recognition election. The terrible conditions in the plant had generated enthusiasm for a union. 77% of Landers workers had been injured on the job, including six with fingers amputated in unguarded machinery. She was then slandered by the bosses for 'sexual harassment' of two male bosses! She allegedly "pulled down the trousers of the two... and made disparaging remarks about their penises". After a long battle, the female worker was reinstated into the Landers Plastics plant. The government had fined Landers for 63 'egregious' safety violations and charged the company with 71 unfair practices. But Landers continues to put off a recognition vote. Disconsolately, this brave union activist declared: "How can I win when women come to me crying, scared for their jobs. Of the 200 workers who signed up for the union over two years only 15 remain."

Another employer took revenge on a New Orleans pipe fitter after he spoke up for union in his shipyard. They made him sit for weeks in a tiny rowing boat in the Mississippi River and instructed him to fish out logs. When he refused, Avondale, a major defence contractor, sacked him and 20 other union supporters. After four years of litigation, the Labor Board ordered that they all be reinstated. Meanwhile, the union's drive for a contract had withered and died.

A whole industry of 'management/labour relations' lawyers in consulting firms are hired by the bosses in massive 'union-busting' drives. They charge upwards of $1m to defeat union recognition elections. One union organiser told the correspondent of The Observer in Britain: "It's surprising we win any elections at all." In fact, the unions have lost 60% of recognition elections in the last seven years. This is despite the fact that the unions only request elections if they have a solid majority of a shop's workforce on record in favour of unionisation. The unions lose because in the months between the government's scheduling of an election and a vote, massive intimidation takes place of workers.

One study found that 62% of US industrial companies threaten to move or shut operations when faced with union votes. Such threats are illegal, but a violation "simply affords another opportunity for law firm consultants to delay the election while the Labor Board investigates". As The Observer comments: "This is a cautionary tale," for the unions in Britain who, under New Labour's 'Fairness in the Workplace' proposals should have union recognition election laws similar to the US on the statute books soon. The trade union leaders in Britain hope this legal structure alone will "help them recover from the devastation of the Thatcher years". But as The Observer continues: "US-style recognition elections are a leaky lifeboat."

Recent bitter disputes

Notwithstanding the huge obstacles in their path, the working class will move into struggle. The unions in the US will be filled out as the mass of the working class, propelled by events, will flood into them and, in the process, begin to transform them. It is true that for the first time in 100 years union membership has dropped below 10% of workers in the private sector. Also, there were only 29 major strikes in the US last year, the lowest ever. In the three decades before Reagan came to power, the unions called an average of 303 major walk-outs each year. Nevertheless, the bitter battles that have taken place in US industry in the last period are a harbinger of the convulsive movements of the US workers to come. The bitterly fought 1997 Teamsters' strike resulted in a partial victory for the workers. However, UPS remain unreconciled to the outcome of the strike and are attempting to take back some of the concessions forced on them last year. A Teamsters spokesman has pointed out: "UPS is still very, very bitter about the strike, and very, very angry at the Teamsters." By deliberately misinterpreting the contract agreed at the end of the strike on the volume of work, the company is trying to nullify the job creation agreement. No full-time union jobs have been created since the strike and the company has been reducing its workforce. UPS have 16,000 fewer part-time and full-time workers than a year ago and several thousand drivers have been officially laid off. The company is undoubtedly engaged in speed-ups, pressurising drivers to work more forced overtime and to work through their lunch hours.

Similarly bitter battles have developed in 1998 between bosses and unions in General Motors, in Bell Telephone, where 73,000 workers went on strike in August 1998, taxi drivers in New York, and in many other companies. The GM strike was one of the most significant. This is the biggest car company in the world, and with more than 200,000 workers on strike, production of a quarter of a million vehicles was lost and GM's profits were reduced by $1.2bn.

The cause of the strike lies in the cutthroat competition between the giants of the auto industry, not just in the US but on a world scale. There is massive overcapacity, which, it is estimated, will be the equivalent of the total auto production in North America by the year 2000. Every car company in the world is involved in ruthless 'cost cutting', that is, wage cuts, speed-ups, etc. GM, which has massively reduced its labour force in the US, has still not been as ruthless in this respect as many of its competitors. It is an open secret that it needs to 'shed' at least 40,000 hourly workers. Little wonder then, as one union representative declared in the British Financial Times: "At the core, it is a feeling of insecurity, a fear of the future and a deep distrust of General Motors."

In competition with "hi-tech, non-unionised Japan" (The British Independent), US car manufacturers have savagely cut 'inefficient' plants, especially in unionised centres like Flint, and have sought to open new ones with non-militant labour forces. GM has moved much of its labour-intensive activities to Mexico, which has reinforced the suspicions of the union, the United Automobile Workers (UAW) that GM wants to move out of the rust belt altogether. Over the last 30 years, GM's market share has dropped from 50% to 30% which, through confrontation with the unions and 'labour costs' savings, it hopes to put into reverse. The strike ended after two months with a stand off but with the ground prepared for further battles. A Flint union activist stated: "GM is claiming communication with the union has been re-established. I can tell you... that is BS [bullshit]. We don't trust each other as far as we can spit."

Labour and Capital battles

The ground has been prepared for an almighty collision between the arrogant US ruling class, bloated by its victories over labour under Reagan, by the fabulous profits piled up in the 1990s, and an increasingly angry US working class. John Sweeney, President of the AFL-CIO, on Labor Day gave vent to the pent-up frustration which is threatening to burst out when he denounced the "cruel, winner-take-all economy", and bitterly condemned the employers for manipulating the labour laws to discourage union organisation.

One of the keys to any fight back of the unions is a concerted drive, particularly in the private sector in which union density has decreased to less than 10% last year from about 27% in the early 1950s. In the public sector, union membership is still growing. It is workers in the 'contingent' sector, some with 'permanent' jobs but in reality very insecure, as well as those in part-time working, who can become a major centre for union organisation.A pointer to future developments is the successful drive by the Canadian Auto Workers Union (CAW) in unionising a McDonald's outlet in Canada.

It is possible that an economic collapse in the US could further undermine union strength. But the accumulated anger of the last 20 years, at low wages and deteriorating conditions, is also a guarantee that huge defensive battles are likely once the bosses attempt to lay-off workers. An actual overall growth in union strength, however, will probably have to wait a further upturn in the US economy after the coming slump. But as in other countries, a politicisation, a greater class awareness, will inevitably develop from the changed situation that will result from this.

Perspectives in the unions are organically connected to the character of the union leadership, which is dominated overwhelmingly by the right-wing. In the Teamsters union, the election of Carey represented a shift towards the left within that union and the trade union movement as a whole. That, however, has now been thrown into reverse by the removal of Carey and his expulsion from the union by the legal intervention of government-appointed US Federal officials. He was found guilty and stripped of his post and barred from the union because of the alleged embezzlement, by his campaign organiser, of union money that was used in his election battle for the presidency with Hoffa. Carey partly contributed to his own downfall because he opted not to fight, as did the former rank-and-file Teamsters, the TDU (Teamsters for a Democratic Union). Hoffa will now probably win the run-off for the vacant presidency. Although Hoffa may demagogically put forward some radical demands, especially in the election campaign, he is the candidate of the right who wishes to return the Teamsters back to the dark days of the past.

Similar battles between the right and incipient left exist throughout the US trade union movement. Sweeney is really on the right of the unions but is more sensitive to the pressures from below than the Kirkland wing of the AFL-CIO.

The right was looking to strengthen its position with a proposed merger between the National Educational Association (NEA) - which is presently outside the AFL-CIO - and the American Federation of Teachers (AFT). In general, Marxists stand for the greatest possible amalgamation and combination of workers in the trade unions. But when it leads to the strengthening of the bureaucratic grip of the right-wing trade union officialdom, then there are occasions when proposals for mergers must be opposed. The NEA is already the largest union in the US with 2.3 million members, and would add 900,000 members to its strength if it merged with the

AFT. The combined union would account for 20% of the membership of the AFL-CIO, and would have been used by the most conservative elements within the AFL to mount an offensive against the current leadership.

However, considerable opposition exists in the NEA to the merger terms which would have ended secret balloting and strengthened the national leadership. This would have undermined the rank-and-file's right to take decisions in committees and assemblies at the base of the union. Moreover, the NEA has opposed merit pay and teacher testing, although in the past it has declared that it is more of a 'professional organisation' than a union. At the same time, it is not affiliated to the AFL-CIO and certainly its members would be repelled from joining a body which is linked to the Clinton regime, which has pursued policies in education of a narrow and reactionary character, which are now being borrowed by Blair in Britain. The opposition prevailed and the merger was rejected at a special union conference in July.

Perspectives for the Labor Party

The looming economic slump in the US will lead to a period of unprecedented ferment and turmoil within the trade unions and the broad labour movement in the US. This will lead, at a certain stage, to the search by workers for independent political representation, a new mass workers' party, in the US.

The present Labor Party could be an anticipation of how things will develop in the future. It is a small, embryonic formation with a union base. The individual membership is 15,000 and one million are affiliated through the unions. Ten small unions and hundreds of local labour bodies have recently joined the Labor Party. At the Labor Party Convention in November, it is expected that the non-electoral stance of the Labor Party will be ended. This will be a step forward with the possibility of the Labor Party in the future standing in elections. However, in the short term, this is unlikely, as the trade union leadership is not yet ready to break decisively with the Democrats.

It is not possible to determine exactly how the Labor Party will develop. Certainly the conditions are being created in the US, particularly in the event of a serious economic crisis, for the evolution of independent workers' political representation. Even Jesse Jackson, currently an adviser to Clinton, has summed up the differences between the Republicans and the Democrats: "What we have got now in the United States is one party, two names. We've got Republicans and Republicans Lite." (The British Guardian, 3 June,1995)

Immigrant communities and ethnic minorities

The US section of the CWI has undertaken serious work within the LP over the past period, actively participating in the building of local chapters. Comrades on the

West Coast have also undertaken important work amongst immigrant workers and communities.

The importance of this work amongst 'minorities' cannot be overestimated. Big changes in the ethnic composition of the US are underway. The rise in the young Latino population has now outstripped that of young Afro-Americans. Fifteen percent of the under-18 age group are Latino, a slightly greater proportion than Afro-Americans. By the year 2020, the Latino share is expected to rise to 22% with Afro-Americans at 16%. The US Census Bureau has calculated that in 2005, Latinos will displace Afro-Americans as the US's largest ethnic minority; by 2050 they will account for a quarter of the population. Shortly after 2050, non-Latino whites will become a North American minority for the first time since the early colonisations by Europeans. The Latino population of the US has nearly doubled since 1980 from 14.6 million to 29.1 million.

The importance of acquiring a base amongst the Afro-American population, particularly the Afro-American working class, is vital. More than at any other time in the post-war period, the Afro-American population now lacks organisation and a voice. The NAACP, which rose to half million members in the 1950s and 60s, articulated the demands of the Afro-American population for the ending of racial segregation in the south and the continued oppression of Afro-Americans in the north. Even those radical organisations from the 1960s and 70s no longer exist and the Afro-American establishment has imposed their own 'leadership' on the Afro-American population.

Anything that threatens the status quo is stamped on, as the recent Million Youth March, in Harlem, demonstrated. Sections of the Afro-American middle class and bourgeois leaders moved heaven and earth to undermine this movement. Farrakhan's Muslims can never attract more than a small minority of the Afro-American population. And yet the brutal murder of James Byrd in east Texas by ex-prisoners with links to the 'Aryan Nation of the Ku Klux Klan' hark back to the Jim Crow murders of the 1950s. This, in turn, led to the mobilisation of Afro-American groups, such as the Black Panthers, which are a pale echo of the movements of the past.

Racial discrimination and conflict between the different ethnic and national groups in the US is woven into the very historical and social fabric of US capitalism and will remain so long as that system exists. Periods of heightened struggle by Afro-Americans are inevitable at certain stages. The same is now true of the growing Latino population, which suffers discrimination in language, jobs and conditions.

These movements, however, tend to take a separatist or 'nationalist' form in periods of stagnation in the class struggle, or of quiescence within the official labour movement because of the grip of the right-wing leaders. Change towards more open class conflict, tends to merge the struggles of the different 'nationalities' in the US

with those of the working class as a whole.
This does not, of course, mean that the class struggle or the basic idea of class unity can simply resolve hostilities and divisions, inherited from the past, between groups of workers from different racial backgrounds. Class unity, solidarity, is absolutely necessary but must be complemented with a programme and action which takes account of the special needs of the different sections of the US proletariat. In this respect, the work which comrades on the West Coast have undertaken amongst the immigrant population is an important beginning.

Economic disaster looming

The US, as the citadel of world capitalism, will be profoundly affected by the coming slump. We have separate material dealing with economic perspectives in the short and medium term, so we will just make a few comments about how this crisis is affecting the consciousness of the US working class. Even before the 'music stops', when the US boom runs completely out of steam, the signs of decay are obvious. In California, for instance, the 'Golden State', and a past model for the rest of the US, all the symptoms of the 'British disease' are manifested. This was at one stage, the "tenth industrial nation in the world", but now suffers from economic stagnation, growing joblessness: some areas have become disaster zones, and there is a net drop in population. There is also the collapse of the infrastructure.

On the East Coast, on the other hand, the city of New York appears, under the right-wing Republican, Mayor Giuliani, to be economically buoyed up. This, however, is largely the spin-off effect of the wealth generated by Wall Street's spiral upwards. It will shortly come crashing down and with it the superficial wealth that has inflated support for Giuliani as well. It should be remembered that one-third of the 35 million population who are officially poor have experienced 'severe poverty', even during a so-called boom,.

A foreboding of what lies in store is reflected in the comparisons, which are more and more drawn, between the present situation and the period prior to 1929. Marx's diagnosis of capitalism has been invoked in this period. Even recent advocates of the 'new paradigm', such as a certain Ed Yardeni, quoted in a British Guardian supplement in July, admits that there is a crisis of overproduction, caused, in his view, because, "capitalism has an arch enemy in corruption. In corruption the rich get richer and the corrupt don't distribute the income sufficiently so that the workers can buy what they make. I think that's one of the basic problems in Asia." Leaving aside the waffle about 'corruption' this is, in the words of another Guardian writer, a justification of Marx, who "warned of a crisis of overproduction."

Other economic commentators have weighed in, warning that the situation if anything is worse than in 1929: "At the time of the great crash, very few Americans were actively involved in the market. It was considered the sort of thing that racy, and rather corrupt, city slackers did. A lot of Americans, if they didn't actually cheer the crash, felt a certain grim satisfaction." (Ron Chernow, a historian of finance). The effects of the depression had a lasting effect both psychologically and also economically. The US market, "did not return to its 1929 peak until 1954, 25 years later."

In the speculative bubble which has gripped the US in the 1990s, an estimated 100 million Americans now own shares. Most, of course, own just a handful of shares, but the tendency has been to invest, either directly or indirectly through 'mutuals', what in the past went into savings. Therefore, a drop in the stock market will have a decisive effect on household incomes and, therefore, on consumption.

In Britain, 27% of the population are 'shareholders', up from 8% in the early 1980s. Many of these 'shareholders' only own one or two shares from the Thatcher privatisations of the 1980s. A drop of 25% in the stock market will have a considerable effect, and a 50% fall, which is possible, will have a decisive effect on household incomes for a big section of the US population.

Lewinsky affair

It is against this background that the crisis arising from Clinton's sexual affairs must be viewed. This is another expression of the political crisis affecting the world bourgeoisie, this time in its most important centre. It points out the contradictions in the US constitutional and electoral system, and the vicious infighting between the major bourgeois parties of the Republicans and Democrats. This infighting is reminiscent of the mutual slaughter of the British feudal aristocracy in the War of the Roses, in the Middle Ages. The Republicans, in a nauseating and hypocritical moral crusade led by the Speaker of the House, Gingrich, have attempted to whip up the 'moral majority'. The Democrats have hit back with similar charges of sexual infidelity against leading Republicans which prompted the British newspaper, The Observer, to write that this was preparing the ground for "laying bare Washington's sex life [which] will make Caligula's Rome look tame". The Democrats have countered with charges against the Republicans of 'sexual McCarthyism'.

The Lewinsky affair was the trigger for demands of impeachment but not the initial reason for the ferocity of the Republicans' anti-Clinton drive. The investigation against Clinton began on the Whitewater issue. The special prosecutor, Starr, stumbled by accident onto the Lewinsky affair. The Republicans, having lost the last two presidential elections, are fearful that Gore, as Clinton's anointed successor, would be elected in the year 2000, thereby establishing a third victory and a virtual Democratic dynasty for the foreseeable future. They, therefore, sought to use their majority of 21 seats in the 435-member House of Representatives and the 10-seat majority in the 100-member Senate. They wish to shatter the base of the Democrats with a campaign of denigration. They hope in the November elections that their grip on both chambers will be reinforced, thereby repeating the control similarly exercised by the Democrats between 1954 and 1980. The aim is to so discredit Clinton and his regime that he is not so much a 'lame duck' as a 'dead duck' for his last two years in office. It cannot be ruled out that the Republicans will proceed with impeachment proceedings, but the situation is very uncertain. Their repugnant moralising has already rebounded on them with increased support for Clinton in the polls. The November mid-term elections will have a profound effect upon which way the Republicans will go. But, even if they increase their support, it may serve them better to leave the damaged Clinton in power rather than see Gore in office in the two years up to the next presidential campaign.

The vicious political infighting between the 'political class' of the US has served to further discredit the presidency and the Congress - vital institutions of the bourgeoisie. The growing disenchantment with fraudulent and meaningless elections is shown by the fact that less than 50% voted in the last presidential elections. Clinton's real crime, the real impeachable offence, is that he has acted as the front man of US big business to the detriment of the working class and poor. He has balanced the budget and Wall Street has boomed. But, as one political observer in Britain commented: "Those are achievements that will be toasted by bankers but not by the children of the ghetto he emoted so effectively about."

The economic, social and political situation in the US is preparing the ground for the emergence of the working class, one of the most important detachments of the world working class. A measure of the success of our ideas will be how, in the mighty maelstrom of events in the US, the CWI and its US section builds a powerful pole of attraction for the best workers and youth who will be moving into struggle.

5 - Russia and Eastern Europe

Capitalist restoration in the former USSR has been an unmitigated disaster for the peoples of this region, particularly for the workers and peasants. The latest crisis is also a big defeat for imperialism, which has invested much political and economic resources in guaranteeing a 'return to the market'. The IMF, for instance, has in the past poured in resources without the usual 'safeguards' and preconditions with which it intervened recently in Asia. (Most of the financial reserves given by the IMF and other western financial interests found their way into private bank accounts before being salted away into secret foreign accounts.) The general processes since the beginning of the 1990s are set out in the excellent programme produced by the CWI section in the former USSR. As that document points out, "We always warned that if capitalism was restored in the USSR, it would be a weak, sickly and corrupt form of capitalism more akin to that found in Asia or Latin America. The likelihood of a new Sweden or Germany emerging was always nil. We can only be accused of over-optimism in that respect."

The figures of economic collapse are at least twice as bad as those experienced by the USA during the Great Depression. Over the whole of the Soviet Union, GNP has plummeted by over 50%. Millions of workers do not get paid for months and sometimes years. In many areas telephones, heating, hot water and other features of a modern society no longer function. Male life expectancy has dropped to 58 years, in some regions it is as low as 43.

None of the republics has been able to resist the process of privatisation, although there are clearly differences of pace. Russia, in many respects, forged the way and is now able to boast one of the highest non-state sectors in the CIS. The Ukraine proved to be not too far behind. Workers have gained no benefit from this as the factories have been privatised and handed over to various crooks and gangsters. The prize for the most callous privatisation programme probably has to go to Kazakhstan, where the Nazarbayev regime has sold off key enterprises to the western companies that pay the largest bribes into the numerous off-shore accounts set up by members of his own family. They, in turn, shut down all the factories that cannot make a profit. Whole towns no longer work, schools can no longer teach children, homes are no longer heated in what the miners of Kentau call, "genocide of the people".

The process of capitalist restoration has been completed in all the former republics of the USSR. Even in Belarus, where pro-marketeers complain that President Lukashenko has held back market reforms, and 'communists' and 'patriots' hold him up as the saviour of 'socialism', it is well on the road to capitalist restoration. The gangster capitalists of the former USSR were able to dream, up to the beginning of 1998, that their 'shock therapy' had laid the basis for a real growth of capitalism. However, even the most optimistic pro-marketeers, such as Chubais, foresaw real growth only beginning in 2002 while in Kazakhstan the government was only prepared to guarantee economic growth by the year 2030!

There are enormous differences between regions in such a vast semi-continent as the former USSR. Moscow during the latter part of the 1990s has been relatively prosperous because 80% of investment from abroad goes through this region. However, absolute impoverishment, mass unemployment and a sense of hopeless- ness has gripped the great bulk of the regions and many towns of the former USSR. A colossal deindustrialisation process has taken place with most investment and growth coming from the fuel energy sector. Now, the collapse of commodity prices, particularly of oil (detailed earlier), is a body blow to the Russian economy and to the bourgeoisie. What 'growth' has taken place has been on the basis of the ruthless exploitation and robbery of the proletariat. As with all nascent bourgeoisies, methods of primitive capitalist accumulation have been tried, the non-payment of wages the most blatant of these.

Kiriyenko 'the brief'

But, even before the financial and economic meltdown experienced by Russia and its political fallout in September 1998, it was clear that a massive mood of opposition was brewing to these measures and towards the Yeltsin regime. This was reflected in the removal of Chernomyrdin from government in early 1998 and his replacement by Kiriyenko as prime minister. We pointed out at the time that while the struggle between the different capitalist cliques or 'clans' was a factor in the change of government, far more decisive was the growing opposition of the working class to the brutal methods employed by the capitalists. The debates, votes and eventual ratification of Kiriyenko in the Russian Duma (parliament) took place against the background of decisive sections of the working class coming onto the streets to demand payment of back wages. Some sections, such as the miners, resorted to the 'arrest' of managers and directors and the occupation of mines and workplaces. Given this situation, we predicted that the Kiriyenko government would be blown away in a matter of months.

The trigger for the downfall of 'Kiriyenko the brief' was the financial and economic collapse in Russia in August-September 1998. It has been estimated that 40% of industry (as opposed to output) has been destroyed between 1990-98 in the former USSR. The underlying economic catastrophe was reinforced by the plummeting price of oil and the effects of the Asian crisis. Russian capitalism and the government of Yeltsin has been sustained by the enormous piling up of debt, both internally and also from loans from foreign banks. This colossal pyramid of debt collapsed as the rouble was devalued, losing 66% of its value in three weeks with prices on the street increasing by 150% in the same period. Bourgeois experts wailed that an area that was supposed to promise a 'rebirth of capitalism', threatened to become the trigger for a new recession or slump. The Wall Street Journal commented that there was some irony in the present situation whereby "the former enemy of world capitalism has now been converted to the cause only to threaten serious damage to the whole system".

The collapse of the debt pyramid has in turn led to a partial default on the $194bn which is owed by Russia to western banks. Some bourgeois experts have tried to pretend that this default will not have a serious effect. They have argued that Russia's stock exchange is puny and is of less value than the British company, Sainsbury's. However, this is a view not shared by Martin Taylor of Barclays Bank which has lost more than £250 million ($410 million) through the Russian default. Some of the bourgeois of the west have suggested retaliation, with threats to seize Russian assets abroad. Taylor has debunked the idea that these events will have no effect on Europe and the capitalist west in general. Already a flight to quality, in the form of government bonds, is under way. In its wake, a credit crunch, a refusal to give risky loans, is materialising.

In desperation, some bourgeois commentators have tried to pretend that the major powers of Europe will not be burnt by the Russian firestorm. After all, they claim, only 2% of German exports go to the former USSR. Much more important, however, are the repercussions of events in Russia on Eastern Europe, which have reinforced the already serious effect of the crisis in Asia (13% of German exports go to this region). Throughout Eastern Europe, the stock exchanges have suffered serious setbacks. The social and political repercussions of the economic crisis in Russia were immediately felt in the Duma's rejection of Chernomyrdin, Yeltsin's nominee for prime minister. During the crisis, the air was thick with warnings from Lebed that the position of Russia was worse than in January 1917, on the eve of the February Russian revolution. Chernomyrdin warned that the country would "be in flames" like Indonesia unless his government was installed quickly. Subsequently Lebed, governor of the Siberian region of Krasnoyarsk and a leading presidential hopeful, has commented that the mood in the armed forces has "reached breaking point". He pointed out that some units were "seriously considering scaling down to two meals a day, and after 26 years in the army I know very well that a hungry soldier is an angry soldier". It is reported also by military sources that the army has already consumed 80% of the food reserves kept in the case of war. Top commanders have suggested to servicemen that they fish, hunt and gather mushrooms in the forests to survive until the government of Russia could afford to pay wage arrears that date back months! Tales have appeared in the media of the starvation of conscripts who have been forced to eat dog food. The mood in the army has been shown by the incident involving a young conscript on a nuclear powered submarine in Murmansk who shot eight fellow crew members before being shot by a special commando squad.

The possibility of a coup cannot be ruled out but does not seem likely in the immediate period ahead, given the installation of the Primakov government. Notwithstanding what happens at the top, the desperate mood from below can result in 'popular uprisings', as food shortages and starvation looms. Even potatoes, the staple diet of Russians when all else fails, will be in short supply it seems because of the bad summer. The position of the poorest, already desperate, now appears hopeless.

The collapse of the rouble means, for instance, that an old age pensioner in the Russian enclave of Kaliningrad, who previously eked out an existence on $118 a month, now receives closer to $41. Desperate old people have appeared on television, having just been turned away from food shops where they cannot afford to pay the price demanded, with one declaring that all that is left for her is to "go home and hang myself". But it is not just the old, the sick and those on fixed incomes that suffer. The working class and the middle class, even in relatively prosperous areas, like Moscow, have been hit hard. Credit cards are just not accepted at cash dispensing machines.

Rejection of consequences of capitalism

There is, in effect, a three-fold crisis in Russia. There is a currency crisis with the devaluation of the rouble. There is also a capital market crisis as loans and credit has dried up. This has repercussions not just in Russia but internationally as we have pointed out. Foreign investors have lost, because of the defaults, an estimated $100bn which is the "biggest credit loss ever imposed on private-sector creditors". There is a financial crisis with the complete collapse of the stock exchange and the market and, last but not least, there is a terrible, endemic crisis in the real economy. On top of this, inflation has increased, with the hard earned savings, particularly of the middle class, wiped out and with the spectre of a Weimar-type situation of hyper inflation, or even of stagflation. The state, the government, is in crisis with no real authority amongst the mass. Eighty-four percent of the population now believe that the 'drunkard who runs the Kremlin', Yeltsin, should be removed. The moral bankruptcy of the government goes together with the financial and economic bankruptcy of the state.

These events signify a massive rejection of the consequences of the introduction of capitalism in the former USSR. However, no clear alternative is posed before the masses. The major oppositional force, the KPRF (Communist Party of the Russian Federation) led by Zyuganov, is not a genuine party of the masses, is not a genuine workers' party. It represents that section of the bureaucracy excluded from sharing in the spoils of the massive 1990s privatisation programme. It combines old-style Stalinists who yearn for a return of the 'command economy' with those, like Zyuganov, who recognise the market and stand for a 'mixed economy', that is, capitalism but with a considerable state sector. Even before the Primakov government was installed, Clinton on his visit to Moscow raised the spectre of a "return to the command economy".

No doubt there will be those 'Marxists', who have been utterly incapable of understanding the processes at work in the ex-Stalinist states, who will take this and the coming to power of the Primakov government as an indication that this is a real possibility. There is no immediate prospect of such a development. Zyuganov does not want this nor do the different elites who have been struggling, sometimes viciously, amongst each other for a greater share of the loot arising from privatisation. Under the impact of the crisis, even Yeltsin was compelled to ratify the renationalisation of eight banks, including three of the biggest finance houses. This does not, however, represent a return to the 'command economy'. These are measures of a state capitalist character. They signify a more 'controlled' return to capitalism. Moreover, serious bourgeois commentators both in Russia and outside have urged the Primakov government to go a lot further and act against "wild or gangster capitalism" by renationalising significant sections of industry. The purpose of such measures, if implemented, will be to renovate such industries, paid for by the state and, therefore indirectly, by the working and middle classes, and then hand them back to the capitalists.

Growth of imperialist appetite

Although weakened by recent events, the Russian bourgeoisie will still attempt to assert itself, particularly abroad. Its growing imperialist appetite and actions are touched on in the programme of our CIS section: "The new Russian bourgeoisie will use the overwhelming weight of the Russian economy to expand their area for exploitation, use the cheaper labour found in other republics, take control of the natural resources and speed up the capitalisation process in those republics that have lagged behind.

"Already the newly established capitalist Russia is acting in an imperialist manner in relation to the former Soviet republics. Russian companies such as Gazprom constantly threaten to cut off energy supplies to the Ukraine and other republics unless debts are paid. Latin America-style debt-equity swaps are being used where the debts of the non-Russian republics are being written off in exchange for shares in industrial enterprises. Russian banks are demanding the right to take over privatised factories and Russian troops are patrolling the border to the Caucasian and some central Asian republics. The pledge that Yeltsin made to support Kuchma in the next Presidential election was directly tied to the latter's promise to allow Russian banks to participate in the Ukrainian privatisation process.

"Moreover, attempts to form a new union are likely to reinvigorate national tensions in regions which see Russia as an oppressor state. President Kuchma discovered soon after his election that his promise to move back towards Russia threatened to cause a breakaway of the West Ukraine.

"In this sense, the demand to restore the USSR is a reactionary slogan. With capitalism restored in the different republics, reunification can only lead to further marketisation and privatisation in those republics in which reforms are lagging those of Russia. Moreover, support for the formal slogan of restoring the USSR by parties that claim to be left, in reality, turns them into supporters of Russian imperialism. This is clearly the case with the Russian Communist Party and, to a lesser degree, the Communist Party of the Ukraine. As a result, parties, which support that slogan are overwhelmingly Russian-speaking and find it difficult to win support amongst other nationalities. Simonenko, leader of the CPU, was heckled and booed as a Moscow man when he recently visited Lvov.

"In each of the republics, only when the working class organise can they defend their interests. They will find that they cannot limit their struggle to their own factory or even their own region, but will soon find that their interests are the same as those of workers in the other republics.

"Workers need to organise to ensure that if economic links between factories in different republics are re-established, they are done so in the interests of the workers themselves."

However, the mood amongst the mass of the working class is a different question. The movements in 1998 signified a massive rejection of the consequences of a return of the market. This is most noticeable amongst those groups who first embraced it nine or ten years ago. The miners, for instance, the shock troops in Yeltsin's rise to power, have reaped a terrible whirlwind in the economic desolation of the mining areas through the return of the market. In the decisive mining areas of Vorkuta and the Kuzbass, these very same miners have swung over into opposition with many of them searching for an alternative.

The significant growth of the forces of the CWI in the CIS is a harbinger of the colossal upheavals that loom. The heroic work of maintaining a toehold in the most difficult objective conditions is now beginning to pay dividends. From the new generation who are beginning to be radicalised by the economic and political developments, have come the new members that have travelled into the ranks of our organisation. Our work with the miners and other workers has established us as a small but extremely energetic and effective force, which can in the future attract wide layers of workers.

Despite the claims of bourgeois experts that, as opposed to Russia, Eastern Europe signifies a success story for the return of capitalism, the reality is very much different. A few countries have done better than the USSR, with some growth, but also with a significant deterioration in social conditions and the economic position of the working class.

Eastern Europe

Two regions in Eastern Europe have experienced growth, as the document of the CIS comrades point out: "Estonia, due to its links with Scandinavia, attracted $295 a head from 1989-94 and the Czech Republic $289. In contrast, Russia attracted $11 a head and the Ukraine and Moldova $9." However, recent developments in the Czech Republic show that "this localised growth is not based on solid foundations. The rainstorms that swept Eastern Europe in May 1997, coinciding with the currency crisis, was sufficient to undermine the economy and trigger a government crisis." The discontent of the mass of the people and the disappointment at the results of a return to capitalism explain the chronic political instability in all the countries of Eastern Europe. In the Czech Republic, for instance, the ODS, led by the architect of reborn Czech capitalism, Vaclav Klaus, was defeated in the general election in July by the Czech 'social democrats'. Under his rule, Prague benefited as well as business people, bankers and young professionals. But there is bitter disappointment at the drop in living standards of older workers, pensioners, the sick and the unemployed that, according to the British Financial Times, felt "betrayed". In desperation, many of these voters turned to the Social Democrats led by Milos Zeman. Even former supporters of Klaus were repelled by the rampant corruption and colossal greed of his closest supporters and the looting of the national treasury by the capitalists.

One of the immediate results of capitalist restoration has been the opening of old racial tensions that were unresolved by Stalinism. The Roma people became one of the first victims of social changes being almost excluded from society when it comes to access to jobs, housing and even public shops or bars. Proposals for an apartheid-style segregation in the city of Pilsen, according to human rights activists, are "reminiscent of the Nazi era when Roma, along with Jews, were separated from the rest of the population". The Roma people are regularly attacked by neo-Nazis who have links with similar groups in Germany and Austria - 32 have been killed in racially-motivated attacks in the Czech Republic since 1989. Moreover, they are harassed by the police and face massive discrimination in housing and welfare. Czech Roma people have been murdered by skinheads with the compliance of the state and, in particular, the police. The general situation has led to total division of Roma and Czech communities and produced a massive emigration wave, unprecedented since the time of the USSR bureaucracy's invasion in 1968.

The election did not give the Social Democrats an outright majority. They are, therefore, reliant on Klaus's party. As one commentator pointed out: "It [the new government] will be swimming in a sea of problems he [Klaus] created. He can bring it down and ride back on a white horse."

On the basis of feeble Czech capitalism the political instability will continue with the parliamentary cradle rocked from 'left' to right and back again without any solution to the underlying problems of the mass of the working class and middle class. The Communist Party retains support, particularly amongst the old pensioners and some sections of the working class. If the Czech Republic is further seriously affected by the Russian and Asian crisis, as is likely, it cannot be excluded that the masses in desperation may, at least on the parliamentary field, give increased support to the CP. At the same time, as with the rest of Eastern Europe, the issue of a genuine mass workers' party will be posed in the convulsive events which will develop.

The soap bubble of Poland's success is also going to be punctured in the next period. Any growth that has taken place in the past has been creamed off by the new Polish elite, many of them ex-Stalinist bureaucrats. The presidency is in the hands of an 'ex-communist', Alexander Kwasniewski, but with a weak constituency of 20-30% of the former 'communist electorate'. The Solidarity-led government has

60% of the deputies in the parliament (Sejm). The dilemma and contradictions within the pro-capitalist Solidarity is summed up by the crisis of the Ursus factory in Warsaw and in the chronic weakness of Polish agriculture. The giant Ursus tractor factory has been targeted by the Solidarity-led government for 'restructuring and privatisation'. They wish to attract foreign investment, but this has brought them up against the opposition of the local Solidarity union. The same conflict is taking place in the loss-making coal industry where, according to the Financial Times, "job cuts are urgently needed", and also in the steel industry. The government is looking to sack 2,500 workers in Ursus from a 12,000-strong workforce. This was rejected by the unions, which has brought the government into conflict with its base.

The position of this factory is aggravated by the crisis in Polish agriculture. Unlike in Hungary and the Czech Republic, where much land was collectivised, Poland remained, even under Stalinist rule, predominantly a country of peasant smallholdings. There are an astonishing two million farms, more than in the whole of the rest of Central Europe combined. Moreover, agriculture accounts for 27% of employment, compared with just 7% in Hungary and 5% in the Czech Republic. Even the Financial Times comments: "Most peasants are worried about the future, fearing capitalism as much as communism."

Under the pressure of the European Union, a process of 'consolidation' has already taken place with the number of farms falling by over 100,000 since 1988. However, opposition to a further contraction has increased amongst the peasantry, which is linking up with the fate of the workers in the Ursus factory. The leader of the Ursus workers declared: "The European Union wants to liquidate 90% of our agriculture," which will, of course, dramatically undermine the sales of Ursus tractors.

Their opposition is reinforced by the knowledge that the rich farmers and agribusiness in western Europe, particularly in Britain, are rushing to buy up cheap land in Eastern Europe. The cost of land on average is one-tenth of what it is in East Anglia in England and, with the expected entry of Poland into the EU by 2002, these foreign buyers can be expected to benefit from CAP subsidies. Although the opposition to the Solidarity-led government can lead, in the first instance, into increased support for the more right-wing, Catholic and nationalist parties, the even greater upheavals which loom in Poland will raise the idea of independent political representation by the working class at a certain stage.

Chaotic and confused

The picture in the rest of Eastern Europe varies only in its degree of 'awfulness' as far as the working class is concerned. Extreme volatility has been demonstrated in Hungary with the 'Socialists', the former Stalinists, led by prime minister Gyula Horn, enjoying a landslide victory four years ago. However, in the elections in May

1998 they lost a third of their seats and were replaced by the Fidesz/Hungarian Civic Party, a right-wing party founded only ten years ago. This resulted from the brutal austerity programme of the 'Socialists' which, while it earned high praise from the capitalists in the west, alienated the mass of the workers and middle class. Economic and political instability is the order of the day as Fidesz is reliant on the votes of the Smallholders Party, which demagogically offered to scrap university tuition fees, build low-cost housing projects, etc. It is unlikely to remain in power for four years.

An even more chaotic and confused situation exists in neighbouring Romania. The country's GDP plunged by 9.4% in real terms in the first quarter of the year compared to 1997. Industry contracted by 7.4% but the biggest drop came in the still sizeable agricultural sector, which experienced a 37% drop. The economy had contracted by 6.6% in 1997 and the 'best hope' economic scenario for this year is a drop of 'only' 2%, which is in all probability a gross underestimate. The major political formations are composed of different pro-market, incessantly squabbling parties with different capitalist politicians acting on behalf of opposing business and industrial interests. The Romanian president, Constantinescu, describes the conflict between the parties as "merely... over the speed of reforms". For "reforms" read privatisation and the introduction of the market.

In the run up to the resignation of the Ciorbea government in March 1998, the foreign minister was forced to resign after failing to substantiate allegations that senior politicians were foreign agents, while the transport minister was sacked for publicly criticising the prime minister.

The Democratic Party (PD), the junior partner in the ruling coalition, in power since 1996, is mostly drawn from the younger members of the former Stalinist elite. After the revolution of 1989, as with many of their cousins in the rest of Eastern Europe, these creatures moved into private business, looted state assets and set up a network of their supporters. Its leader, Petre Roman, was a close associate of former president Ion Iliescu, and was prime minister in the first post-Stalinist government from 1990-91. They are opposed in particular by the Peasant Party, which purports to represent the rural population, but stands for the restoration of agricultural land to its former owners, which would be a catastrophe for Romania.

Stirring of the masses

The political deadlock in Romania has halted the process of privatisation for the time being but international capital, through the aegis of the IMF, is exerting enormous pressure for the process to be stepped up. In all of this the condition of the masses sinks lower with endemic unemployment and inflation reckoned now to reach 151% by December.

The next period in Eastern Europe is likely to see a stirring of the masses. Even in what is left of former Yugoslavia, the largely Serbian state, the working class has begun to move into opposition to Milosevic. The ethnic conflict with Croatia and then with Bosnia and now with Kosova acted to dampen down mass protests against Milosevic despite the catastrophic fall in living standards. But conditions are so bad that opposition is now visible and growing. The economy has been crippled by years of international sanctions imposed for Belgrade's role in the Bosnian civil war. This has resulted in more than 30% unemployment. Many workers are on forced leave with little or no pay.

In recent months across Serbia, teachers, health and transport workers, as well as arms workers have held partial stoppages. This is despite the fact that there is no coherent nationwide labour movement threatening to bring down Milosevic's Serbian coalition of 'socialists' and ultra-nationalists. However, the grip which Milosevic's Socialist Party machine has over the trade unions is beginning to weaken. In mass demonstrations workers have denounced the Milosevic leadership: "They are sick with amnesia, they eat caviar and drink whisky. How long will it last? The devil's blood runs in their veins."

Stoppages of two hours, and week-long partial hunger strikes by some workers are resorted to in desperation at the fact that many have not been paid for more than a year. Poverty wages which amount to $27 a month and a bus pass are the norm for many. The working class is still not ready for all-out strike action but the regime is obviously concerned that the protests which have taken place so far have been led by the Alliance of Trade Unions of Serbia (SSS) which up to now has been allied to the Socialist Party. One trade union leader declared: "The Socialists want to control us but can't... our trade union is trying to join the streams of discontent into one river that will sweep away the leadership that brought us this crisis."

The independent trade union federation is, it seems, gradually increasing its strength but is confused politically and looks towards the model of Walesa's Solidarity trade union movement in Poland. In their confusion and desperation many workers have turned to the extreme nationalist Radical Party with its demagogy and anti-western rhetoric.

The picture of spasmodic small protests by workers can change given the further collapse of the already battered economies of Eastern Europe in the period that is opening up. Difficult though it has been for the CWI to maintain tenuous contact and a foothold in some countries, with the exception of the excellent work that has been done in the Czech Republic, in the next period greater opportunities will exist for our ideas - those of genuine Marxism. Ideological confusion is undoubtedly the major feature in the consciousness of the mass of the working class. But it is events, and mighty events at that, which will demonstrate the incapacity of an already discredited capitalism to show a way forward.

Albania perhaps best typifies the collapse and the lack of an alternative. Albanian wages, it is now estimated, are lower than the average for Africa while 70% of the workforce is unemployed. Primitive barter, payment in goods, is now the norm as the country visibly disintegrates into a 'Mad Max' scenario. Most of the population is sustained by cash, which is sent back by Albanian exiles in Greece, and elsewhere in Europe. At the same time imperialism is penetrating and seizing the assets of the country: 500 Italian companies already operate in Albania.

Ideological confusion still persists amongst the broad mass of the working class in Eastern Europe and Russia, nevertheless an important group of advanced workers will become more open to the ideas of genuine Marxism and socialism, and the programme of the CWI in the period that we are going into.

A Socialist Millennium

We have seen that as the 1990s draws to an end, the promises made by capitalist strategists in the early part of the decade have turned to ashes. The new millennium, which was supposed to have begun with a strong triumphalist world capitalism preparing for a new century of domination, will instead begin against the backdrop of unprecedented world disorder, ethnic, national and racial tension, as well as a devastating world recession or slump. The viability of any system ultimately depends upon its ability to develop the productive forces. It will gradually dawn on the proletariat in the tumultuous events which impend, that outmoded capitalism promises only unrelieved misery. In these events, the possibility of building mass parties of the working class on the basis of a socialist and revolutionary programme will be posed.

As important, a new mass International, as envisaged by Lenin and Trotsky, can take shape. Our task is to draw all the necessary conclusions to lay the foundations for building such a force, which can introduce the greatest liberation in history, world socialism.

First draft circulated September 1998
Resolution adopted by World Congress November 1998

Europe at a Turning Point

The new global crisis of capitalism will have a huge impact on future developments in Europe as it takes place against a different background than the last recession in 1989-91. At that time, the problems of capitalism were overshadowed by the collapse of Stalinism and its negative effects on the consciousness of the masses.

The process of globalisation has meant that the repercussions of a crisis in one continent, or in one major country, could spread across the world more rapidly than before. Dramatic changes in one part of the world can cause a domino effect. The illusion that Europe could somehow manage to avoid being affected by Asia's deep slump, a downturn in the US and international financial turmoil will be shattered. The world economy is dangerously dependent on the US at the same time as the recovery in the US and the European Union is running out of steam. This in turn points towards an a world slump or a synchronised deep recession.

The US economy is already slowing down and is moving into a recession in the course of 1998. A slowdown in the US will mark the end of the weak recovery in the EU countries. The impact of a US recession on Europe would be particular marked if the value of the US dollar begins to fall. Europe's exports have up to now been boosted by the depreciation of the western European currencies against the US dollar and the British pound, but these trends will most likely be reversed during 1999. The deustchmark has already regained strength against the US dollar and the British pound is set to fall as the country moves into a recession this year.

The recovery has reached its peak

A downturn in Europe has already begun in Britain, where a fall in manufacturing output and a profit squeeze have been accompanied by a slowdown in the service sector. Latest reports from both France and Germany indicate that the recoveries in both those countries are looking more and more fragile.

The situation in the world economy is more volatile then at any stage since the 1930s. There is a strong possibility that the world economy will experience a similar, disastrous crash-landing as in 1929. The factors that point in the direction of a crash are: the over-valuation of shares at the same time as the economy is slowing down, and companies are experiencing weaker sales and lower profit growth. This contradictory situation cannot last. Profit growth is a pre-condition for the continuation of the stock market boom. The longer this contradiction lasts, the bigger the fall. Whenever in the past the stock market reached such heights as today, it has fallen sharply. A crash could be triggered off by the banking crisis in Japan, a default on loans by a debt-ridden country or a new wave of competitive devaluations. Even a minor, accidental event could, given the present instability, trigger off a crash that will spread throughout the world.

Europe will, most likely, move into a slump rather than a recession in 1999, when the full impact of the global crisis is going to be felt. However, it is not possible to give an exact timetable, neither can we at this stage foresee how deep and how long this slump will last. Our prognosis has to be conditional in that respect.

A classical crisis of capitalism means...

The upheaval which erupted first in Asia is a classical crisis of capitalism, expressed in over-capacity and even over-production.

The present excess of unsold goods or capacity that cannot be used, what the bourgeois economists used to call a "a glut-economy", will give way to an enormous destruction of productive forces and job cutbacks on a global scale as the capitalists try to "balance" the market's "supply and demand". The level of unsold goods in, for example, Japan is higher than any time in modern history. This is compelling Japanese companies to cut production and slash prices.

... Tougher competition from abroad

The European monopolies are facing tougher and tougher competition from abroad. Japanese capitalism and other crisis-ridden economies in Asia are bound to try to capture a bigger share of the market in Europe. The US market, especially when it is heading towards a recession, cannot absorb all the cheap goods exported from Japan and other crisis-ridden countries in Asia. On top of that, a widening of the US trade gap with Japan in particular can give rise to protectionist sentiments and growing demands for trade regulation, as in the 1980s.

This will give Japanese capitalism no choice other than to turn to European markets and the prices of Japanese goods are falling, due to deflation and a weak yen. The rapid increase in Japanese car exports to Europe (up 32 per cent in the first 11 months of 1997) is just one example.

As was pointed out in the British Financial Times 15 November 1997: "For Japanese car-makers, expansion in Europe is important at this point in their global business strategy, mainly due to the mature domestic market. The share of Japanese sales in the US has reached the politically sensitive level of about 24 per cent. Raising exports to expand sales (in the US) has become increasingly risky. The situation raises the importance of Europe as an export market to soak up excess production in Japan.." World-wide overcapacity in the car industry is on its way to becoming the equivalent of the entire North American car industry. According to the European Metal Workers Federation: "Hundreds of thousands of workers in the European car and auto components sectors are set to lose their jobs over next few years, because of overcapacity, stagnant demand and cheap imports."

In addition to that, US capitalism, after losing sales in Asia and faced with the prospect of falling profits, would try to increase its share of the European market. A weaker dollar would benefit US exports at the expense on its European competitors. The outcome of tougher competition from abroad and slower export market growth will take its toll on European output in the coming period. In the words of the US Wall Street Journal 24-25 July 1998: "Declines on Wall Street and falling consumer demand have fuelled fears that the good times in the U.S. are nearing an end. The alarm is beginning to cause sectors (industries in Europe) to hold back on invest-ment...and leading many analysts to believe that the rest of 1998 and beyond could prove a rough ride."

Consumption inside the EU, depressed by years of cuts, tax increases (on ordinary people) and persistent mass unemployment, cannot overtake exports as an engine for sustained growth. This will especially be the case if the majority of EU countries are trying to implement the strict financial framework laid down for European Monetary Union.

"The EMU would be particularly vulnerable during an economic downturn" The austerity measures stipulated by the Maastricht convergence criteria in order to prepare for EMU prolonged the last recession in Europe. Now the majority of the EU governments have a dilemma. They have a lot at stake, both financially and politi-cally, in making EMU work. But if they continue the same strict policy as before they will run the risk of puncturing the recovery in Europe.

The economic convergence inside the EU is mainly superficial. It is primarily the recovery and the relative stability of major world currencies since 1994 that have made it possible for the ruling classes and governments in Europe to take the first step towards EMU in May 1998. This was at a time when the EU was experiencing the fastest growth rate of this decade in many countries, aided by quite fast growth in the broad money supply.

The EMU has currently got full support from the ruling classes, the political elite and the top trade union leaders. But "Europe's people are against it. There is a marked lack of popular enthusiasm for the euro in Europe", wrote The British Economist 11 April 1998. Even Ireland's vote on the Amsterdam Treaty showed that there is little popular support for EMU despite the Irish Republic receiving the equivalent of nearly five per cent of its GDP from different EU funds in 1997. No government can in the long run just ignore this lack of support.

The last recession in the early 1990s led to the collapse of the EU Exchange Rate Mechanism (ERM) and a wave of competitive devaluations across Europe. A new recession, or more likely a slump, would once again make it impossible to maintain a fixed exchange rate and an all-European interest rate set by the new European

Central Bank (ECB). This will mean that the EMU will most likely break up before 2002. Nevertheless, as The British Financial Times Guide to Economic & Monetary Union, July 1998 wrote: "The constraints of EMU could lead to extreme economic and financial tensions in time of crisis. EMU would be particularly vulnerable during a economic downturn."

There is a huge difference between the currently booming Irish economy and, for example, the slow growth rate that German and French capitalism have enjoyed in the recent years. On top of that, Italy, one of the countries that wants to be part of the EMU, is already on the verge of a recession and no chain is stronger than its weakest link. A pre-requisite for a single monetary policy, or a stability pact, are similar conditions in the different countries. Without this, a single economic policy, particular in the context of an impending global crisis, is not workable. The EMU project will therefore tend to blow apart when the world economy moves into a slump and the EMU countries diverge more and more.

The real test for the euro is still to come. It is one thing to bless the EMU project while the economy is recovering and another thing to implement the necessary changes in the face of economic storms (including the first post-EMU recession), political instability and social turmoil. The tendency towards a world market divided by the three blocs, Japan, US and the EU/EMU, is undoubtedly compelling the countries inside the euro-zone to try, repeatedly, to go ahead with EMU. But not even the existing clique of EMU members is fully integrated, let alone Europe as a continent. The British Observer, 3 May 1998, described what it called "The nightmare scenario": "With mounting economic turmoil and little popular support for the single currency, governments - particularly newly elected ones, untarnished by the euro - are likely to want to pull out. History shows that every significant currency union that hasn't been backed by full political union has fallen apart. Fund managers in the city are already working out how to take advantage of this. As with the collapse of the ERM in 1992, huge profits can be made if you play it right. Many are forecasting speculative attacks on the single currency in its first years of existence. ...But if a country does want to pull out, it will not be an orderly process. There is no mechanism in the Maastricht Treaty for withdrawal... The row over the European Central Bank will seem like a teddy bears' picnic compared with the rows as members countries fight for economic well-being. All will be pursuing different agendas, and all will want to amend, or simply break, the treaty."

For a socialist Europe – a workers' Europe

Capitalism is still rooted in the nation state, which is not an economic category but a social formation that includes historical elements such as territorial property, a common language and culture, etc. Each different national bourgeoisie still depends on the various forms of protection provided by its state apparatus and government, despite globalisation and the fact that the EU has developed beyond being just a trade bloc. The barriers on the development of productive forces put up by the national state cannot simply be overcome by purely economic changes. It is a social question, which means that only the working class can bring the borders down and unite Europe on the basis of socialism and workers' democracy.

However, the national state and national governments' power and ability to act independently, against the will of the market (particular the global financial markets), have been reduced by the process of globalisation. That process has been accelerated by political decisions, such as the dismantling of capital controls, de-regulation, privatisation and the drive to create the most favourable conditions possible for capital. The Single European Act ("the single market"), various EU legislation and uniform regulations, tax-harmonisation, etc. have acted as means of stimulating further integration inside the EU. This, together with the political consensus established throughout Europe during the 1990s, has given rise to the illusion that EU is on its way to become a "super-state". This is certainly not the case. The new global crisis has already to some extent halted the process of globalisation. This could also spill over to Europe and thwart the process of further integration in the EU/EMU, particular when national governments are faced with economic problems that correspond to widespread political and social unrest.

But there is no solution on a national basis. Lasting, fundamental changes will only come about as part of an international socialist revolution. The need for an international programme and an International is more crucial than ever. The struggle against the bosses and the bourgeois governments will have to take an all-European shape. This will reinforce the need for an international outlook on the behalf of the working class. One effect of globalisation is that there is an increased awareness amongst workers that the struggle needs to be organised on a global or all-European plane, that workers will have to look for solidarity from brothers and sisters in other countries.

Globalisation has become a reality, thanks to the development of the world market, world trade, monstrous financial markets and the speed, size and interconnections of the movements of goods and information across the world. To counterpose to this fact the false argument that "the world economy was more integrated at the beginning of this century" could feed illusions of "a national, reformist road out of this crisis". Even the bourgeois left economist John Gray, from Britain, is much more correct when he writes: "Today's world economy is inherently less stable and more anarchic than the liberal international economic order which collapsed in 1914. Like the hyperglobalizers, whose Utopian fantasies they effectively criticise, globalisation sceptics are trading in illusions. They cannot accept that globalisation has made the world economy today radically different from any international economy that has existed in the past; that would spell death to their hopes of a revamped social democracy. They are right in their belief that a more radically globalized world is less governable - such a world economy makes their vision of 'continental Keynesianism' unworkable. In truth a much less governable world is the inevitable result of the forces that have been at work over the past two decades". (John Gray, "False Dawn - The delusions of global capitalism".) From a bourgeois point of view, "today's world is more ungovernable" this is why the global crisis of capitalism is also a crisis of imperialism, of all international bourgeois institutions of trade - and inter-governmental blocs such as the EU.

The EU countries, North America/NAFTA and Japan are the dominant powers or blocs in the capitalist world. Europe is the largest of the three blocs, but also the one that, so far, has experienced the weakest expansion since the mid-1970s. According to an article in the US Wall Street Journal, the annual growth rate inside the EU averaged 4.8 per cent from 1961-70, 3.0 per cent from 1971-80, 2.4 per cent from 1981-90 and 1.7 per cent from 1991-97. Moreover, unemployment has been persistently higher in Europe than in the rest of the advanced capitalist world, despite the fact that EU has a lower rate of employment than Japan and the US.

"Mass unemployment has become a scar across the Community (EU), threatening the social and political cohesion of a single market in which 10 per cent of the labour force are excluded from its supposed rewards ... The EC countries (now EU) have good reason to feel worried when they look beyond recovery to the future. For unemployment appears to be 'ratcheting up' from each cycle through the next. And the malaise runs deeper. Europe has high unemployment but also a miserable record of job creation compared to other developed countries. Twenty years ago the percentage of the US population of working age was very much the same as the EC. Since then the US has succeeded in increasing the numbers in employment by 30 million - three times as many as the Community", wrote Financial Times in Britain 21 June 1993. Since then the situation has gone from bad to worse.

Six million EU jobs were lost between 1991 and 1994, which was twice the size of any other contraction in employment since before World War II. Even an official report issued on employment by the EU commission in 1995, has to confess that: "On the evidence of the last 15 years, a high rate of GDP growth is not a sufficient condition for maintaining a high level of employment". This is just another way of saying that the European labour market that once provided full employment has turned into its opposite and unemployment will stay high whatever capitalist policy is adopted. It also explains why structural unemployment is as high as 10 per cent in the EU, and in the words of Leon Trotsky: "Structural unemployment is the most deadly expression of the decline of capitalism".

Overall unemployment inside the EU reached 11.2 per cent in 1997 and, according to the OECD, will just drop to 10.5 per cent in 1998, despite a recovery in investment, increased exports and rising domestic demand. Unemployment in the 11 countries that are taking part in the EMU project will be even higher, 12 per cent in 1998. On top of that, half of the EU's unemployed have been out of work for more than a year. Youth unemployment (under 25s) is more than 20 per cent.

Casualisation and job insecurity

In "Capital" Karl Marx drew the conclusion that: "The greater social wealth... the greater is the industrial army... the greater is the mass of consolidated surplus-population... the greater is official pauperism. This is the absolute general law of capitalist accumulation." The crisis of European capitalism has meant that a huge section of the unemployed can no longer be described as part of the industrial reserve army but as the socially excluded, without any chance of entering the labour market. Many are no longer counted as unemployed. As many as 1 million withdrew entirely from the EU labour market in the recession of 1990-94. The industrial reserve army today is mainly made up by those in temporary and casual work.

The response from the bosses and the governments to the persistent high structural unemployment in Europe has been the move "to a more flexible labour market". A flexible labour market has meant: de-regulation (i.e. removing workers' safeguards), low-wage employment, anti-trade union legislation, "flexibility" (e.g. annualisation of working hours, "zero-hour" contracts), workfare systems and the replacement of permanent jobs with temporary jobs. Those measures have been introduced as part of a general offensive against workers' rights in order to push down wages, weaken the trade unions and create divisions inside the working class. The threat of mass unemployment and job insecurity together with the lack of an organised national fight-back (or globally if necessary) on the part of the trade union movement has not made it easy for workers to resist the bosses' offensive. But the battle is far from over. A resolute stand from a group of workers against de-regulation and/or privatisation, as was the case with the bus drivers in the Danish town of Esbjerg in 1995, can spark off a movement from below despite the vacillation at the top of the trade unions.

Nevertheless, the European labour markets have changed in the past few years and "European companies are pushing Europe toward de-regulation much as American corporate titans led the way to de-regulate America a decade ago. And nowhere is the trend more evident than in Europe's labour market, which is now seeing its biggest-ever rise in temporary contracts... the temp boom has spawned a dual labour market, split between full-time workers and the temps or part-timers", wrote the Wall Street Journal, 4 June 1998. De-regulation of the labour market is now a top priority as far as the bosses and governments are concerned. The policy of "flexibility and de-regulation" was endorsed by the EU at its "Job Summit" in Luxembourg in 1997. Jospin went to the US in June 1998, "to assess the sources of American dynamism".

In the 1980s, the bosses in Europe tried to copy the Japanese model (the "just in time" system, lean production, various forms of employment, etc.) but that model was no more when the bubble burst in Japan in the end of 1989. A slowdown in the US economy accompanied by higher unemployment will also strike a blow against the new model. The implementation of a "flexible labour market", despite the treacherous role played by the union leaders, will force workers and the unemployed to step up the struggle to maintain welfare and workers' rights. This is because more and more workers realise that what is lost will never come again and what is at stake is the very essence of a social welfare system - public education and health, unemployment benefit, job security, etc.

The traditions of organised struggle, collective action, are stronger in Europe than for example, in the US. This is not a guarantee of victory, but it shows the potential for huge battles in Europe, along the lines of the 1988 Wharfies' (dock workers') struggle in Australia. The existing flexibility clauses, negotiated or forced on the workforce by the law will act as means of squeezing the workers when production and productivity growth start to slow down. Many workers, including skilled workers in full-time jobs, will learn that all the concessions made today, in order to "safeguard jobs", were made in vain.

The bourgeoisie will not intensify their attacks from a position of strength, but more out of desperation and against the background of an impending economic and political crisis. All these factors, together with the fact that there is a beginning of a more outspoken mood against capitalism and the dictatorship of the market, point in the direction of a struggle that will become more political. This in turn will pose the question of forming left wing opposition movements to organise the fight-back against the bureaucracy in the trade unions and the creation of new workers' parties.

Millions of jobs can be lost in the next recession

According to calculations made by the authors of the book "The global trap", Hans Peter Martin & Harald Schuman: "A further 15 million white-collar and blue-collar workers in the European union will have to fear for their full-time jobs in the coming years. That is almost as many again as the registered jobless in the summer of 1996." After several years of jobless growth there is now, at least, a sign of a fall in the number of unemployed inside the EU. But this has occurred towards the end of the recovery and, as The Economist in Britain pointed in an article 13 June 1998, "Europe's problem has been that with each economic cycle unemployment has hit bottom at ever-higher levels. It is unlikely that the pattern has been broken."

The drop in unemployment has been accompanied by an increase in the number of part-timers, most strikingly in Britain and the Netherlands. Overall, one European worker in six is now a part-timer. This rises to one in four in Britain and nearly two in every five Dutch workers. The trend to more "flexible jobs" has gone farther in Britain than in other European countries. According to a report published by the Business Strategies consultancy, nearly half of the workforce will soon be covered by "flexible" arrangements, such as temporary contracts, self-employment and part-time jobs. It is not a coincidence that Britain is also the European country with the longest working hours, the most vicious anti-trade union legislation in the advanced capitalist world, and the EU country that has the biggest proportion of people counted as poor.

An upsurge in the struggle

It may appear paradoxical that capitalism enjoys its fastest growth rate just before a downturn. The reasons for that are, in short, that industries have reached full capacity utilisation and stocks are low, workers in jobs receive increases in real wages, more people are in work, and the better-off start spending their savings.

This can also have a positive effect on the confidence of the working class and stimulate offensive struggles by workers for increases in living standards. This was shown in Denmark when workers in April-May 1998 went on strike, in fact a partial general strike, in support of six weeks' paid holiday. Similarly in Spain there is a movement for a 35-hour week and in France, where the return of fat business profits and the enrichment of the millionaires under Jospin (the present Prime Minister), has forced the union leaders to call for a substantial increase in wages and the minimum wage.

It is the struggle and the conditions today that prepare the working class for what will take place tomorrow. How the workers will first react when faced with a new recession or slump depends on many factors. These include: what is the existing mood amongst the workers, how confident is the class, and what is the level of consciousness when the new crisis set in?

The developments in countries already hit by the recession and the slump are showing what can happen in Europe as well. What is the most striking feature is how fast the consciousness has changed in those countries. The economic meltdown in Indonesia has been followed by a social collapse and the beginning of the Indonesian revolution. The workers in South Korea have launched an offensive against job losses and social insecurity. In Russia, where the coal industry is facing an agonising death under capitalism, the miners have organised several strike actions against the failure of privatisation. In all those struggles the masses have started to raise some anti-capitalist demands, including nationalisation, or re-nationalisation, and expropriation of companies and the capitalists' wealth.

The capitalist crisis of the former Stalinist states, where Russia is on the brink of economic collapse and widespread social upheavals despite the latest IMF bail out in July 1998, tends to undermine the position of the EU countries even further. On top of that, the reaction against the market and mafia-capitalism in eastern Europe and the former USSR will also have an effect on the outlook of workers and youth in western and southern Europe. This time the effects on the consciousness will be of a fundamentally different character than in the beginning of the 1990s. The change will be directed against capitalism and the dictatorship of the market. The impending crisis is the most serious that the bourgeoisie in Europe have confronted since the 1930s. At the same time, the working class in Europe is, on the whole, intact and remains the most powerful social force in society. So far its strength and ability to fight have only been partially demonstrated.

A new political terrain

The collapse of the Stalinist states neither fundamentally strengthened capitalism, in the sense of providing the opportunity for a long period of growth, nor fundamentally weakened the working class in the advanced capitalist countries. Now the political and ideological effects of the collapse are becoming less and less of an obstacle in re-building the workers' movement on socialist lines, and in building the forces of genuine Marxism, that is Trotskyism.

Today's crisis of capitalism has been accompanied by a deepening of the crisis of reformism and the remaining Stalinist parties. The crisis of reformism in the 1990s has expressed itself in the bourgeoisification of the old traditional workers' parties. Increasing layers of workers and especially youth no longer regard Social Democracy as "their" party. While still being able to score electoral victories as workers vote against the openly right-wing parties, workers are coming to expect less and less from the Social Democracy in the way of social reforms and better living conditions. The monolithic character of the old Stalinist parties, the southern European Communist Parties, has eroded at the same time as these parties are moving rapidly towards reformism. This is a recipe for new divisions and splits in those parties. The workers' movement, and the Marxists, are in a new and uncharted political terrain. The present situation facing the working class as well as our organisation, has no real precedent in history.

The protracted death agony of reformism and Stalinism has created a big vacuum on the left. This will, at a certain stage, give rise to the development of new broad socialist parties, that will reflect and express in an organised form the ongoing change in the consciousness of the masses. However, it is impossible to predict when and under what conditions such formations will appear. The task of Marxists today is not to wait for such a development. The best way to prepare for such a decisive change in the process of radicalisation, which will only come about after a change in consciousness, big upheavals and experience from the living struggle itself, is to build strong revolutionary forces today that can make an impact on the workers and youth who will constitute new mass formations. However, these new formations will not have the same stable character as the old former traditional workers' parties, which after all were operating on the basis of the post-war 1945 upswing. The new formations will be more unstable and fluid. The pressure from capitalism, and the fact that reforms can only come about as result of a conscious and determined struggle, will mean that these formations will soon face the moment of truth. We see this, for example, with the PRC in Italy, the most left-wing mass party in Europe, which is heading towards a split on the question of what should be the party's attitude to the Italian government.

For revolutionary Marxism, the coming years will be more favourable than the previous years. The youth will almost certainly be the first group in society that will react to a changed situation and many youngsters are going to be prepared to join a revolutionary party. The key for building the CWI and its European sections is therefore a turn to the young workers, school students and students.

Europe after the collapse of Stalinism

The collapse of Stalinism redrew Europe's political and social map. The old division between the Stalinist East and the capitalist West is thing of the past. Capitalism has been restored in the former Stalinist states of Europe and the former USSR. The emerging bourgeoisie in those countries, though weak and corrupt, are eager to establish close economic, political and even military ties with the EU countries and NATO. Today's Europe is foremost a continent divided by capitalist exploitation (the struggle between capital and labour), inequality, race and sex discrimination, national oppression and a growing gap between the richer and the poorer countries or regions. The existence of a Stalinist bloc acted as a superglue that brought the capitalist countries together and locked the US into the European continent. But in the present new world disorder there is no such superglue, and old rivalries and tensions have re-emerged. At the same time, US imperialism is striving to expand its world influence and maintain its military presence in Europe.

The Balkan wars of the 1990s - a warning

The restoration of capitalism in the Balkan peninsula and the eastern part of Europe created instability and uncertainty. Yugoslavia's disintegration meant wars and civil wars, for the first time since 1945, on Europe's doorstep. The tragedy in Bosnia created the biggest refugee catastrophe in Europe since the end of the Second World War.

The intervention from the EU in former Yugoslavia was a disaster. It helped start the war in Bosnia and exposed the EU as being utterly incapable of formulating a common foreign or security policy. This was once again repeated in the EU's failure to work out a common response to the spontaneous and confused revolt against gangster-capitalism in Albania in 1997. The only thing on which the EU could reach an agreement was support for a military intervention by Italy in order to stop refugees fleeing from poverty-ridden Albania. The intervention was a military adventure with the aim of strengthening the foundation of a fortress Europe.

The Balkan crisis and the development of a civil war in Kosovo in 1998 have shown that the national question in the Balkans cannot be solved on the basis of capitalism, and there is a tendency towards barbarism in the weakest links of the European capitalist chain. The horrifying wars in former Yugoslavia have sent a dire warning to workers and youth throughout Europe of what can happen if the workers fail to combat racism and reaction. If the working class suffers defeat after defeat, all the dark forces in the society will emerge and drag civilisation closer to barbarism.

The proposed extension of the present EU, the so-called enlargement process, will, if it ever takes place, eventually turn the newcomers into second-rate members, who will be held to ransom by the dominant powers inside the EU. An enlargement would increase the EU's population by around 30 per cent - but its GDP by only 4 per cent. In the words of The Economist in Britain, 31 May 1997: "This would certainly be a big drain on the EU budget, with the potential to bankrupt the common agricultural policy and to cause regional and structural aid to rocket". This explains why the present EU members are in fact very reluctant to extend the EU eastwards. The outlines of a fortress Europe shows that dream of a capitalist united Europe, of a single European entity, will never come through. The special crisis of European capitalism is giving rise to centrifugal tendencies inside the present EU as well as amongst some of its members. The June 1998 Cardiff EU summit showed that the governments inside the EU are navigating without a compass and are retreating from the previous illusions of EMU as the springboard for political union. Both France and Germany (and not only because Kohl needed help in the election), supported by other nations, declared that the era of big European government is over and the power of the EU Commission has to be reduced. This was a confirmation of what has been obvious for some time: there is a growing political division inside the EU and the bourgeoisie in Europe has still to decide what role the EU should play in the post-Stalinist world. There is a growing, untenable contradiction between the proposal of a single economic policy and the national governments' drive to diminish the influence and authority of the EU bureaucracy.

Crisis of confidence

The downfall of the Stalinist regimes in 1989-91 meant an international victory for capitalism, mainly in a political and ideological sense, and marked the end of the old post-war world relationships. A wave of bourgeois triumphalism swept over Europe in the early 1990s. The collapse of Stalinism was hailed as the ultimate success of the so-called free market and liberal capitalism. The consciousness of all classes and sections of the society was affected by the historic events that took place in the former USSR and Stalinist Europe.

The ruling class in Europe hastily concluded that the old capitalist policy of easing class conflicts and recession; state-intervention, public works, "welfare-policy" and the traditional "social partnership" was totally outdated. Neo-liberalism was declared as an official global doctrine and shock therapy was ordained for Russia and the ex-Stalinist parts of Europe.

Nevertheless, even sections of the European bourgeoisie have now started questioning the alleged success of neo-liberalism and could be compelled, like the Japanese bourgeoisie, to implement some Keynesian measures as a response to a looming recession and social upheavals throughout the continent. Although these measures, or a "dose of inflation", will be short-lived and with little effect.

Today, the world bourgeoisie is facing a deep crisis of confidence. What was supposed to be a new world order has been a new world disorder which breeds crises with increasing speed.

The false idea of the superiority of the "free market" also penetrated the labour movement and the left. In general, consciousness fell back. Bourgeois propaganda was echoed by the leading cliques inside the traditional workers' parties (Social Democratic as well as Communist) and the trade union movement. The right-wing turn on the part of the leadership was summed up in the words of Dennis MacShane, a former International Metalworkers Federation official and now a British Labour MP: "The choice of the left is no longer what kind of socialism it wants, but what kind of capitalism it can support." (quoted in "One World Ready Or Not", by William Greider).

Europe was the continent that gave birth to modern capitalism and the independent organisations of the working class. The post-war upswing and the strength of organised labour were the main reasons behind the creation of the welfare state. But another reason was the existence of a Stalinist Bloc based on a planned economy, although bureaucratised, in the "other half of Europe" (which for a time in the 1950s and 1960s was on the way to narrowing the gap with the West). Social reforms in Western Europe were one way to overcome the legacy of the 1930s depression and to avoid workers being too impressed by the achievements then being made in Eastern Europe and the USSR on the basis of state ownership and a planned economy.

The power of organised labour and the radicalisation that swept all over Europe in the 1970s made it possible to maintain, and in some cases strengthen, welfare and workers' rights, despite the ending of the post-war upswing in 1974-75.

This 1970s radicalisation of workers and youth was reflected in the formation of left currents inside the trade union movement, the traditional workers' parties and youth organisations. This particular expression of the process of radicalisation probably arrived at its highest level at the beginning of the 1980s, when the left became a dominant force inside the British Labour Party, and after the historic election victories scored by the Socialist parties in Greece and France in 1981.

From reforms to counter-reforms

However the U-turn from reforms, nationalisation, etc. to counter-reforms made by the Socialist-Communist government in France within a year of its 1981 election symbolised that traditional reformism had reached an impasse. At the same time, Thatcherism in Britain and Reaganism in the US signified that the bourgeoisie was preparing a class war against the working class and its organisations.

Generally, the reformist and the Stalinist leaders of the labour movement failed to organise a fight-back against the counter-offensive launched by the bourgeoisie in the 1980s. Instead they turned to the right and started to advocate or implement counter-reforms. The workers were taken by surprise and were not prepared for this development. Even where struggles did break out the national leaders usually settled for a rotten compromise or isolated the militant sectors. Many activists became demoralised and disorientated, and subsequently dropped out of activity.

The relationship of forces was changing inside the European labour movement, to the advantage of the right. This, together with the failure to defend jobs and living standards even when the economy was recovering or booming, alienated ordinary working-class people and youth. A trend towards a decline in trade union membership or level of organisation started to set in, particular amongst working-class youth.

The seeds of the last steps in the bourgeoisification of the European Social Democracy and left parties were sown in the 1980s. A new upsurge in the class struggle as a response to the downturn in the economy in 1989-90 could have cut across or halted that process, but the opposite took place. The fall of the Berlin Wall reinforced the right-wing trend inside the labour movement and marginalised the old left.

The collapse of Stalinism put a temporary brake on the development of a socialist consciousness and caused widespread confusion. In the ideological and political sense the working class was disarmed. Moreover, with the collapse of Stalinism, many reformist and also so-called communist leaders, particular inside the Italian PCI (then the biggest Communist party in the "West"), saw no reason to pretend that they were still committed to the idea of a socialist transformation of society. The process of bourgeoisification accelerated and became almost irreversible when it became obvious that the new generation of workers did not regard these parties as their parties or as a vehicle for serious social changes.

The breakdown of the Stalinist bloc and the restoration of capitalism in eastern

Europe and Russia was a historic watershed. Its negative effect on the level of consciousness is still a complicating factor in the process towards a general revival in socialist consciousness and the belief in the viability of an anti-capitalist alternative. But the consciousness and the conditions that exist today are different from the situation that existed in the beginning of the 1990s.

The Social Democratic/Socialist parties' roots inside the working class, in the trade union movement and the firm electoral support enjoyed were mainly sustained on two factors: (1) The unique post-war upswing that gave rise to reforms and full employment and (2) A reaction against the crimes of Stalinism. These twin pillars have crumbled away and the character of Social Democracy has changed, fundamentally.

These parties are now on the centre-left (it is questionable if some can be described as even being on the "centre-left") in bourgeois politics. This is why the development in the 1970s, when the class struggle and the radicalisation led to a turn to the left inside the labour movement, did not repeat itself in the 1990s. Instead, every main class battle in Europe since 1993 has had a tendency to expose the huge gap that exists between the leaders and ordinary workers.

A big vacuum to the left

An enormous vacuum to the left has been created in European politics and this has made it possible for Communist parties in countries such as France, Portugal and Greece to at least maintain an important level of electoral support amongst organised workers.

The vacuum to the left and the potential support for a socialist working-class alternative has partly been shown in the important electoral gains achieved by the revolutionary left in France; the increased vote (from two to five MPs) for the Socialist Party in Netherlands (not on the revolutionary left) in the May 1998 general election; and above all in Ireland where, in 1997, Joe Higgins (representing the Socialist Party, the Irish section of the CWI) won a seat in the parliament on a clear socialist ticket. But in this volatile political situation there is a danger that the reaction against the EU/EMU and globalisation could, under certain conditions, take the shape of an upsurge in right-wing populism, nationalism and racism.

The coming years will feature elements of a pre-revolutionary crisis as well as the menace of the extreme-right and neo-fascist terror. But the most striking features will be the intermediate and transitional stages between a non-revolutionary situation, that could even feature elements of mild reaction, and a situation moving in the direction of a pre-revolutionary crisis.

A pre-revolutionary situation arises when - as Trotsky explains in his book On France: "The nation stops going forward, when modern technology has advanced to a point where it can assure a high standard of living to the nation and to all humanity; but the capitalist property system which has outlived itself, dooms the masses to ever-increasing poverty and suffering.

"When the bourgeoisie find itself in a blind alley, a political crisis erupts and the petit-bourgeoisie is in a state of instability and fluidity". The situation today features many of these characteristics. However, the present level of consciousness and the political weakness of the working class will result in a protracted development towards a situation that can fully be described as pre-revolutionary.

Distrust for the establishment

The level of distrust and contempt for the capitalist Establishment and the undermining of support for bourgeois institutions has reached an unprecedented level. Only 17 per cent of the people questioned in an opinion poll in Belgium said that "they live in a working democracy". Corruption scandals, the constant abuse of power and positions, a widening democratic deficit, and the idea that there is one law for the rich and another for the rest has exposed the rottenness at the heart of the system.

The erosion of support for capitalist institutions and state authority is also an indication of a change in consciousness. Events like the horrifying paedophile scandal in Belgium can trigger off a mass movement that calls for far-reaching social and political changes. The discontent that has accumulated is on its way to being transformed into a more widespread anti-capitalist mood, although not in a straightforward way but in the context of a deepening social and political polarisation.

The fact that struggles have become more bitter and often lead to clashes with the police has steeled the new generation as well as the old. Even sections of the middle class and farmers have experienced attacks from the repressive forces of the state. Further experience from the living struggle itself, extraordinary abrupt turns in the domestic as well as the international situation, will tend to diminish the legacy from the past. Europe is on the eve of such abrupt change as the continent is approaching a new millennium just as the crisis of global capitalism will start to be felt.

Workers' movement in the 1990s

Our last World Congress in December 1993 took place against the background of an upsurge in the class struggle in western and southern Europe. The strikes and mass demonstrations, that began in France, spread across Europe. As the US magazine Business Week commented at the time: "Trade union militancy is on its rise in Italy and Belgium, two countries always under the strong influence of events in France. Workers have been inspired by their successful French colleagues. There seems to be a domino-effect, although every national protest is caused by domestic events." This movement reached its peak when Belgium (during the Congress itself) saw its biggest strike movement since the general strike in 1936.

These strikes and protests exposed the discontent and anger over economic and social hardship that existed and showed that the masses were prepared to struggle. It was the starting point of a new phase in the extremely complex process of radicalisation in the 1990s. This process has its own conjunctural ups and downs, and these fluctuations have become sharper in the aftermath of Stalinism's collapse. The strength of the working class and the limit of right-wing reaction in this period was seen in Italy at the end of 1994, when a ten-million strong general strike and the biggest demonstration in Rome (organised by the trade unions) since 1945 forced the right-wing government to resign after only a few months in office.

In 1995, workers and students in France took to the streets in a movement that the French paper Le Monde described as: "A mass reaction of the French against financial globalisation – a collective attack on anxiety over threats to the good life which has prevailed since the Second World War." This strike against a proposed wage freeze in the public sector, social cuts and de-regulation (the Juppé plan) and further action paved the way for defeat of the right-wing parties in the general election held in 1997.

But what was laid open in the strikes was that workers and youth did not trust the main opposition party - the so-called Socialist Party. Workers rejected the Juppé plan and the proposed austerity measures, but they doubted that a government led by the Socialist Party, the only governmental alternative, would have meant a real change in the running of the country. This, together with the role played by the trade union leaders, explains why the struggle did not develop into a struggle to overthrow the government, despite its unpopularity and the huge popular support for the strikers.

The French workers are undoubtedly at this moment the most advanced detachment of the European proletariat. The movement of 1995 and the lorry drivers' strikes and blockades have been followed in the run-up to the world cup by a strike wave involving pilots, airport baggage handlers, Paris Metro workers and rail workers. One-day protest marches by workers from six different industries brought the capital's traffic to "a fuming, honking standstill". Even the biased bourgeois press has been forced to concede that there is widespread support for the strikes and the right to strike. Even a middle-class 'marketing executive' at a Paris airport commented to a British Guardian reporter: "France is about the only place left in Europe where we still believe that taking to the streets or walking off the job can make a difference... Governments come and go, political parties rise and fall, and yet there are still strikes here more or less all the time. Good luck to them if they're not being treated fairly."

At the same time, the right fumed at the strike wave, with Raymond Barre (ex-Prime Minister) calling the Air France pilots' strike "profoundly scandalous". He was joined by 'socialist' senator, Michel Charasse, who said that anyone who went on strike during the world cup was "an egotist who loves himself more than his country". The position in industry is matched by the social frustration of the victims of French capitalism, particularly the unemployed and above all the unemployed youth.. They live in the 'doughnut of deprivation' around most large French cities. In the US and Britain towns tend to rot from the centre, but in France, the poor, the unemployed, the second- and third-generation immigrants have, in the words of an Independent (British newspaper) reporter, "been swept into the first ring of suburbs". Here, youth unemployment is more than 40% and sometimes is well in excess of 50%.

The national unemployment rate is 12.5% and under the Jospin government there has hardly been a dent made in this figure. Despite the radical gloss of the government, it has moved to implement the general policies of the European bourgeoisie, of introducing flexibility and deregulation. Jospin's policy has been a combination of appearing to make concessions, like the largely empty proposal for the 35-hour working week (accompanied by flexibility and a worsening of working conditions), while systematically attempting to undermine the rights and conditions of the French workers. This is a harbinger of his government's intention to begin to dismantle state control of industry and 'restrictions', that is, the defence of workers' rights. In the Air France strike, the government held out against the strikers until they agreed a deal which was, in the words of the Financial Times (Britain), "in marked contrast to past experience, when the government had all too often caved in". At the same time, there have been small steps, but nevertheless important ones, in the direction of deregulation. These include privatisations and "emphasis on encouraging entrepreneurship". In fact, the Jospin government is the best that the bourgeoisie can hope for at this stage.

The lack of a clear political alternative has not stopped workers and youth from taking the road of struggle, but has undoubtedly acted as an obstacle in developing the movement beyond the point of making a determined stand against cuts, worsening living conditions, corruption and the Establishment (including the politicians) in general. It has been the anger from below that has compelled the trade union leaders to call, sometimes very reluctantly, for action.

The present trade union leaders are not leading, they are misleading and derailing the movement. This explains why the bosses and governments have been able to continue and even intensify their attacks against the workers throughout the 1990s. This is why the working class and its organisations have not been able to defend the previous level of social welfare, jobs and its former position at the workplaces, and why there have been setbacks.

Only resolute and consistent struggle can force the bosses and the government to make at least temporary concessions. But even small victories in this situation of a general trend towards a decline in living and working conditions can have an electrifying effect on the mood and spark off a broad movement. This is not only on the national arena but also on an international plane. The tendency for struggles to become more global has been expressed in the Euro-strikes against cut-backs in the car industry, the rank-and-file support for the Liverpool dockers, the mobilisations against Maastricht in Amsterdam and Luxembourg 1997, and the all-European impact of the successful strike action by the French lorry drivers in 1996. That strike has had a lasting impact and inspired, for example, the Norwegian transport workers to organise an historic strike, including both national unions, in June 1998. As one Norwegian trade union official said: "France is showing that it is worth fighting".

Germany and France are key countries

Neither France nor Germany has yet experienced such drastic slaughter of welfare and cuts in public spending as, for example, Britain or Sweden, the latter a former capitalist model of welfare. France and Germany are key countries as far as the European revolution is concerned.

The German and French ruling class, particularly the latter, always haunted by the spectre of "a new 1968", have tried to act in a less provocative way than some of their foreign colleagues. However, a new downturn in the economy will tend to compel the bourgeoisie in those countries to adopt more brutal measures. In the beginning, their counter-attacks will probably be directed against singled-out sections of the working class.

The fact that those attacks will be carried out by a Socialist-led government in France and probably a Social Democratic-led government in Germany will have profound effects on consciousness. This, of course, will be a risky affair for the French and German bourgeoisie as the whip of counter-revolution can provoke a mass revolt. The workers in France and Germany have not suffered the same defeats recently as, for example, the British workers, and will therefore organise a fight-back marked by confidence. The French workers have collected a lot of experience from their industrial and political struggle over the last ten years and have kept alive the tradition of taking to the streets in a period when the official dogma from the European trade union leaders was that "mass actions belongs to the past". The power of the German working class has only started to be shown. The most likely defeat of Kohl and the CDU will mark a breaking point in the situation, that will be the case even if the election will give way to a grand coalition between SPD and CDU. Although, it cannot be ruled that the impotence of the SPD and Schröders "Blairism" could result in the re-election of Kohl. However, a possible new SPD government under Schröder will enjoy little breathing space before having to confront an economic down-turn and an EMU that lies in disarray. Huge class battles in Germany will have repercussions throughout Europe. Particularly the eastern part of Germany, former DDR, is facing the future risk of rapid social deprivation and sharp political polarisation. The growth of the east German economy is already lagging behind the national growth rate and unemployment has reached 18 per cent in the east. The problem of absorbing the former DDR has become increasingly apparent over the past two years, despite the recovery and despite the net transfers of more than $570 billion dollars from the west since 1991

A new phase - worsening social conditions

Both struggles in Europe and consciousness are passing through a new phase, from expressing what workers "don't want" towards a struggle that shows what "we want": a shorter working week, minimum wage, an increase in social benefits, etc. A change in consciousness is on its way. Europe today is not the same continent as in 1993, at the time of the last World Congress. Europe is heading towards a situation that will include elements of a pre-revolutionary crisis, restricted to elements only because of the weakness of the subjective factor.

Casualisation and the creation of a dual labour market are going to give birth to a counter-reaction from workers and unemployed. Mass unemployment and impoverishment of a big section of the population is tearing society apart and is a permanent source of social instability. The existing social conditions in working-class estates, immigrant areas and de-industrialised cities are so depressed and the mood so desperate that it will simply explode into riots if an organised movement, like the action by the French unemployed (supported by those in work) at the end of 1997, does not show a way forward.

The unemployed teachers in Greece, in June 1998, occupied 30 schools being used as examination centres. Their action was joined by others, including teachers in work, an indication of the bitterness of the struggles which lay ahead. The demonstrations were attacked by riot police, in many towns with a brutality never experienced. Huge defensive battles lie ahead, which can on occasion, take the form of local civil wars where whole villages or towns come out in support of workers fighting to save their jobs and communities. The example from the struggle put up by the Spanish miners could be repeated in other countries. In the beginning of 1998, miners on strike "strewed flaming pit props and upturned coal wagons across Asturia's new motorway to Madrid trying to make the region a no-go area", reported the British Independent 17 January 1998. Several times the miners were attacked by riot police. One was killed by a car, others were hurt on the barricades. However, the miners received huge support from the region's population, with many youth joining them on the barricades.

The struggle against unemployment and job insecurity will once again raise the question of workers' control, of nationalisation of companies that are proposing cutbacks or closures. It will also bring back demands to open the books, for a programme of public works and the need for a plan in order to create millions of new jobs. Instead of the bosses' and the governments' false proposals for a mis-named shorter working week, which are often nothing more than "annualised" working hours accompanied with a wage decrease, the demand will be for an immediate cut in the working week without loss of pay and under conditions set by the workers. Those are the demands that we as Marxists need to stress and put in our programmes for action.

The death agony of capitalism has made it virtually impossible for the trade union leaders to act as mediators in the struggle between labour and capital. This has reinforced the tendency, described by Trotsky, as towards, "the trade unions growing close to and growing together with the capitalist state". However, even if this tendency has been particular marked in countries like Sweden and Austria, it has not been completed. The trade unions, despite their bourgeois leadership, still have a dual character. That means that we have to avoid both the danger of being too much restricted by the limits set by the structures of the unions: we have to be prepared to go beyond those structures if that is needed in order to develop the struggle, and the danger of simply dismissing the unions as "hopeless bureaucra-tised organisations". The imminent crisis of European capitalism will have profound effects on the trade unions, especially when the class struggle makes its inroads into the unions and the members start to fight back against the leaders' right-ward turn. The task of forming and organising opposition groups or more informal networks will be posed, even in countries where there has been no tradition of rank-and-file movements.

The crisis of capitalism is also reflected in a crisis of bourgeois democracy. There is no stable or "strong" government in Europe. Nearly every established party has experienced a sharp decline in, and ageing of, its membership over the last 10-15 years. Official politics have become a matter of careerism and enrichment.

The "Americanisation" of the political system in Europe is not only reflected in the fact that there is little difference between the established parties, but also in lower turn-out and the fact that official politics alienates ordinary people.

No party enjoys the same firm support as they did in the past. Voters today cast their vote more against something than in favour. This has meant that election results just mirror the existing mood on the polling day and is the reason why the pendulum can swing so sharply in a short period of time.

Alienation of workers and youth

The British Conservative Party, once the most successful bourgeois party in the world and with a mass membership, has seen its membership collapsed from one million to around 300,000, with an average age of 64 years. "By the time the Conservatives will next be fighting for a government, the party will, on a straight-line trend, have ceased to exist. It will have no members. Most will have thrown in the towel. One quarter will have died", according to a report presented at the Conservative Party Conference 1997.

The German Social Democratic Party (SPD), once the strongest and best-organised workers' party in Western Europe, is becoming more of a pensioners' society. More than a quarter of its membership is over-60 and its membership has been in continual decline for 20 years. The position of the CDU (the main right-wing party in Germany) is even worse: nearly 40 per cent of the membership are over 60.

CDU will probably lose the coming general election in Germany and Kohl's government will be replaced by a Social Democratic-led government. If this happens, it is yet another devastating defeat for the European conservatives. First Major in Britain, then Juppé in France and now Kohl in Germany. Moreover, the Dutch conservatives, who were in power from 1918 until four years ago, were also defeated in the last general election (1998) in the Netherlands.

The bourgeoisification of Social Democracy does not mean that these parties will just disappear from the scene. Workers will still vote for them as a means of stopping the right, if there is no other mass alternative available in the elections.

The reaction against neo-liberalism has undermined the support for the traditional right-wing parties and boosted Social Democracy's electoral support. However, this is a temporary phenomenon. The newly elected Social Democratic governments can soon, when faced with a new recession and aggravating class contradictions, become even more unpopular than their predecessors.

However, the crisis of the traditional bourgeois parties has also compelled the ruling class to become more and more dependent on the Social Democrats or, in the case of Italy, the PDS. It was the PDS, whose leaders now do not want to call themselves a party any more - just "Democrats of the Left" - which made it possible for the Italian bourgeoisie to carry out a massive programme of budget restraint to qualify for the EMU. It was the Social Democrats that implemented Thatcherism on an all-European scale, something the traditional right was not capable of doing.

It is the combination of the bourgeoisification of the traditional workers' parties and the disarray of the traditional right-wing parties which is shaping a new political landscape in Europe. Social Democracy has captured the ground that earlier was occupied by liberals or bourgeois centre parties.

The traditional right is squeezed from the right by right-wing populists, who are winning votes on an anti-immigrant platform and through demagogic attacks on globalisation. They are also squeezed in "the centre" by the Social Democrats, who are becoming more like the Democratic Party in the US under Clinton.

It is a sign of the times that on the one hand, Clinton and Blair are trying to set up a new international organisation with the aim of giving "formal direction to the general trend in which liberal, labour and socialist parties are abandoning government ownership and tax and spending programs" according to the press. On the other hand, the conservative parties in Europe are lining up with Berlusconi's Forza Italia. The former French Prime Minister Balladur has come out in support of the National Front's demand for "national preference", another word for sacking immigrants, restricting their allowances and rights. This policy is already carried out in towns controlled by the National Front. Throughout Europe, the openly right-wing bourgeois parties are politically redundant as far as the bourgeoisie is concerned. In Britain, for the time being, the Tories remain shattered after their general election defeat and saddled with an inept leader who is widely perceived as a stop-gap before a more serious figure emerges to lead the Tories out of the wilderness. In France, the right-wing parties remain defeated and divided, with a section of the Gaullists flirting with the semi-fascist Front National.

Racism and the 'Hard Right'

Two factors have acted to undermine the traditional right-wing bourgeois parties. On the one hand, the bourgeoisification of the former social democratic parties and some of the ex-Stalinist parties such as the PDS in Italy, has meant that they are now reliable props for the maintenance of bourgeois rule. They have the added advantage, at least in the initial period when in government, that they can give a radical gloss to the implementation of the programme of the bourgeoisie. If the same policies were tried by the traditional right-wing bourgeois parties, they would immediately provoke mass opposition, as was the case in France in 1994-95. On the other hand, the traditional bourgeois parties have been outflanked on the right by the extreme right, neo-fascist and semi-fascist organisations which have re-emerged in the past period.

The worsening of the social situation has undoubtedly led to a strengthening of racism and on its back, the parties of the 'hard right'. In five countries in Europe, Austria, Italy, France, Belgium and Denmark, parties with pronounced neo-fascist or fascist tendencies have scored more than 5% in elections. In three countries, Austria, Italy and France, they have taken as much or more of the vote as, for example, the Liberal Democrats in Britain at this stage. In addition to this, in Germany, the German People's Union (DVU) netted almost 13% of the vote in the eastern state of Saxony-Anhalt on an 'anti-foreigner' platform. They have been assisted by the similar 'anti-foreigner' approach of the CSU, the CDU's partner in Bavaria. A Turkish couple who had lived in Germany for 30 years have been threatened with deportation twice, because of the alleged criminal record of their son, aged 13.

It is in the main the worsening social conditions, and the lack of any socialist and revolutionary alternative at this stage, which has given success to the DVU and other fascist organisations. Only 2% of the Saxony-Anhalt population are immigrants, whereas there is 25% unemployment in the region. Recently, the neo-fascist organisations have given their propaganda a 'worker-friendly' slant. They marched on May

Day linking their anti-immigration propaganda for the defence of 'German labour': "There are six million Germans unemployed and seven million foreigners in the country. It's not hard to see the connection."

For want of any other explanation and alternative, this propaganda has found an echo amongst sections of the youth. A quarter of the voters under the age of 25 in Saxony-Anhalt voted for the DVU. These developments undoubtedly reinforce the need for us to continue with our anti-racist, anti-Nazi work, particularly through the YRE. We have to consider whether we can take initiatives on an all-European scale to counter the fascists and neo-fascists. Our sections in Belgium and France, as well as in Sweden, have recently conducted excellent and very effective anti-fascist work.

Main Trend to the Left

At the same time, we have to maintain a balanced approach towards perspectives for the fascists and far-right. We cannot underestimate the significance of recent successes for the neo-fascists. But at the same time, the main trend in the next period, particularly under the blows of recession and slump, will be towards the left. One of the consequences of an economic collapse is not just social polarisation but the development of the political 'extremes'. The re-emergence of the hard right must be set against the background of the recent dramatic success of the Trotskyists in France. Overall they got 5% of the vote in the recent regional elections, but 8% among the under-25s and in some regions this was in excess of 10%.

The re-emergence of the proletariat will be the main feature of the coming situation. This is shown not just by events in France, but even in traditionally sedate Switzerland the trade unions have recently rejected the labour accord that goes back to the 1930s, because of an increased militancy amongst workers arising from significant job losses in Swiss industry. Switzerland's record of being one of the most strike-free of any developed countries could be broken by the actions of the trade unions in the next period.

Even more significant is the near-insurrectionary anger of Greek workers at the brutal austerity programme implemented by the 'socialist' PASOK government. The Simitis government has announced a widespread privatisation programme which began in the banking sector. Workers in the state-owned Ionian Bank promptly went on strike for six weeks in protest against a decision to sell off a 51.4% stake in the bank. The governor of the bank fled from a shareholders' meeting in terror clutching his underwear and shoes after outraged union members 'shredded his suit'. Workers at Olympic Airways and dockers at Greece's two main ports have been involved in the fight against measures from a government which is clearly seen as bourgeois by the Greek workers.

This is a harbinger of the future. There is a vacuum which can be filled, for a time at least, by the right. But the main trend throughout Europe is to the left which, in the first instance, will limit the development of the ultra-right. At the same time, one of the consequences of a rapid change in conditions, predicated on the economic calamities which loom, is a polarisation between revolution and counter-revolution. The flirtation of the traditional right-wing bourgeois parties with some of the ideas which have assisted the rise of the hard right is an indication of the way that the bourgeois parties as a whole will move in the future.

With their traditional territory now occupied by the ex-social democrats and ex-Stalinists, the traditional right have flirted with the idea of moving even further to the right. Thus in France, Eduard Balladur, the former Gaullist prime minister from 1993-95, believes that nationality and immigration are the only issues that clearly separate the opposition from the 'left-wing' government of Jospin. Since the emergence of the Front National 15 years ago, a section of the Gaullists have toyed with their ideas and even with an alliance with them. Ten years ago, right-wing Gaullist, Charles Pasqua, proclaimed that Gaullists and extremists "had the same values". Now Balladur, supported by the Gaullists' secretary general, has called for a commission to consider withdrawing "family and medical benefits from mainly north African and black African settlers who do not hold French citizenship". He is opposed by the Gaullist president, Jaques Chirac, and the national chairman of the party, Séguin, and other Gaullists. Former defence minister, Charles Millon, has formed a popular movement called La Droite, seeking closer links with the Front National (FN).

The process of political polarisation and fragmentation tends to drive the right wing further to the right or give room for the development of new extreme right-wing parties. In France the traditional right, the Gaullist RPR and the UDF (Union for Democracy), moved into a deep crisis after losing its big majority (four-fifths of the seats) in the 1997 parliamentary election with endless rivalry at the top, plus being rocked by corruption scandals, etc. It is an open question whether the right will come out of this shambles. This is raising the possibility of regroupment on the right, including National Front without Le Pen, as one possible outcome of this crisis.

A reaction to the crisis the capitalist states are facing will be also a stronger move towards racist measures. This means they will try to deepen the division of working class along "racial lines" in order to "divide and rule". Racist policies are also carried out by the social democratic governments in Europe. But the absence of a mass socialist alternative and further social deprivation could pave the way for a temporary upswing and support for the extreme right beyond the level of elections. Which in turn will encourage fascist groups to step up their attacks on socialists, immigrants, homosexuals and disabled people, a serious threat to workers and youth, which we have to oppose. This is particularly so in a period when the struggle is on a low level and in the aftermath of a setback or defeat. The answer of the socialists to this threat is the mass mobilisation by workers, and anti-fascist and immigrant organisations. Our responsibility is not just to appeal, for example, to the unions to act, but to act in organising anti-racist campaigns, also against state racism. We also have to take into account that a massive anti-racist movement may quickly develop into a more generalised anti-capitalist one.

The formation of national governments or broader coalition governments, something that could be posed in several European countries in the near future, could also give way to an increase in support for the far-right.

There will be years in the future that will include elements of mild reaction. It could take the form of right-wing governments that could be on the lines of Berlusconi's short-lived government in Italy in 1994 or a future right-wing government in France based on regroupment of the right. But that is not the most likely perspective in the short term.

Workers and youth against the market

The coming crisis in Europe will first of all be reflected in a change in the consciousness of the masses. That change has already started, and at the time of writing, most notably in France. France is the most advanced country in Europe, as far as the class struggle is concerned. A very wide section of the population in France has been out in struggle. The movement of the unemployed, at the end of 1997 and at the beginning of 1998, got support from two-thirds of the population and shocked the establishment, despite the fact that this particular movement was small in numbers. We are moving away from a situation where workers and youth are reacting against the effects of the market towards a phase in the complex process of radicalisation where the reaction will be more directly against the market, the capitalist system. Consciousness, which is lagging behind events, will begin to catch up with reality. This will open up a new chapter in the history of the struggle for socialism in Europe.

First draft circulated July 1998

Resolution adopted by World Congress November 1998

The Former Workers' Parties

The last World Congress (6th) of the CWI undertook a thorough reappraisal of the role of, and perspectives for, the former traditional workers' parties. At that time in some countries there was a clear process towards the complete bourgeoisification of these parties. This was at an initial stage of development but since then it has become an international trend. Since the 1993 congress there has been a qualitative change in many of these parties. It has been necessary for us to develop our tactics and methods for building open independent revolutionary parties as a consequence of this changed situation.

The resolution adopted at the 6th World Congress, 'The traditional workers parties' explained: "The leadership has swung further to the right. In general they have embraced the bourgeoisie to a greater extent than before..." As a result of this development it concluded that: "In the minds of important layers the traditional parties are no longer associated with 'reforming' governments. To a greater extent than ever the 'reformists' have become the vehicle of counter reforms and consequently in opposition to big layers of the proletariat. They are even hated by a layer of the most combative elements, especially the youth."

The resolution went on to point out, "...the class basis of the traditional parties always assumed a two-fold character with both bourgeois and proletarian elements within them. We would make a mistake to approach the class basis of a party as being set in stone for ever.."

The majority of the sections of the CWI are currently undertaking open, independent work in order to intervene in the class struggle and win the new generation of workers and youth to Marxist ideas. This does not mean that the CWI has adopted "one world tactic". We have always been extremely flexible in developing our tactics. The tactic/s that are adopted by our sections are worked out after a careful evaluation of the concrete situation that exists in the relevant country. This was reflected in the discussion about launching an independent, open organisation in Scotland in 1991/2. The CWI majority at that time argued that in Italy it was correct to undertake work inside the PRC. Since then we have adopted numerous tactical turns in some countries such as Brazil where our section undertook work for two years in the PSTU. Our section in the USA is working in the Labor Party. Although it is not a mass workers' party this, together with the other examples illustrate our flexible approach to tactics.

Traditional workers parties transformed

Following the Sixth World Congress the process of "bourgeoisification" of the former traditional workers' parties in western Europe has qualitatively transformed most of them. The leadership of these parties has swung even further to the right and fully embraced capitalism. This, combined with the collapse of the left reformists/centrists inside these parties, has meant that there is nothing to attract the most conscious working class and youth to these parties.

There is no prospect of a revival of a mass left reformist or centrist current within the social democracy in this period. Although in some countries small "left" fragments may break from these parties these will not represent a major left/centrist split. The degree this phenomena may develop will of course vary from country to country. In the British Labour Party there is no real left-wing. In France, from the PS there may be the prospect of a relatively larger split to the left. Even here the "left" in the PS is a shadow of its former self. Elements of these may play a role in the formation of new workers' parties that will emerge at a certain stage. This does not contradict the predominantly bourgeois character of the PS or Jospin's government.

The process of bourgeoisification has also taken place in the former colonial world amongst the workers' parties. In addition the radical bourgeois nationalist forces that enjoyed the allegiance of the working class in some of these countries have dramatically swung to the right and adopted the programme of the "free market". The ANC in South Africa and the Peronist (Partido Justicialista) in Argentina are two examples of populist bourgeois formations that have embraced the "neo-liberalism" of the past period. The same process has affected the guerrilla organisations of the 1970's and 1980's like the FSLN in Nicaragua and the FARC in Colombia. The latter has continued a military campaign but, like the FSLN and others, have openly embraced "social democracy" and the ideas of the free market.

In some countries the process of bourgeoisification may have been slightly slower than in others and may take a somewhat different form. In Brazil the process is still unfolding in the PT and has not yet been completed. In the light of the recent Presidential elections, it may result in a split from the PT to the right - with some similarities to the "neo-socialists" who split from the SFIO in France in 1933. The terminology of the party leadership may also have been more restrained in some countries than in others. However, the direction they are heading in is clear.

Tony Blair has undoubtedly been in the vanguard of this process. He has the conscious objective of transforming the class character of the former workers' parties. The objective he has is to roll back the wheel of history and change the traditional workers' parties into liberal capitalist parties and thereby rob the working class of independent political representation. As the bourgeoisification of the former workers' parties is completed in more countries it means that a similar task is posed to that which has existed in the USA, where only bourgeois parties exist and it is necessary to pose the need for an independent workers' party . Although the process of bourgeoisification of the former traditional parties is being completed the more general idea of Blair (to rob the working class of independent political representation) will fail when it confronts the objective reality.

The British Labour Party was born because of the failure of the capitalist Liberal Party to satisfy the needs of the strengthened working class that developed. This took place at the end of the last century as the curtain began to fall on British imperialism's global supremacy. In the more recent history, in Greece, PASOK was built in the 1970s because of the failure of the Centre Union to satisfy the interests of a strengthened proletariat that also was looking for an alternative to Stalinism. The current intensification of capitalism's global crisis is certain to ensure that none of the existing pro-capitalist parties is able to satisfy the interests of the working class and will pose the question of the need for the working class to establish its own independent political party. This process has already been seen in South Korea and other countries of the Asian region where the question of the need for a party to express the needs of the working class has emerged as an important issue.

'Third Way'

The international forum of the "Centre-Left" which has been established linking up the Democratic Party of the USA is a reflection of how far the leaders of the former workers' parties have gone in attempting to link themselves with capitalism. For Blair and some others this represents an attempt to break totally with the past and even move towards the break up of the Second International. The fact that Jospin and the French Socialist Party did not attend was more out of his concern to defend his own particular interests than out of any principled ideological opposition. The "left-wing" Jospin, outlining his version of Blair's 'Third Way' has declared that: "We say yes to market economy but no to market society."

The recent election victories of social democratic parties in Western Europe represents two processes. Firstly, because of the undermining of the basis of the traditional bourgeois parties, they are the most reliable instruments through which the capitalist class can rule at this conjuncture. Secondly, despite the pro-market programme of the social democracy, for the masses they signify (in a distorted way) a left-ward protest against the "neo-liberal" policies that have been implemented during the 1990s.

The new social democratic governments in Europe are all regarded as "safe" by the ruling class and they have willingly embraced the programme of capitalism. In the past the ruling class also regarded the leaders of these parties as defenders of capitalism. However, the bourgeoisie feared that they could be forced, under the mass pressure of the working class, to take measures which threatened the capitalists. This is now less and less the case as the parties have become more and more bourgeoisified.

One of the most dramatic illustrations of this process is the Chilean Socialist Party. Under the Popular Unity government of Allende the party leadership was compelled to go much further than its leaders intended because of the pressure of the revolutionary aspirations of the working class and party rank and file. Today, without this pressure, its leaders sit in coalition with the Christian Democrats and support every reactionary step taken by the government. This year PSCh ministers even defended the killings and repression by the state forces that took place on demonstrations marking the 25th anniversary of the military coup in 1973.

In France also despite a certain "radical" phraseology, Jospin is regarded as a reliable defender of capitalism. His pledge to introduce a 35-hour week has been revealed for what it is - a cover to attack conditions and labour rights. Jospin, although avoiding the word "privatisation", has in fact privatised more than the previous Juppé administration.

Amongst the decisive questions for Marxists when determining the class character of a party are: its programme; tradition and how it was formed; class character of the leadership and membership; and the attitude of the working class and the masses towards it.

The former traditional workers' parties are now increasingly seen as simply part of the established society and no longer as parties that defend the interests of the working class and most exploited layers of society. The hostility by sections of workers towards these parties was reflected in Spain where striking miners in the Asturias attacked the offices of PSOE.

In the case of the British Labour Party the membership is now unrecognisable compared with what it was only a few years ago as workers have been replaced by various layers of the petty bourgeoisie and even some individual capitalists and financiers. The influence of the trades unions has been slashed and the financial basis of the party has become increasingly dependent on big business. Most importantly the possibility of the working class changing the party is cut off as every avenue has been blocked by a series of bureaucratic obstacles that have concentrated power and policy decisions into the hands of the parliamentary leadership.

In Japan the process of bourgeoisification of the former Socialist Party (initially renamed the Social Democratic Party) has taken a somewhat different route. After politically swinging to the right the SDP has followed a path of splits, fragmentation and then virtual disintegration of the party. The party voted to disband itself. This process ended in big sections of the SDP merging into the Democratic Party and a small section even joined the LDP.

'Safe' but not stable

These processes now mean that there is no prospect of a movement by the working class and youth to join these parties. The hostility towards these parties is set to increase in Europe because now in government they will become the instrument through which the attacks of the ruling class are carried out.

Although the ruling class regards the new governments as "safe" this does not mean that they will be stable. The hopes that greeted Blair's election in Britain are beginning to turn into opposition, as the pro-capitalist programme of the new government becomes more apparent. This is not contradicted by the high support Blair is getting in the opinion polls. These reflect the fact that economic recession has not yet fully hit home. The total collapse and disarray of the Conservative Party means that it is not seen as a viable alternative. The same has also begun to take place in Jospin's France, especially after the protests by the unemployed. Schröder in Germany will be subject to the same development, especially with the onset of a recession in Europe.

The process of bourgeoisification of these parties does not mean that they will not be able to win electoral support. The elections in Britain, France and Germany and the victory of the social democratic formations were undoubtedly greeted with a great relief by the working class and big sections of the middle class. The vote was mainly fueled by the prospects of defeating the established parties of capitalism. This was particularly the case in Britain and Germany after a prolonged period of rule by the Conservative Party and the Christian Democratic Union/Christian Social Union. The CDU got its worst result since 1949 and the combined vote of the "Left" (SPD, Greens and PDS) was the highest ever. In France, after a relatively brief period of government by the traditional right-wing parties, Jospin's election was also a by-product of the mass movement that took place in 1995. Internationally there has been a pronounced tendency to vote against all governments in order to punish them.

The striking feature of the process that has developed is how quickly the mood has begun to turn to opposition to the governments in France and Britain. Any honeymoon enjoyed by the social democratic governments will be short lived. This reflects the programme of these governments and the increasingly changed attitude of workers towards these parties. In Greece, the PASOK government of Simitis has seen a massive erosion in its support following savage cuts in public expenditure, labour reform laws and a massive privatisation programme that has provoked strikes of bank workers, a national strike of transport workers and protests by other others sections of the working class.

The consciousness of the masses usually lags behind the demands of the objective situation. A layer of older workers may still continue to harbour some illusions in these parties. This is based upon the memory of the history of reformism - in particular the period of reforms that were conceded after the Second World War. The reality of the new situation will be burned into the consciousness of the masses as the new governments are forced to attack the proletariat because of the economic crisis that is currently unfolding. This will not allow lasting reforms anything like those of the 1950s, 1960s and to an extent the 1970s to be implemented by these parties. Any concessions that they are forced to make will rapidly be taken away and accompanied by further cuts and attacks on living standards.

This does not mean that these parties will simply disappear. They can maintain an electoral basis for a period, especially given the absence of viable alternatives being formed in the short to medium term. This was illustrated in Spain where, despite losing the general election, PSOE was able to maintain an important electoral base mainly due to the hatred of the right-wing PP and its association with the Franco period in the eyes of many Spanish workers and youth. The Izquierda Unida, led by the Anquita of the PCE, did not put forward a left alternative to PSOE and failed to win the support that potentially existed for it.

Electoral gains for 'Left' parties

However, the recent general election in Sweden illustrated how even the electoral support for the Social Democracy can be rapidly eroded as its pro-capitalist programme is exposed. The vote for the Social Democracy was the lowest received by the party since 1922!

The dramatic increase in the vote of the Left Party (former Communists) to 12% illustrates the rejection of the openly capitalist programme of the Social Democracy. Big sections of blue collar workers, the unemployed and youth voted for the Left Party because they perceived it as representing something to the left of the Social Democracy. Amongst the unemployed the Left Party won 28.3% of the vote compared with 33% for the Social Democrats. Amongst first time voters 19% voted for the Left Party and 22.4% for the Social Democrats.

This took place despite the Left Party having moved to the right and having supported the cuts that have been carried through by local councils. The perception of the party amongst the mass is that it is to the left of the social democracy, despite the programme it has defended and the cuts it has carried through.

A similar phenomena was also seen in the German election (although to a lesser extent than in Sweden) in relation to the PDS which despite its role at local level still managed to increase its share of the vote in eastern Germany. For the first time it obtained over 5% of the national vote and increased its support in the west by 100,000 votes. However, this was significant and has boosted the PDS so that it could be seen more as an all-German party. In the semi-colonial world the Chilean Communist Party also increased its electoral support in elections during 1997.

The votes for both these former Stalinist parties by a significant minority should be distinguished from the electoral swings to the social democracy in Britain, France and Germany. Those who voted for the former CPs are looking for a more "left-wing" or socialist alternative to the right-wing policies of the social democracy. In this sense they reflected in a distorted way a higher level of political consciousness. Despite the swing to the right in policy by the Japanese Communist Party, the dramatic increase in its vote to more that 14% also reflected an element of this. However, the programme, role and methods of these parties will, in the main, prevent them from attracting significant layers of workers and youth into their ranks.

In France, this element of a protest vote to the "left" of the Socialist Parties has partially been reflected in a different way. The vote of the PCF (French Communist Party) has generally continued to decline in part because of a rejection of its association with Stalinism and also because of the role it has played in France i.e. during its period in government under Mitterrand, in the mass movement and now in its participation in Jospin's government. The PCF remains an important force because of its influence in industry. However, the left protest vote against the PS has mainly gone to Lutte Ouvrière and to a lesser extent the LCR. (The LO and LCR because of their policy and wrong methods will not be able to fully capitalise on this increased electoral support. The sectarian ideas and methods of LO was illustrated by its refusal to take an initiative after the success of their candidate in the last Presidential elections. The wrong methods and programme of the LCR are reflected in a more opportunistic direction).

The role of the PCF leaders has resulted in the development of opposition groupings amongst the rank and file. This reflects the more 'open' situation that has developed in most of the Communist Parties since the collapse of Stalinism. In Portugal a similar development has also taken place because of the role of the CP in carrying through cuts at local level where it has controlled the local councils. This provoked strikes against the councils, often with the active participation of rank-and-file CP members. The CP subsequently lost control of some local councils around Lisbon in 1997. The opposition currents often have a proletarian make-up. Where relevant we should undertake joint work and a certain political orientation towards them. However, they are frequently made up of older workers who still have an allegiance to some of the ideas and methods of Stalinism making it difficult to recruit them to the CWI.

Where ex-Stalinist parties like the PDS and VP (Left Party, Sweden) do win a significant degree of electoral support it may be necessary for our sections to undertake a certain political orientation towards them. This political orientation would mainly be required to reach those who had voted for such parties rather than to win the existing members. We must follow the development of these parties closely and equip our own comrades to take full political advantage. The support for these parties is more in the nature of a protest on the electoral plane, which hasn't translated into any growth of membership, roots in the working class etc. It is a very fragile base, entirely because of the political vacuum in society. These parties will rapidly disillusion those who voted for them, especially as they are increasingly drawn into local and even national government coalitions etc. We approach these parties for "united front" type initiatives in the anti-racist work, for example. At the same time we engage in implacable criticism of their political representatives, attempt to draw them into debates and politically expose them. We adopt a friendly attitude to those who voted for them, patiently but clearly explaining our criticisms of these parties.

New Left parties unstable

At the last World Congress the Socialist Left Party in Norway and the then recent "left" split from the Labour Party in New Zealand, the New Labour Party, and other parties in other countries, were featured during the discussion. The resolution,'The traditional workers' parties' stated, " Whilst such left splits are likely to be posed as a central part of our perspectives in many countries, in others they can be delayed or may not develop for various and diverse factors". It also pointed to the limited nature of the programme put forward by the left splits that had taken place.

Since the last world congress an important feature in the situation has been the incapacity of the new formations that have been established in some countries to consolidate a stable and firm basis. Most, although initially opposing cuts in welfare spending and "neo-liberalism", did not assume a clearly defined left reformist or centrist character. They failed to oppose capitalism and defend the ideas of socialism and rapidly also moved towards the right.

This was the case with the Democratic Social Movement (DIKKI) in Greece that split from PASOK in Greece but adopted a mildly "left" policy that was heavily coated with Greek nationalism. This formation failed to develop significantly or gain any major base. In New Zealand the New Labour Party (NLP), after eventually making some electoral gains, developed in a rightward direction. It has recently re-established some relations and a pact with the Labour Party from which it originally split. The Socialist Left Party in Norway quickly moved in a rightward direction and the support it was winning evaporated from having 20% support in the opinion polls to 5.9% in the election that took place in 1997.

The reason that these formations have developed in this way was because of developments in the international economic and political situation. Most importantly is the inability by national governments to withstand the enormous domination of the world market. The abandonment of the reformist measures of the Mitterrand government in 1981/2 were an anticipation of what was to follow later internationally. The internationalisation of the capitalist world economy made it impossible to adopt an independent "national road" and oppose the "neo-liberal" programme that has been implemented by all governments during the last decade. This was the situation during the recent economic conjuncture in which the programme of "neo-liberalism" was the policy that was applied internationally by capitalism and its representatives. In this period only the adoption of a revolutionary and internationalist socialist programme could offer a viable alternative to capitalism and "neo-liberalism". The leaders of the new formations were not prepared to embrace the alternative of Marxism.

In the former colonial world the radical bourgeois nationalist formations fell into line with this trend and opted for the adoption of a "free and open market" and opposed state intervention. In Mexico, even the PRD, a radical bourgeois party established by Cardenas, initially won massive support and aroused high expectations. Although it has maintained electoral support it has also gone back to the right and the tremendously high illusions in it that existed have substantially declined. Its leadership is dominated by former leaders of the PRI and it has now supported the idea of a governmental pact with the PRI and the right-wing PAN to deal with the developing economic crisis.

The onset of the current economic crisis will partially check the increased globalisation of the economy and even reverse the recent trends that have taken place in this direction. The left-reformist/reformist leaders and others are raising "neo-Keynesian" ideas of capital control and other means of state intervention. The capitalists themselves will resort to these and other measures in order to try and protect their interests during the rapidly developing crisis and new conjuncture in the world economy. These processes will be one factor that will again lead to the re-emergence of new mass reformist currents and parties.

PRC in crisis

In Europe the exception to the lack of any left-wing or socialist alternative appeared to be the PRC in Italy. The PRC was (and probably still is) the most left-wing of the new parties. This party grew and developed an important basis. By the end of 1997 it had a registered membership of 130,000. It contained within it important elements of centrism as well as Left-Reformism. The youth within this party formed an important basis for the most left-wing of the tendencies within it. However, the party has now entered into a crisis and its future is far from certain.

The absence of a Marxist programme and a clear decisive leadership has meant that the party has been unable to face up to the tasks that confronted it in Italy. The PRC was left with the worst of all possible worlds when, firstly, it withdrew support from the Prodi government without preparing its own members and supporters. Lacking a clear alternative, under intensive pressure from the PDS and trade union bureaucracy that had mobilised important sections of workers against it, the PRC leadership then reversed its decision, within twenty four hours, and returned to prop up the Prodi government. It subsequently voted for the biggest public expenditure cuts that have been implemented in Italy since World War II. The IEC resolution 'The Current Situation and Tasks for the CWI' (adopted in November 1996) warned that if the PRC "...fails to distance itself from the policies of the Prodi government it could begin to see its base eroded".

A section of the PRC apparatus led by Cossuta is now clearly opposed to Bertinotti and is intending to remain with the Prodi government. This opens the prospect of split in the party and the possibility of Cossuta and his supporters returning to the PDS. An important feature in the development of the PRC has been the relatively low level of activists in the party. According to one report out of 130,000 party members only 20-30,000 are active. Of these 5,000 hold either regional or local government positions!

These developments in the PRC are important because they illustrate one feature that new parties of the working class are likely to have when they are eventually established. They will tend to be less stable, more transitional and have a more precarious existence than the former workers' parties. It will therefore be a mistake to assume that they will enjoy the relatively secure and stable basis of the old workers' parties in the post Second World War period. The new parties will be established in a period of sharp economic and social turmoil. The former workers' parties maintained an extended lease of life for two main reasons, apart from their historical roots amongst the working class.

Perspectives for new workers' parties

Firstly, the prolonged period of capitalist boom after the Second World War allowed a lengthy period of reforms to be conceded by the ruling class in the advanced capitalist countries, especially western Europe. Secondly, they appeared to offer an alternative to the totalitarian regimes of Stalinism to the working class.

The decade of the 1990s has shown that the formation of new workers' parties will be a complicated and quite protracted process. Many of our sections have got a good response amongst a layer of workers for the idea of forming a new party of the working class. This was the case in Belgium during the struggle of the steel workers at the Forges du Clabeqc and during the 'white movement' in 1996. The masses were disgusted at the corruption of the traditional parties and the role they have played. The question of a new party arose during a specific struggle. Numerous "parties" were in fact launched although none of them were workers' parties and were launched on specific social issues. Because of a lack of programme and leadership none of them developed.

However, although a sympathetic response to the idea of a new party illustrates the loss of a solid base by the traditional parties and a certain development in consciousness, a greater leap in consciousness is required by the most class-conscious workers before they take the necessary steps to actually build such a party. Before reaching this conclusion workers and youth will need to pass through further experience of both industrial and political struggles.

The formation of new broad workers' parties, even on a reformist basis or in some countries without even initially adopting the idea of socialism, would represent a step forward. Such a development would represent the working class establishing its own independent political organisation. This provides an umbrella under which the most conscious workers can engage in political struggle. With the audacious intervention of revolutionary Marxists it can assist in raising the political conscious-ness and confidence of the proletariat.

Although the onset of a deep recession and crisis can speed up the process towards the formation of new workers' parties it is still likely to be a more protracted process in most countries. The issue can develop in the consciousness of important sections of the working class but it still can initially be delayed for subjective reasons. This has been illustrated in South Korea where the question has featured in the KCTU as an important issue during the recent upheavals. However, the union leadership has thus far derailed the formation of a combative independent party of the working class. A ferocious struggle is taking place on the issue but even the new a militant leadership seems to have accepted the vague concept of a "people's" movement.

The steps towards the formation of new broad parties of the working class will develop more rapidly in some countries than in others. Some forces from the CPs in some countries may play an important part in the process. Initially they can also hinder the formation of a new party. In general this development will still tend to be of a more protracted nature because of subjective weaknesses and obstacles.

The subjective weaknesses relate both to the existing consciousness of workers and to the role played by Stalinists, ex-Stalinists and some trade union leaders. In Britain the attempts to form a new broader workers' party were effectively blocked by the role of the Socialist Labour Party (SLP) and Scargill's Stalinist methods.

In Indonesia the PRD is an important force with a self sacrificing membership. It still needs to build a mass membership, which if it fails to do could result in other formations arising during the revolution. The leadership of the PRD has also embraced ideas such as "the two stage theory" which can derail the Indonesian revolution. The CWI needs to argue for the party to adopt a Marxist alternative.

Role of the CWI in developing new workers' parties

Where appropriate we should put forward the demand for the formation of a new workers' party. We should propagate and fight for this demand in those countries where it is relevant. Under the new Social Democratic governments we can also begin to raise the question of the trade unions withdrawing financial and political support for the social democracy in countries where this is relevant. At the right moment it is correct to raise the idea of the trade unions giving financial support to other socialist candidates in elections and other struggles (including our own).

When raising this demand we must ensure that we do not reduce our own section/party to merely campaigning for the establishment of a new workers' party. In some countries through this demand we can reach a layer of workers and youth. Our German section (SAV) was able to do this during the recent general election by featuring this demand and linking it to the need to join our party and support our programme and ideas.

We must guard against the risk of neglecting the building of our own organisation and reducing our forces to a campaigning body for a new workers' party. We cannot build and recruit on a solid basis without convincing workers and youth of our general programme and ideas as well as our intervention in the class struggle.

When the opportunity does present itself and where the forces exist we should go further than simply raising the demand for a new workers' party in a propaganda fashion. Our sections should be prepared to take initiatives and propose concrete steps to participate in launching a broader party of the working class. The British section (SP) attempted this in 1995. An opportunity arose when Scargill was launching the SLP. We approached the SLP and proposed concrete steps to launch a broader umbrella formation. The opportunity that existed to establish a substantial party was lost because of the sectarianism of Scargill and the SLP.

In Greece at the end of 1995 our comrades had numerous discussions with Tsavolas, a "left" PASOK MP who prepared the split from PASOK and formed DIKKI. We tried to convince him of the need to launch a new workers' party with socialist ideas. Unfortunately he restricted himself to trying to construct a "movement" rather than an organised force of the most advanced workers and embraced a nationalistic programme. As a result of his role this opportunity was also lost at that time.

The World Congress stresses to all sections that when such an opportunity arises and the forces exist we should seize it in an audacious but correct fashion.

Any proposal or initiative that our sections take to establish a broad workers' party must also ensure that we fight to win support for own independent programme and recruit new members of our section/party. It will only be possible to do this effectively if we ensure that we maintain our own clearly distinct and coherent party and structure.

Many tactical turns will be necessary as mass left reformist and centrist currents develop. It will not be possible for us to intervene in them effectively if we only have a loose political cohesion and organisational structure. It will be vital for us to have the necessary political cohesion and clarity and a well organised structure if we are to win the best workers and youth involved in these formations to genuine Marxist ideas and methods. An important aspect of winning such forces will be the question of the need for a revolutionary international.

Building CWI forces

At this conjuncture in the majority of countries our sections are not yet confronted with this development. Nevertheless, we need to be alert to the prospect and possibilities of new workers' formations being established, and the CWI and its sections reject any idea of passively waiting on such developments. On the other hand it is not correct for us to conduct a fruitless search for small worn out forces and individuals thinking that they will constitute the basis for a new workers' party. The situation that is opening up will enable us to building substantial revolutionary formations. In some countries at national level these can become small mass parties. In others, initially we will be able to achieve this at a regional and local level. The development of our party (Socialist Party) in the south of Ireland and the election of a member of parliament are an indication of how we are already strengthening our forces there. This can be repeated in other countries.

The main task we have is to intervene and undertake initiatives to reach fresh layers of workers and youth independently as an open organisation. We need to intervene in the struggles of the masses with a view to recruiting the fresh generation of workers and youth. Through this emphasis we can win the most combative and radicalised sections and introduce them to revolutionary socialist and Marxist ideas. Initially many of those we reach will be attracted to us by our interventions in the class struggle and the initiatives we take amongst the workers and the youth. These can begin on very basic questions. The most politically aware and combative layer we must try and recruit and then systematically introduce them to our programme and the nature of national parties/sections and the international. The recent success of our Swedish section (RS) is an indication of what we can achieve elsewhere in the near future.

This emphasis on building our own independent forces does not mean that we adopt a sectarian approach.

'United Front' methods

Most of our sections have adopted 'united front' methods of work with other groups in order to try and reach a broader layer. This has applied to struggles of workers and youth, in the trade unions and in our revolutionary electoral work. The Sri Lanka section (USP) is currently participating in a left-wing electoral block, the New Left Front. Our Swedish section participated for a short time in a block, the Justice List. When doing this work we have maintained our own independent political and organisational profile and publications.

The flexibility of our tactics has been shown in the work of our Nigerian comrades

(DSM). Our work in the National Conscience Party (NCP) has involved elements of both a united front character and a certain aspect of entrism. After the recent upheavals it has been possible for us to launch a publicly open organisation and continue to work in and around the NCP. In the past, in some countries of the former colonial world we have conducted work in and around radical bourgeois formations that have had an important basis amongst the working class and other exploited layers.

For a period our sections conducted work in and around the BNP in Sri Lanka, the PPP in Pakistan and others. Because of the changed attitude of the masses towards these organisations and the swing to the right that has taken place in them, this tactic has not applied in recent years. However, the emergence of new radical bourgeois formations in some countries of the former colonial world will mean we should be prepared, where necessary, to work in and around them. If we had forces in Mexico it may have been correct for them to orientate in/around the radical bourgeois PRD when it was launched at the end of the 1980's.

Although the majority of our sections are undertaking open, independent work, this does not prevent us from joining and working within parties when the situation justifies it. The re-joining of our Brazilian section into the PT in the recent period is an indication of this. This may be only a short term situation. However, if the right-wing do split from the PT it may develop for a period of time, under the impact the deep social and economic crisis that is taking place. Our Brazilian section, in such a situation, may need to continue to work in the PT.

The application of the method of the united front has been beneficial to our work in some countries. It has enabled us to develop our influence, build our own forces and take the struggle forward. At the same time the World Congress stresses that when applying 'united front' methods we must ensure that we maintain a correct balance. In undertaking this work we must ensure that we do not lose our own independent programme or party profile.

'United front' methods will inevitably mean conducting a joint struggle with other forces on specific issues and in support of concrete slogans. It is important that we apply the transitional method when taking our ideas to the new generation of workers and youth during this activity. We must also ensure that when participating in 'united front' methods of work we do not lower our own political and organisa-tional banner. We must maintain our own independent publications explaining our programme and the need to join our own organisation. The old maxim of 'march separately but strike together' must continue to be applied.

The twin dangers of sectarianism and opportunism need to be guarded against. We must combat any tendency towards a sectarian attitude towards the working class and the youth that may develop in our international. However, sectarianism should not be mistaken for adopting a principled stand to defend our programme and build our organisation in opposition to other political groups who are presenting a wrong programme, analysis and method of work which confuses and disorientates the proletariat.

It is important that we maintain a sense of proportion when applying the method of the united front. In the main the activity some sections have participated in has not been the application of a classical united front which related to the mass organisations of the working class. It is important that when sections discuss these type of initiatives we seriously consider what investment in time and resources we put into them and what benefits we are going to get out of them. Formal alliances with other political groups are inevitably temporary and may not be long lasting.

Trade unions

This Congress emphasises to all sections the importance of our work in the work places and the trade unions. We face an entirely new situation even in relation to the trade unions due to: (1) a parallel process of bourgeoisification of the union tops; (2) a crisis of falling membership; (3) a failure to defend old positions in the face of 'globalisation', neo-liberal attacks, mass unemployment etc. This is the point of departure for the industrial work of the CWI in the coming period.

While there are important differences in our characterisation of the trade unions, as distinct from the bourgeoisified ex-workers' parties, primarily that they are still based in the working class, it is nonetheless clear that this process has affected the unions, albeit to varying degrees in different countries. This has transformed the conditions in which Marxists and other worker militants are forced to work, raising new political and tactical problems

The tendency for the trade union apparatus to become integrated with the 'market' has gone further than in the past. This is manifested in numerous ways: big union investments in stock markets; massive growth of bureaucracy and privileges, seats on company boards, pension funds etc and even bigger retreats in relation to anti-strike legislation, new versions of social contracts etc.

During the 1990s the officialdom have been a huge break on workers' resistance, have collaborated with and sponsored privatisations, redundancies etc and acted to hold down wage levels. The unions have acted as an important pillar for the bosses' EMU process, this is especially clear in Italy.

All this has had a big effect on consciousness. While the idea of trade unionism - as an ideal - is popular, workers generally have less allegiance to their unions than in the past and, in particular, the authority of the union leaders is, with some exceptions, on the same low level as for the "politicians". Especially in Europe, dominated by social democratic governments, which we characterised as bourgeois parties, is of special interest.

This does not mean that we 'write off' the existing union organisations, even where the character of a union has changed. We must avoid a sectarian and ultra-left attitude towards the official trade union structures. It is necessary to combine work at the base with the building of opposition currents to the trade union bureaucracy. Even if the intensified pressure from the bosses and the process of bourgeoisification of the trade union officials penetrate down to the lowest levels; they cannot eradicate an elemental class-consciousness in and around the local unions closest to the membership. Marxism, especially in this period must demonstrate great flexibility in its approach and tactics. Lenin argued that communists must be prepared to work in the most reactionary trade unions - the key question is consciousness, and where the workers can be reached. The Bolsheviks even worked in a Black Hundreds-led union in order to win the workers involved.

The only factor that can arrest and, under certain conditions, reverse the process of ever deeper integration (with capitalism) is mass struggle - and this of course is our perspective. However, this does not settle the question in advance of in which direction the union apparatuses, subjected to the blows of a mass movement, will be pushed. The character of the trade union structures, opportunities for rank and file influence, traditions of opposition groupings, are important factors in determining this. In some cases the existing structures can be 'rejuvenated' as partially occurred within the US Teamsters. In others the perspective will be one of splits or new formations, small examples of which we have seen in Australia, South Africa, and most clearly in South Korea. Splits will be a stronger feature than previously the case. Even where new formations emerge, however, these too will arrive at an impasse without a political re-orientation.

Our tactics will depend on the concrete situation: What is the best means to take the struggle forward? In most cases our intervention will involve a combination of a "hybrid" involving parallel official and new, unofficial structures.

Two key tasks

Marxism is faced with two key tasks in the new period that began with the collapse of the former Stalinist regimes. Firstly, to face up to the new features present in the situation and draw the necessary conclusions for the tasks of revolutionary socialists. One crucial task in this period is to assist in the process of rebuilding the idea of socialism as an alternative to capitalism. It is important for us today to explain the reasons for the emergence of Stalinism and the collapse of the Stalinist system.

Secondly, to defend the method and fundamental ideas of Marxism from the ideological offensive that has been launched against them. A crucial aspect of this is the need to educate and train a new generation of cadres and members in the political and organisational methods of Marxism. This does not mean repeating Marxist ideas as dogmatic formulae but of applying the Marxist method to the new world situation.

The decade of the 1990's has been marked by a period of ideological confusion and collapse on the left, including some of the revolutionary left. The CWI has withstood this pressure far more effectively than other organisations. However, in this period a danger exists of diluting the programme of Marxism in order to find a short cut and to reach a general accommodation with other forces/individuals on the socialist left. This process has been re-enforced in the recent period because of the absence of a cohesive left-reformist current in many countries. This can lead to a blunting in the presentation of our programme and ideas if we do not guard against it.

Powerful centrist and left-reformist currents and parties will develop in the future. Even when we are in a minority Marxists have a responsibility to explain to workers why our programme is necessary. In periods of ideological confusion it is even more important that we patiently explain to workers our analysis and why our programme is necessary.

If our cadres are not steeled in our programme and how to defend it we will pay a heavy price in the next period as reformist and centrist ideas are expressed in a more formulated way. The ideas of popular frontism and the stages theory that have emerged again during the Indonesian revolution are an indication of the need for us to sharpen the understanding of our sections on all aspects of our programme and ideas.

The 7th World Congress of the CWI recognises that we must avoid the twin dangers of opportunism and sectarianism. It is necessary that we apply the maximum flexibility when developing our tactics. At the same time it is necessary to combat any attempt to water down our programme and to accept an opportunistic adaptation.

Lenin and Trotsky fought to differentiate themselves politically, programmatically and organisationally from left-reformism and centrism. As the experience of the POUM in Spain demonstrated, at critical moments in the class struggle the most fatal role can be played by centrism and left-centrism.

The 7th World Congress instructs the IEC/IS to review these aspects of the work and to ensure that the experience of each section is fully discussed throughout the CWI. This will strengthen the work and experience of all sections and help ensure that we are fully prepared to face up to the tasks that we have at the present time.

First draft circulated October 1998
Resolution adopted by World Congress November 1998

CWI Contingent on Euromarch Demonstration, Amsterdam, June 1997

The World Economy

1 - A Global Crisis

❝ Consider the big picture: an east Asia of toppling currencies and bank insolvency: rising unemployment in Latin America's largest economy (Brazil) and falling real wages throughout the region: stagnation and unemployment in Europe: a rapidly approaching limit to the capacity of US consumers to take on more debt. As the global economy slows, social unrest threatens. This global ... contraction could lead to a deflationary cycle."

Robert Reich, former US Secretary of Labour, in the British Financial Times 15 January 1998.

A turning point

The ongoing turmoil and financial meltdown in east Asia, has confirmed the perspective put forward by the CWI at its last IEC meeting, in November 1997, that world capitalism is moving into a new, synchronised downturn. This is a turning point in the post-Stalinist period.

The crisis in Asia became acute in July last year when Thailand, after spending $25 billion in a desperate move to prop up the value of the baht, was forced to devalue and asked for assistance from the IMF. But this is not simply an "Asian crisis"; it is a crisis of global capitalism which will cause economic, political and social instability all over the world.

The crisis is not restricted to finance and banking, but also to what used to be called "the real economy". It is not only banks and financial institutions or investment- and pension funds that are active on the financial markets; the big companies - the multinationals - are also active players in the global 'casino' economy.

The collapse in east Asia and its aftermath have shattered the illusions built up in the so-called "emerging markets" and is striking a political and ideological blow against the bourgeoisie. These economies were held up as models of capitalism, but what is now left of that model?

The last recovery (from 1991) was the weakest recovery in world capitalism since 1945 and in Europe it has been a jobless recovery. World capitalism is heading towards a new recession and is in a more volatile and fragile position than before. East Asia and Japan will hardly experience any growth this year. Indonesia, Thailand and South Korea will suffer an absolute fall in output. Millions of east Asian workers have already become unemployed. In South Korea alone, one million jobs could be lost this year - 12 per cent of the workforce - in a country that does not have a social safety net. As one placard read in a demonstration in South Korea: "IMF = I'M Fired". The latest figure given is that 7 million jobs will be wiped out during this year in the region. The unemployed will be plunged straight back into poverty. In Indonesia alone, the number of people classified as poor could swell from 24 million to 42 million - one in five Indonesians. "East Asia is heading for 'a social catastrophe'", warned a spokesperson for the ILO in Bangkok. The existing political order in the region can not survive the present crisis; it will be turned upside down.

Over the last couple of months the world has experienced a general slow-down in growth rates, shrinking demand, production cut-backs, mass lay-offs and increased competition on the world market. The financial system is balancing precariously on a tightrope. The credit crunch is causing a wave of bankruptcies throughout east Asia.

Along with that, the present financial turmoil "is perhaps the most serious crisis since the break-down of the Bretton Woods system in the early 1970s. Its repercussions are global and much serious than the financial crises we've seen in the past 15 or 20 years", said Yilmaz Akyuz of the UN Conference on Trade and Development in an interview in the US Wall Street Journal, 19 January. In the same interview, he stressed that this crisis is "certainly more serious" than the 'peso crisis' in Mexico 1994-95 and the Latin American crisis at the beginning of the 1980s "because we have much greater integration financially. And these (Asian) countries have a much higher share in the world economy in terms of trade and production".

At the end of 1997, the debt-ridden economies in the region were on the brink of default. The amount of short-term debt that could not be re-paid - in the case South Korea, $65 ban - forced the IMF to step in. Part of the IMF's so-called rescue package was to ensure that at least some of this money would find its way back to western banks and funds. The IMF acted on behalf of western imperialism. Its actions strangled these economies. At the same time, the imperialist powers used the opportunity to strengthen their influence in the area.

This new recession will develop against the background of a completely different world situation compared to that of the last crisis, in the beginning of the 1990s. Then the slowdown was overshadowed by the historic changes that followed the collapse of Stalinism. The world bourgeoisie hailed the collapse of Stalinism as a final triumph for capitalism and western imperialism - the planned economy had been beaten by the superiority of the so-called free market and liberal capitalism. In that way, the beginning of the 1990s was becoming, despite the crisis facing the world bourgeoisie, dominated by capitalist triumphalism reinforced by the imperialist victory in the Gulf war and the proclamation, by president Bush, of a "new world order".

All over the globe the message was being spread: there is no alternative to the so-called free market. This idea was echoed by the leaders of the labour movement and penetrated the minds of the masses. In general, consciousness was falling back and the workers' movement became disarmed in a political and ideological sense. This played into the hands of the bosses, who intensified their attacks on every gain the workers had achieved during the long post-war upswing.

However, the 1990s were also characterised by an increased social and political polarisation, a growing distrust in the capitalist establishment and an undermining of confidence in bourgeois institutions. The political and social discontent that has accumulated even during the latest recovery will now come to the fore and give way to an anti-capitalist mood. This new recession is developing at the same time as there is a beginning of a global popular reaction against neo-liberalism and the capitalist establishment.

Over recent years the bourgeoisie has constantly repeated that the process of globalisation, de-regulation and the rapid development of new technology was going to generate prosperity all over the world. There has also been much talk about the "new paradigm" in the world economy: That instead of inflation and low productivity gains, as in the 1980s, the world has entered a period of sustained growth and low inflation, in which capitalism was on its way to overcoming the "productivity paradox". However, investment in 'IT' (information technology) did not boost overall labour productivity throughout the advanced capitalist countries. Instead of producing a new paradigm, the world economy was breeding a classical capitalist crisis, expressed in overcapacity and, to some extent, even overproduction.

The blind and chaotic market forces, fuelled by speculative capital, have created a worldwide overcapacity in several key industries - from semi-conductors to cars. This excess of goods, or 'glut' - in the sense of profitability rather than real need - will lead to an enormous destruction of capital (productive forces) and wealth.

Every continent will be affected by this new world recession. The events in Asia, according to the IMF, could knock nearly 1 per cent off potential growth in the developed world in 1998. However, the drop in world production is likely to be bigger than this figure, given the fact that there is a lot of wishful thinking based on the assumption that after the 'bail-out' things will start to get better. But the latest events contradict this: the severe crisis in Indonesia, the collapse of the Hong Kong merchant bank Peregrini. In a recent speech, Alan Greenspan, chairman of the US Federal Reserve, said: "We have as yet experienced only the peripheral winds of the Asian crisis. But before spring is over, the abrupt current account adjustments, that financial difficulties are forcing upon several of our Asian trading partners, will be showing through here (USA) in reductions in demand for our exports and intensified competition from imports".

East Asia acted as an engine of global growth in 1990s. The region generated 60-65 per cent of the growth in world output between 1990 and 1995. The same region has been responsible for 70 per cent of the increase in world investment in the 1990s. Asia as whole accounted for a bigger share of global investment than the US and the EU put together in the mid-1990s. Rising exports and increased demand in SE Asia have been important factors behind the recovery in the 1990s. That, in itself, indicates that shrinking demand in Asia, drastic cutbacks in imports and much slower growth will have a huge impact on the rest of the world.

It seems that the world is moving into a new recession at a speed that could not have been foreseen in November last year. No one can predict in advance how deep the crisis is going to be and how long it will last before a new recovery begins to develop.

A crisis was brewing

The private capital inflow into the region was based on the assumption that economic growth and a rapidly booming property market could be sustained indefinitely. However, as pointed out by Marx and Engels a long time ago: Capitalist expansion always comes up against the resistance "offered by consumption, by sales, by the market for the products of modern industry... The markets cannot keep pace with the extension of production. The collision becomes inevitable".

Already in 1996 there were signs that the investment boom in SE Asia was leading to 'overinvestment' or overaccumulation of capital. It had created overcapacity in goods and property. The return on capital began to fall and the value of exports started to go down.

What took place in South Korea is a graphic illustration of how this process - towards overcapacity and a deflationary spiral - developed. In the words of the British Financial Times, 15 January: "South Korea enjoyed an investment boom 1994-95, but at a cost. The chaebol, always heavily reliant on borrowing, now had huge debts - four times equity on average - and excess production capacity. Prices for computer memory chips, Korea's largest export, collapsed in a global glutted market. Earnings of chipmakers fell by 90 per cent. Cars, shipbuilding, steel and petrochemicals were also affected.... The corporate debt bomb was primed to explode. The first detonation came in January 1997 when Hanbo Steel collapsed. By now a wider crisis in Asia was under way."

Later on, in 1997, an outflow of foreign capital started. "The South Korean currency, the won, dropped sharply. Foreign banks began refusing to roll over short-term loans to South Korea. By early November, the slide in the won was accelerating. Foreign currency reserves started the month at $30 bn, less than three months' imports. They fell by half in two weeks."

Balancing on the edge

Due to many factors the crisis in SE Asia immediately worsened the crisis for Japanese capitalism (see other material such as the last two issues of Socialism Today, the theoretical and discussion journal of the Socialist Party, the British section of the CWI). 43 per cent of Japanese exports were going to other countries in Asia, up from 30 per cent in 1990. During the 1990s, up to 70 per cent of the increase in Japanese exports has been to the rest of Asia.

Japan is already in a recession. In fact, the country has not recovered since the 'bubble economy' burst at the beginning of the 1990s. In December 1997 the Bank of Japan said, "The economy is undergoing a severe shock". Unemployment could reach 5 per cent this year - the highest figure since the second world war. Retail sales dropped 4.7 per cent from November 1996 to November 1997 - the biggest drop since 1955. Domestic demand in Japan continues to fall as consumer spending goes down. Japanese capitalism is therefore compelled to try to export itself out of the crisis, but meanwhile their competitors in other Asian countries have devalued their currencies and are trying to do exactly the same.

The wave of competitive devaluations that has followed the financial 'meltdown' is also affecting China and Hong Kong. The Hong Kong dollar is still pegged to the US dollar. Despite the impending crisis in the finance and property market, the Hong Kong dollar is becoming increasingly over-valued. Asia's weakened currencies have nearly wiped out all the competitive advantage China gained from the yuan's 33 per cent devaluation in 1994. Increased competition from abroad and a general slow-down in the growth of world trade could force the Chinese government to devalue again, whatever the Government is saying today. A devaluation in China would make the Hong Kong dollar's peg to the US dollar unsustainable. In the words of the British Observer, 11 January: "The devaluation of both currencies is now a real possibility rather than a vague fear".

Asia as a region is now becoming a net exporter instead of a net importer. Asia's slowdown means less demand for Japanese capital goods. Japan must therefore try to increase its share of markets in the USA and Europe. This will build up tension in the world market and cause even bigger problems for Japanese capitalism.

The Far Eastern Economic Review at the end of 1997 asked the question: "How bad can Japan's economy get? Consider this scenario for 1998:- Stock prices plunge, causing a number of banks to collapse. Consumers cling to their savings in fear of the future. The economy descends into a full-blown recession... The prime minister resigns and political turmoil reigns. The nightmare is already turning into a reality". The Finance minister in Japan has already been forced to resign, after yet another corruption scandal and the arrest of numerous officials at the Finance Ministry. The present government may have to go before the end of this year.

The financial meltdown in Asia sent shock waves into the already extremely fragile banking system in Japan. Japanese banks have lent the rest of Asia $275 billion.

Many of the Japanese banks would already have been wiped out (the official figure for the banking system's bad loans is $600 bn.) if it was not for the fact that they are fiddling the figures. Unlike other banks they can count over-valued equity portfolios as part of their own capital. But that also means that if the Japanese stock market index (Nikkei) starts to fall again, as it did throughout 1997, and if the Nikkei plunges beyond 14 000, Japan's 20 biggest lenders would face $96 bn. in losses. That figure is from November last year and is probably much higher today.

The spectre of a world financial crash, as the outcome of a severe banking crisis in Japan, cannot be ruled out. If the Japanese stock market continues to go down during this year and the economy contracts even more, then there is a risk that Japanese banks will start to go bust. That can happen despite two government rescue packages. (The first one worth $250 bn. has already been announced; the second one will be announced in February.)

In the three years up to 1995, the Japanese government pumped $500 bn. into the economy but it continued to stagnate and Japan ended up with the largest budget deficit in the G7 group - 7% of GDP. If these new packages fail to stimulate growth and ease the financial crisis, then the Japanese banks may be forced to eat into the reserves they have abroad and to start withdrawing their holdings in the USA and Europe. Such a development can trigger off a worldwide dip in share prices on the stock markets and cause severe turmoil in the currency markets.

One of the reasons the US government is putting pressure on Japan to boost its economy is that the North American capitalists are facing the threat of an actual capital outflow, if the dollar starts to fall. This will happen, especially if the Japanese banks start to take back their holdings in the US and Europe.

The threat of deflation

The new recession will aggravate the confusions, splits and divisions that are already evident inside the bourgeois camp. A section of the bourgeoisie will undoubtedly, for their own reasons, come out in favour of increased public expenditure - a reflationary policy to prop up demand - and for more regulations to protect markets.

The most far-sighted section of the bourgeoisie has started to draw parallels with the situation before the 1929 crash. As the former US Secretary of Labour, Robert Reich, wrote in the British Financial Times January 15:

"The seeds of depression were sown in the late 1920s, when demand began to fall. By 1927 sales of houses, cars and consumer durables were in decline, commodity prices had turned downwards and industrial production began to fall. We are entering a similar era.

"Even before the Asian currency crisis, world prices were falling for basic goods such as food, energy, steel and other commodities. A large... global contraction is under way. We are experiencing only the beginnings".

However, it is too early, at this stage, to conclude that the world is heading towards a slump on the scale of 1929-33. There are no exact parallels between today's position and the one that existed in the late 1920s and the decade after. Every crisis and period of depression has its own historical peculiarities.

Nevertheless, if the present stagnation turns into an absolute fall in world production, as in 1974-75, the entire world will experience the most severe crisis of capitalism since 1929-33. Many countries, both in the underdeveloped and in the advanced capitalist world, will experience a similar catastrophe to that which took place in the US in 1929 when the economy, in the words of Trotsky, "catapulted itself into the abyss of monstrous prostration".

Trotsky's description of what happened in the USA in 1929 can be applied to what is now happening in Indonesia, a country with nearly 200 million inhabitants, the 4th most populated country in the world. The currency, the rupiah, has lost 85 per cent of its value against the US dollar in seven months. Interest payments are over 100 billion rupiah a year, twice as much as the government receives in income from tax and VAT. According to the magazine Far Eastern Economic Review, January 29: "At least 6 million people are newly unemployed, and over the next few months untold millions more stand to lose their jobs". Ninety per cent of listed firms are technically insolvent and they have stopped paying their debts. Indonesia has sunk into stagflation and price increases are now running at an annual rate of 60 per cent.

In the search of food, shops are being rioted and looted. The food crisis is becoming increasingly acute in Indonesia. The days of Suharto are numbered - he will have to go.

No wonder a section of the bourgeoisie is now saying, as expressed by Martin Wolf in the British Financial Times, 20 January, that: "One important lesson from the east Asian crisis is that international capital flows can threaten economic stability. Some regulations are required.".

A cynical joke spread amongst the world's speculators sums up the reaction of the market after the events in east Asia: "What is the definition of an emerging market? Answer: A market that you can't get your money out of in an emergency!" This is one way of saying (and it is certainly not funny) that capital flow into the so- called emerging markets is slowing down as a result of what happened in east Asia, Brazil and even the Czech Republic last year.

The speculative character of this capital has been shown in east Asia. South Korea, Indonesia, Malaysia, Thailand and the Philippines suffered a net private capital outflow of $12 billion in 1997 - "The first 'major retrenchment' by international investors in emerging markets in the 1990s", according to the US Wall Street Journal, 30 January. In 1996 these countries were recipients of a net inflow of $93 bn. In total, net capital inflow to Asia will sink to $62 bn. in 1998, from $90 bn. in 1997 and $150 bn. in 1996. Latin America will slip to $65 bn. in 1998 from $82 bn. 1996.

Under the hammer of US imperialism and the IMF

Under the policies that east Asian countries have been forced to implement by the IMF, they have been ordered to balance budgets, raise interest rates, abolish subsidies on food and electricity, accelerate de-regulation and privatisation and to put their banks and industries up for sale. This is enormously aggravating the social and economic crisis in the region. Not only the masses, but also the petit-bourgeoisie and a section of the national bourgeoisie, will come under the hammer of the IMF.

Western imperialism is acting in a very arrogant way; the description now widely used of "a new form of neo-colonialism" is accurate. The IMF is a direct tool of US imperialism.

The IMF and western imperialism were compelled to act, when South Korea was just days away from "having to default on its maturing short-term dollar (loans) at the turn of the year", (British Observer 11 January). A Korean default would have triggered off a banking crisis in Japan, which held $25 bn. Korean debt, and caused enormous financial turmoil in countries where South Korean banks had invested money. South Korean banks were large investors in, for example, East European junk bonds. The US, with 37,000 troops in South Korea, realised that a default on the part of that country would have huge geo-political repercussions throughout the region. But the IMF and imperialism did not act just to avoid an acute crisis. Wider and strategic factors were behind this so-called bailout, worked out in a special 'war room' in the White House.

This time, US intervention took the opposite form from that in the aftermath of the 1949 Chinese revolution and the Korean War of 1950-53. Then, imperialism was prepared to give full support - financially, politically and military - to South Korea and other east Asian countries.

The backing of US imperialism, together with the active role played by the state - even protectionism to support developing industries and reserve domestic market for them - laid the basis for the transformation of South Korea into a highly sophis-ticated economy. These special factors explain why South Korea enjoyed an export growth of 34 per cent a year in the 1960s and 23 per cent in the 1970s.

However, the situation changed dramatically after the collapse of Stalinism. In the new world order, western imperialism, for a long time now challenged by the performances of these countries on the world market, saw no reason why domestic markets in SE Asia should be restricted or why the state should continue to protect - through laws and regulations - banks and industries owned by the national bourgeoisie. Western imperialism's denunciation of "crony-capitalism" in east Asia has to be seen in that context. The very same "crony-capitalism" was build up with the support of US imperialism as a bulwark against social revolution.

The IMF's programme and the outcome of the debt crisis will give western monopolies an opportunity to buy cheap assets in these countries. Banks and industries will now be 'on sale' and, in the words of the US Magazine Newsweek, 2 February, "The Americans have returned with a vengeance. This time they have taken the form of U.S. investment banks, asset and hedge funds and speculators like George Soros, all of them riding a tide of triumphalism as the West's powerful capital markets overwhelm the closed financial system that Japan inspired throughout Asia. As the Asian contagion topples economy after economy, the U.S. firms are prising open these systems with a ferocity that 150 years of U.S. trade negotiation could not achieve". In short, western imperialism is going to plunder the region. This will provoke a strong mood of anti-imperialism, which will also be directed against those politicians and capitalists seen as responsible for this surrender to IMF and US imperialism.

We have to see the revolutionary potential in such a move in an anti-imperialist direction and big struggles that might develop. However, there is also a danger that, if the working class can not lead the struggle, this anti-imperialist mood could be exploited and diverted by chauvinists or even racist demagogues. The recent attacks against the Chinese minority on the Indonesian island of Java is a warning of what can happen in the future.

Nevertheless, the policy of the IMF, together with the arrogance of imperialism, is a recipe for social unrest and workers' revolt in east Asia. A new generation of workers will enter the arena of struggle and try to form their own independent organisations. However, in the initial stage, the proletariat in east Asia could be stunned by the speed and depth of the crisis.

Even new bourgeois governments could be forced, during the course of a deepening crisis and under pressure from the masses, to implement measures that challenge western imperialism and the IMF. Such measures could include refusal to pay off debts, nationalisations, controls over foreign exchange and reintroduction of food subsidises. This happened in Venezuela in 1993-94, when a new government came to power after a banking collapse and a revolt from the masses. The present triumphalism of imperialism will cause its own backlash.

US imperialism is exploiting the crisis in Asia and is trying, at the expense of other advanced capitalist countries, to conquer a bigger share of the region's shrinking market. The Australian government has, for example, accused the US of "stealing its traditional export market", particularly in Indonesia. The head of Australian cotton growers said recently, "The US has behaved like looters after an economic cyclone". Australia supplies about 40 per cent of Indonesia's cotton and is the largest supplier of numerous commodities. The growing trade friction between the US and the

Australian government reflects the rising tensions that have built up in the sphere of world trade due to the economic collapse in east Asia.

The alleged miracle in Mexico

The bourgeois commentators are now saying that Asia should 'learn from Latin America and Mexico'. The alleged Mexican miracle, after the devaluation of 1995 and the IMF rescue package (to save US investors), resulted in:- another million workers on the dole, 20 million more Mexicans pushed below the poverty line, huge sections of the middle class ruined and an uprising in Chiapas! The PRI (the ruling party) and the state-controlled union federation ended up in complete disarray. The peso crisis broke down the old political order in Mexico. Still, GDP (in US dollar terms) has not reached its 1994 level. Mexico today is even more dependent on the US than it was then. More than 85 per cent of Mexico's exports go to there. A slow-down in the US and a fall in the value of the dollar will immediately hit the Mexican economy.

Growth in Latin America as a whole will not exceed 3 per cent this year - down from 5.5 per cent in 1997. Brazil is already in a recession. The J P Morgan Bank is forecasting that the Brazilian economy will drop 0.5 per cent in absolute terms this year. In the wake of the government's last $18 bn. austerity package, unemployment soared to a record level - 16 per cent in Sao Paulo. If the Brazilian government fails to uphold the value of the currency, the 'real', and is forced to devalue, then a whole series of competitive devaluations could erupt throughout the continent.

The recession in Brazil has been accompanied by a slow-down in Chile. One third of Chile's exports went to Asia. The loss of markets in Asia, together with the collapse in the price of copper - Chile's main export, has caused stagnant growth and soaring deficits.

The fall in commodity prices will tend to undermine the economies in the less developed countries even further. Some countries that have only one source of income, like Nigeria with its oil-exports, are going to face a nightmare.

The West is sliding into recession

In the West, the bourgeoisie is becoming more pessimistic about the future or as Financial Times wrote January 27: "Asia's financial crisis is starting to have knock-on effects on companies around the globe". North America is now the only major economy that is a net importer and inevitably the US trade gap will soar. This could "arouse protectionist sentiments", in the words of The Economist 17 January. However, given the development of world trade and the process of globalisation, a move towards protectionism or "regulated trade" will probably be on the basis of the main trading blocs rather than individual nation states.

As long as the US economy is growing at its present rate, there is not an acute danger of a return to protectionism. Anyway, the US cannot on its own act as a locomotive in the world economy, especially not at this time, when the recovery in the US has reached its peak. The latest forecast by the Federal Reserve is also warning that there are signs of weakening demand in the US and that Asian exports are gaining competitiveness.

Weakening demand means lower profits and ultimately a fall in share prices. The Wall Street Dow Jones Index is bound to come down this year from its lofty heights and, "A dramatic drop in the Dow could squash consumption and investment and drag the economy into recession". The British Economist, 17 January.

A crash on Wall Street could trigger a worldwide stock market crash. This is not 1987. Then, the world economy was still in a recovery stage and, with the injection of more than $ 100 bn. by the governments in Japan and West Germany, the fall of the dollar was halted and the crisis was postponed for two years.

This can not simply be repeated. World capitalism is in a much more difficult position today than it was in 1987. The economic conjuncture - the upturn - has reached its peak. German and Japanese capitalism no longer have the enormous surplus they had in that period and the market in Asia is shrinking. Although, faced with the prospect of a slump, governments and central banks will have to intervene and pump in more money. This will not necessarily have anything like the same result as in 1987, given the difficulties that exist.

Since 1995, nearly every country has experienced an effective devaluation of its currency against the US dollar. The appreciation of the dollar has boosted, for example, German and French exports. A strong dollar is making US firms less competitive and is increasing the USA's current-account deficit. This, together with a tendency towards slower growth, could start to bring the dollar down which, at a certain stage, will cause a flight of capital from the US. However, for the time being, the US dollar is regarded as a "safe haven". The capital inflow into the US, partly motivated by an assumption that interest rates there may raise, is holding up the value of the dollar, despite a soaring trade and current account deficit. Nevertheless, an opposite process could develop when the speculators, for one reason or another, fear that their assets in US dollars are at risk. Then they will look for other "safe havens", such as the deutschmark or the Swiss franc. This could trigger turmoil on the European currency market. It would be impossible to maintain an all-European fixed exchange rate mechanism under such circumstances.

As was pointed out in an article in The European, 19-25 January: "The impact of an American downturn on Europe would be particularly marked if, as expected, it sends the dollar into reverse. The pick up in Germany and France has been export-led as the deutschmark and other EMU currencies have fallen against the dollar. Domestic demand has hardly picked up at all. Should the dollar be weakened through 1998, the main impetus for Europe's encouraging growth rate could be removed. Forecasters are already starting to anticipate this as 1998 is progressing". If, the article continues, this becomes a reality, "growth in Europe will quickly fall back to the dismal level of the early 1990s. Would the euro survive?" We have to answer 'no' to that question.

It is becoming increasingly likely that Europe is heading for a recession during this year. The effect of the Asian crisis is lagging behind a bit, but the latest reports and warnings from industries in, for example, Sweden and Germany are saying that exports and output will go down. A new recession in Europe will, in the end, wreck the EMU project or compel the EU-countries to postpone it to the distant future.

Exactly when this would be is another question. Nevertheless, the EU-countries are still trying to bring themselves together and go ahead with the project. The struggle against the Maastricht austerity measures will therefore continue to be a feature in any major class battle in Europe.

 The repercussions of the Asian crisis on European exports, output and banking could be much bigger than anticipated by the bourgeois media. European banks lent heavily to east Asia even in 1997, when all the other banks were pulling out. Europe's banks combined have $365 bn. loaned to Asia. It can not be ruled out that the taxpayers of Europe (in many countries for the second time this decade) will be asked to pay for the losses incurred. In addition to that, slower growth will increase budget deficits throughout Europe and "take the gloss off the predicted recovery in 1998", according to the Observer, 25 January. New austerity measures will be needed in order to meet the Maastricht criteria. This, together with job losses, is going to pave the way for an upsurge in the European class struggle. As one Guardian journalist put it: "There is a risk that the financial meltdown in Asia will be followed by a social meltdown in Europe".

The gap between rich and poor is now greater than at any time in the history of capitalism. Mass unemployment and under-employment in the world are now on the same level as in the 1930s, although in western Europe still 'cushioned', to some extent, by social security provisions. Wage inequality in many countries, one of them Britain, is now bigger than at the beginning of the Industrial Revolution. In 1997, 1.3 billion people on the globe lived in absolute poverty (according to the United Nations definition). Even in the developed capitalist world, there are now 100 million people that the UN regards as poor.

The recovery in the 1990s was mainly based on the super-exploitation of workers and the oppressed masses in the less developed world. Capitalism in the 1990s has all the features that Marx describe in the volumes of Capital: "Accumulation of wealth at one pole is therefore at the same time the accumulation of misery, agony of toil on the opposite pole i.e. on the side of the class that produces its product in the form of capital". For a huge section of the working class, especially the most oppressed - the low paid, part-time and un-skilled workers, women and immigrants

- there has been an absolute decline in their living standards, despite the recovery. A constant re-distribution of wealth and incomes, from ordinary people and the public sector into the pockets of the capitalists, has taken place during the last 10-15 years. Over the last fifteen years the earnings of about half of all working people in the US have dropped in real terms, while the share of profit of national income rose from 4.8 per cent to 8.4 per cent 1995.

The contradictions in society, which were deepened during the last economic recovery, will pave the way for social explosions in the future. The movement of the unemployed in France is an indication of what can take place. Such a movement can act as catalyst and inspire other sections of workers and youth to take to the streets.for the parties, sections and groups affiliated to the CWI, the coming period will open up new possibilities for growth, both in membership and influence. The most burning issue now is to prepare our forces, theoretically, politically and organisationally for the turmoil and social unrest that lies ahead. The greatest danger is that our programme, slogans, tactics and day-to day work reflect the past and not the present or the future.

Back to socialism and Marxism

The bosses will try and put all the burden of the crisis on the shoulders of workers and the poor: that is a recipe for bitter class struggle of strikes, occupations, etc. In the movements that will erupt - in defence of jobs and welfare and for shorter working hours and a living wage - the ideas of socialism and public ownership will be back on the agenda. A strong feeling will emerge against the dictatorship of the market and those who argue that it should be replaced by a democratically planned economy based on people's needs not profit will find a ready response. We have to be seen as the champions of international socialism and transform our sections into combative organisations that can intervene in struggles and show the way forward. Recent events have exposed the crisis of capitalism and bourgeois ideology. The question that follows from that is: Why is capitalism not working and what are the origins of this crisis? To find an answer and a rounded out explanation, youth and advanced workers will turn to the ideas and methods of Marxism.

This year sees the 150th anniversary of the Manifesto of the Communist Party, written by Marx and Engels. The Communist Manifesto was written in order to arm and prepare the members of the Communist League for impending revolutions that swept across Europe in 1848. It still stands out as one of the most important works ever written. Its last words are more resounding than ever: "Let the ruling class tremble at a Communist revolution. The proletarians have nothing to lose but their chains. They have a world to win. Workers of all countries, unite!"

First published by the CWI, February 9, 1998.

2 - The nature of capitalist crisis

Russia's economic collapse at the end of August 1998, one more broken link in the chain of international crisis, marked a qualitative turning point. Bourgeois strategists were at last forced to confront the stark reality facing them.

Asia whose inter-regional and external trade makes up a third of the world total, has entered a deep slump, which is remorselessly spreading around the globe. Warning the US Congress against complacency, the financier George Soros said (15 September, 1998): 'The global capitalist system which has been responsible for our prosperity is falling apart at the seams'. Some commentators are now warning of the onset of a world depression.

The capitalist ruling elite is also realising another nightmare: they are now facing not only economic disaster but also the beginnings of a deep social and political crisis. This is already clear in Asia. Far from being merely a cyclical downturn, cumulative losses are leading to a breakdown of society's productive capacity, opening the door to social turmoil and political upheavals. The fall of Suharto in Indonesia is just the overture. It has also began to dawn on the gurus that, just as the economic contagion is spreading, political turmoil will also become a world-wide epidemic. In the sphere of international relations, the Indo-Pakistan nuclear tests and the US missile strikes on Afghanistan and Sudan are early symptoms of increased volatility.

The intoxicating aroma of capitalist triumphalism which flourished after the collapse of Stalinism has evaporated in a few turbulent months. The 'new economic paradigm' (model) - recently so popular on Wall Street and in academia - has been shattered. Conjured up by the born-again disciples of unfettered market forces - in reality, the advocates of the multinational corporations and banks - the new model was based on the claim that liberated market forces, combined with new technology and globalisation, have given rise to a prolonged period of unlimited economic growth and rising prosperity. This has proved to be a fantasy, more an hallucinogenic trip stimulated by the super-profits of the 1990s, than the product of rational economic thinking.

Despite repeated claims from the economic pundits that the 'fundamentals' (meaning high profits, low inflation) were now much sounder than in the bad old days, the real performance of the advanced capitalist countries (ACCs) during the 1980s and 1990s has never approached the levels of the post-war upswing(1950-73). Average annual growth in real terms (i.e. allowing for inflation) has been about 2.3% in the 1990s, compared with 5% during the upswing. Rates of capital accumulation (net increase of capital stock) and productivity growth have also been markedly lower. At the same time, total unemployment in the ACCs climbed another 10 million every decade, and now totals over 35 million (according to official figures, which understate the real levels).

New features of world capitalism

There were undoubtedly new features in the world economy which appeared in the last two decades and were linked to the hollow, finance-driven booms of the eighties and nineties. But far from overcoming capitalism's long-term trend towards stagnation and decline, they have ultimately given rise to new contradictions which are aggravating the present crisis.

(a) New technology:

Microprocessors, new communications technology, and other innovations, it was claimed, would produce new products and processes, allow much more flexible methods of production, and would produce a productivity miracle. In reality, new technology has had contradictory effects. The growth of new high-tech sectors has far from compensated for the de-industrialisation and structural unemployment arising from the labour- and material-saving effects of new technology (combined with new management methods).

Microtechnology, especially in the field of communications, has served as a vehicle for globalisation, especially of financial markets. It has also allowed multinational corporations to locate plants and secure outsourcing in cheap-labour countries, with minimal taxation and negligible environmental, health and safety, or labour regulation. Through accelerating some areas of production (motor vehicles, computer equipment, etc), while causing de-industrialisation and unemployment in traditional manufacturing areas, the new technological systems have helped give rise to over-production.

Even in the US, new technology has not produced the long heralded productivity revolution. Despite a cumulative investment of $630bn (1987 constant dollars) on computers between 1980 and 1994, the US could not lift productivity growth above its pathetic post-1973 trend rate of 1.1% a year (compared with 3% between 1960-73). In the developing countries, it is also doubtful whether new technology has significantly raised productivity levels in the new plants above world averages. Multinationals have primarily relied on the intensive exploitation of plentiful cheap labour. Growth was mainly investment-driven, with the influx of capital mobilising enormously increased inputs of labour, materials and energy into production. (Ironically, this is analogous to the grossly inefficient investment-led growth during the last period of the state-planned economy in the Soviet Union.)

(b) Globalisation:

Facilitated by new technology, globalisation was increasingly finance-driven. It was an outgrowth of the relative decline of industrial production in most advanced capitalist countries. Wealthy investors sought new fields of investment for their super-profits, seeking higher profit levels than they could achieve at home. In the 1990s speculative investment in property, financial services, and shares and company bonds, became the fastest-growing sector. True, under globalisation multinational corporations seized opportunities of locating plant and securing outsourcing in about two dozen semi-developed countries, mostly in East Asia. But even investment in new production plant was increasingly through shares and company bonds, and became more and more speculative.

During the 1980s net private capital flows from the ACCs averaged $13bn a year, but rose to $90bn a year in the early 1990s. By the mid-1990s $300bn a year was flowing to about twenty-five 'emerging markets'. About 9% of this was invested in commodities, 37% in manufacturing, and 53% in services (a third of it in financial services). Globalisation, however, works both ways. The flood of highly mobile capital to the emerging markets produced a speculative bubble, especially in Asia. This collapsed last year when inflated share and property prices and high debt levels could no longer be sustained. The rise of the US dollar, moreover, made it impossible for Thailand and the others to keep their currencies pegged to the dollar (as it raised their export prices to uncompetitive levels). However, the devaluation of the Thai bhat and other regional currencies last July shattered the confidence of foreign investors. The resulting flight of capital triggered the opening of a world crisis. The globalisation of financial markets, under which a shock in one region is rapidly transmitted to other centres, has ensured that, in less than a year, the Asian crisis has spread across the continents.

(c) Capitalist restoration in the former Stalinist states:

The capitalist re-colonisation of the former Soviet Union, Eastern Europe and the massive penetration of foreign capital into China, it was claimed, would not only prove the superiority of capitalism but play an important part in a world-wide capitalist renaissance. In reality, capitalist restoration has been a catastrophe for the people of the former Stalinist states. Russia has suffered a drop in production of between 50% and 80% since 1989. Following the collapse of the rouble and the government's default on dollar loans, the peoples of the former USSR are facing the spectre of mass starvation.

The rapacious antics of capitalism's infant prodigies, former bureaucrats and mafia turned robber barons, has provoked an economic and financial collapse which will inflict serious damage on international finance capital. Bad loans to Russia make up 20% to 25% of the loan portfolios of many US and European finance houses. At the same time, the international ambitions of Russia's emergent bourgeoisie are causing serious complications for US imperialism on the world arena. China, recently hailed as a key component of the Asian miracle, also faces serious economic problems which will soon spill over into political turmoil.

(d) Neo-liberalism:

Free-market policies (privatisation of state industries, deregulation of markets and business activity, and the undermining of work-place rights and organisation to establish labour 'flexibility') liberated big business from its Keynesian fetters (full employment, high social spending based on high taxation, strong workers' organisations). (See endnote on Neo-liberalism and Keynesianism.) The invisible hand of free-market forces, it was claimed, would regulate economic activity far better than governments. Far from being a 'natural' evolution, however, neo-liberal policies were forced through by capitalist governments using economic and state coercion, legitimatized by an array of neo-liberal legislation.

The capitalists turned to neo-liberalism after the high inflation of 1974-79 which followed the exhaustion of the upswing. The turn away from Keynesianism provoked big clashes with the working class, but the labour leaders were incapable of defending past gains. Then the collapse of Stalinism, which despite its deformations had acted as a certain counter-weight to capitalism, allowed the ruling class to abandon all restraint in its switch to uninhibited free-market policies. Events like Reagan's defeat of the air traffic controllers' strike in 1981, and Thatcher's defeat of the year-long miners' strike in 1984-85 in Britain, were crucial.

By increasing the bourgeoisie's share of the wealth, however, these policies inevitably accentuated social inequalities, ultimately undermining the market for capitalist goods and services. This inevitably sharpens one of the most basic contradictions of capitalism: the tendency of capital accumulation to outpace the growth of the employed labour force, which restricts the ability of the working class to purchase the goods they produce in the course of the capitalist production process. In the late 1980s and 1990s the neo-liberal package appeared on the surface to have successfully provided an escape route from the contradictions of the post-war upswing period (1950-73). That period was also the era of the Cold War between imperialism and Stalinism. The increased strength of a working class enjoying full employment, together with the achievements in that period of the planned economies of the Soviet Union and Eastern Europe, compelled the capitalists to make significant concessions to the working class in the form of state welfare services and relatively high living standards. There was no shortage of demand for capitalist goods and services. On the contrary, high and sustained demand combined with new methods of mass production stimulated a prolonged investment boom and high profits, despite increased taxation.

In the early 1970s, however, that virtuous circle of economic and political factors gave way, through the internal contradictions of the system, to a crisis of capitalist profitability. As post-war technological systems (mass production of motor vehicles, chemicals, electrical equipment, etc) reached their limits, and a strengthened working class increasingly fought further intensification of exploitation, the unprecedented growth of productivity (output per worker/hour) slowed down. Rising real wage levels were therefore no longer compatible with high profits. Moreover, the workers used their industrial strength to increase their share of the wealth produced. It therefore became imperative for big business to increase the share of the wealth produced (from workers' labour power) going to profits - which could only be at the expense of wages.

After the shock of the 1973 oil price rise, which triggered a world slump (1974-75), the capitalists therefore turned away from Keynesian policies to neo-liberalism. Step by step post-war concessions were reclaimed through privatisation, cutting back the 'welfare state' and, most decisively, through attacking workplace rights and trade union organisations.

There was a similar rolling back of concessions by the advanced capitalist powers to Third World countries. Through agencies such as the IMF, the World Bank, and GATT, a free-market 'restructuring' was imposed in order to open up 'developing' countries to the free-ranging activities of the multinational corporations and banks.

Neo-liberalism restored the profitability of the capitalists in spectacular fashion. The tiny layer of wealthy capitalists reaped hyper-profits, with much reduced taxation into the bargain. Much of it came from speculating in finance and property rather than production.

But like every other capitalist 'paradigm', neo-liberalism has created the conditions of its own destruction. Hyper-profits were excavated from the chasm of inequality. In the US, the neo-liberal model, the top 1% now owns as much wealth as the bottom 90%. The earnings of a majority of workers have steadily declined since 1973. For a time, the capitalists could develop new markets for luxury goods and services amongst the affluent strata and also exploit new markets in a handful of rapidly developing economies in Asia and elsewhere.

Accelerating inequality, however, inevitably undermines markets. So the strong demand but diminishing profits of the post-war upswing have been replaced by booming profits combined with increasingly inadequate demand. The result is the currently developing world slump.

A general crisis of the system

All the contradictions of the neo-liberal adventure are manifest in the current downturn. It is not merely, or even primarily, a financial crisis: it is a deeply rooted crisis of capital accumulation, now expressing itself as a crisis of production.

(a) Over-production:

There is a classical crisis of over-production. This is associated with the contraction of production and trade, and a general fall in prices - all coming together in a deflationary spiral. Even last year it was already clear that in Asia there was serious overcapacity (of probably 30% or more), especially in computers, electrical consumer goods, and motor vehicles. The Asian slump almost immediately caused a sharp fall in the prices of oil and other commodities (down 30% this year to a twenty-year low), transmitting the crisis to mainly commodity-exporting economies.

East Asia is, in any case, part of the US, Japanese and European multinationals' global production complex. As the crisis deepens and spreads, rising unemployment, reduced income levels, mounting business and consumer debt defaults, and government cuts, will further erode demand and accentuate over-production on a world-wide basis. Over-production will hit the advanced capitalist economies too. This must lead, according to the anarchic logic of capitalism, to a massive destruction of productive capacity and even higher levels of mass unemployment.

(b) Financial instability:

The acute instability of global financial markets is accelerating and will, at a certain stage, provoke a major crash. There has been continuous volatility since the 1987 crash. But in the last three or four years the volume and volatility of world capital flows has increased enormously. The recent flight from 'submerging markets' in Asia, Eastern Europe and Latin America has dramatically increased volatility. The flight to 'quality' (i.e. 'safe' investments in the US and Europe) has temporarily postponed a crash on US and European stock exchanges. In fact, for a time some of the capital returning from 'emerging markets' went into US and European shares, leading to further rises. In the last few weeks, however, there has been a series of sharp falls. The traders now acknowledge that, after sixteen years, the (rising) 'bull' market has given way to a (falling) 'bear' market. Nevertheless, leading shares, especially in the US, are substantially over-valued in relation to companies profit performance. It is only a matter of time before the US slow-down (which will be followed by Europe) will precipitate a much bigger stock-market 'correction' - i.e. an almighty crash.

At the moment, exchange rates between the US dollar and major European currencies are relatively stable (though there are some signs that the dollar is beginning to slide). But a marked decline in the dollar, which is likely in the next few months, will once again provoke world currency turmoil. Among other things, this will sink the EMU.

(c) Excessive debt:

Neo-liberal policies, despite their emphasis on sound money and balanced budgets, have not overcome the problem of excessive debt which first emerged after the 1974-75 slump. The world debt mountain (both private and government) is rising rapidly and will sooner or later collapse under its own weight.

Credit is essential for capitalist production and trade. The relative decline of production and the turn towards financial speculation, however, has produced a disproportionate burden of debt. Much of the investment in emerging markets - in shares, company bonds, privatisation, etc - has been financed on the basis of loans (i.e. debt). Consumer spending has relied heavily on credit cards and consumer finance. All's well when business is booming. But a downturn inevitably produces a chain of bankruptcies, a so-called credit-crunch.

The sharp fall in prices of commodities, the main exports of many Third World countries, is drastically undermining their ability to repay debt and interest. At the same time, increased unemployment and reduced incomes will make it impossible for many consumers, especially the new middle class which enjoyed a short burst of prosperity, to repay consumer debt.

'Bad debt' is a world-wide problem, but the Japanese banks excel all the others with unrepayable loans of at least $1,000bn. An implosion of the Japanese banking system and/or cumulative defaults around the world will have a devastating effect on the US and European banks and finance houses.

These are the interlocking elements of a critical chain reaction. The sequence and timing of events cannot be accurately predicted. The leaders of the major capitalist states are powerless to reverse this process and, on the basis of their current policies, are unlikely to slow it down or mitigate the effects of a major slump. Japanese capitalism, as its leaders now admit, is sliding into a deep slump. And it is only a matter of time before the US, which is already experiencing a marked slow-down, also enters a serious downturn. Given the importance of the US as a world market and the pivotal role of the dollar internationally, a slump in the US may well open the door to the deepest economic depression since the end of World War II.

A crisis of bourgeois economic policy

The leaders of the advanced capitalist countries have been plunged into a crisis of policy. Buoyed up by the apparent continuation of the rising 'bull market' on US and European stock exchanges, bourgeois strategists (with a few exceptions like George Soros) were resolutely denying the seriousness of the Asian crisis and its global effects. Earlier this year Clinton said it was just a 'glitch on the road'. Greenspan, head of the US central bank, even described the Asian crisis as 'a salutary event' which would dampen the markets' 'irrational exuberance' and help counter inflationary trends. It took the August collapse in Russia to jolt most of them out of their blind complacency.

Even now, the G7 leaders have no idea of what measures they can take to avert the onset of a world slump. Despite Clinton's call for decisive leadership, there is no real agreement on policy co-ordination by the leading capitalist powers. They are still tightly laced in the ideological strait-jacket of neo-liberalism.

The G7 governments are (a) still bound to the minimalist, non-interventionist role of the state in the capitalist economy; and (b) their thinking is still dominated by the anti-inflation policies which reinforced the financial booms of the late 1980s and early 1990s but which are counter-productive in the present situation.

(a) The role of the state:

Privatisation of previously state-owned industries and the cutting back of state investment in infrastructure projects, social welfare, and so on, has to some extent reduced the ability (in any case limited) of capitalist governments to influence economic trends. With the free movement of capital and commodities across frontiers, not even the major capitalist economies can, under present conditions, escape the pressures of world financial markets.

In fact, the ideologists of capitalism have in the recent period elevated 'market forces' to the level of mystical forces operating above the social and political relation-ships through which real economic activity develops. Some even hail 'the market' as society's ultimate - and of course benevolent - governing authority.

Government is seen merely as a ringmaster maintaining the circus arena for a troupe of private performers. If they all pursue their own individual profit (it is claimed), the 'hidden hand' of the market will ensure that everyone is better off as a result. The ringmaster, of course, is expected to use his whip when necessary against the workers outside the privileged bourgeois circle. And despite the globali-sation of finance and trade, capitalist governments are still charged with the task of maintaining the apparatus (including the armed forces) of the national states, which remain capitalism's basic territorial units.

In the 1980s and 1990s it was no wonder that the major capitalist powers willingly accepted the dominance of the global market, when they operated as a siphon sucking profits from the whole world into the coffers of the metropolitan bourgeoisie.

Through the IMF, World Bank, GATT, and other agencies, backed up with threats of financial sanctions, the imperialist powers forced the underdeveloped countries to open up their economies and drastically scale down state intervention in their economies. Third-world countries, which had previously been allowed some protected national economic development, were opened up to plundering by the multi-national corporations and banks. As a result, globalisation has not only produced a slump but provoked deep social crisis, already posing the threat of revolution to the ruling class in a number of countries. That is why Mahathir Mohamad, Malaysia's president, has turned against the free market, reimposing controls on capital, foreign currency exchange and imports. This is a pointer to the future. Other governments, faced with economic collapse and the prospect of revolution, will resort to similar measures to defend the national interests of the ruling class.

The leaders of the advanced capitalist countries are, at the moment, unanimous in their condemnation of Mahathir's rejection of globalisation. But when the economic crisis hits the US and Europe with its full force, they will undoubtedly move in a similar direction. They will not be able to preserve an 'open' global economy any more than they could after 1914, when the 1870-1913 world upswing gave way to a period of depression and intense inter-capitalist rivalry.

When the US national economy faces devastation, its capitalist leaders will once again turn to controls of capital and protectionist measures against foreign imports. This will not prevent US imperialism from continuing to preach free trade to the rest of the world. In the next period, the return to protectionism will most likely be on the basis of the main trading blocs rather than individual states. Both NAFTA and the EU, while relatively open at present, have all the reserve mechanisms needed to establish a continental siege economy behind protective walls. The looser Asian block dominated by Japan would also raise protective walls.

When the capitalist class is faced with the threat of social explosions and mass political movements, it will be forced to turn back towards state intervention to prop up big business and banks. Spending programmes will not primarily be social programmes (though they will also be forced to concede temporary reforms) but the 'socialisation' of big business's liabilities. Such policies will not provide a way out for capitalism, any more than similar measures did in the Great Depression of the 1930s.

For the moment, however, the capitalist powers are still locked onto free market policies. In relation to the Asian slump, these policies, imposed through IMF intervention, have exacerbated the crisis.

(b) Neo-liberal orthodoxy:

The new orthodoxy, which took over from the early 1980s, is that the 'freeing up of markets' will overcome every problem. Clearly, this corresponded with the interests of the finance capital based in the major centres. The only real danger, it was argued, was that posed by monetary and fiscal laxity (that is, excessive money supply or budget deficits). This reflects the capitalists' phobia about inflation, which above all erodes the wealth of finance capital (price rises reduce the real value of borrowers' repayments to lenders). After all, it was the high rates of inflation which infected the world economy in the late 1970s, when the Keynesian order was crumbling, that impelled the capitalist class towards the sound money policies of monetarism and neo-liberalism.

When the Asian crisis broke out with a round of currency devaluations in July 1997, the IMF intervened on the basis of anti-inflation policies. As the price of rescue loans, the IMF demanded that the governments of Indonesia, Malaysia, South Korea, etc, should shut down insolvent banks, raise interest rates, and slash government expenditure - in other words implement a severely deflationary policy.

This was a classic case of incompetent generals fighting the last war rather than the one engulfing them. Monetarist policies which preserved currencies as a store of value and a sound medium of exchange served finance capital well in the 1980s and 1990s. But in Asia today, and the world tomorrow, the capitalists face, not an imminent threat of inflation, but the reality of a deflationary spiral. The collapse of banks, a flight of capital abroad, falling prices, drastic cuts in employment and wage levels, all combine to bring about a massive reduction of liquidity in the economy. The cash flow required to finance production, trade, and all forms of commerce dries up. Government measures like interest rate increases and spending cuts can only exacerbate the problem.

Some capitalist policy-makers are now beginning to recognise this. In recent months, the IMF has begun to come under severe criticism for the policies it tried to impose on governments in South East Asia. Joseph Stiglitz, chief economist at the World Bank, complained that the IMF was pushing East Asia into a severe recession: 'virtually every American economist rejects the balanced-budget principle during a recession. Why should we ignore this when giving advice to other countries?'

Now, while they would never dream of advocating such policies at home, some economists are advocating a reflationary policy for Asia, especially for Japan. In effect, they are turning back to a form of Keynesianism.

A return to Keynesianism?

Could a return to Keynesian-type policies provide a way out of the slump for capitalism? The continued paralysis of Japan shows that it will by no means provide a quick fix. Despite the complaints of western governments that Japan was not doing enough to stimulate growth, since 1993 the Japanese government has introduced six government spending packages, estimated to total over $651bn. True, a large share of it went to subsidise big construction companies to build 'roads to nowhere'. The spending packages were also undermined to some extent by the government's attempt to claw back some of the cost through increased taxation in order to prevent a further rise in the budget deficit. Nevertheless, these packages constituted the biggest Keynesian-type stimulus in modern times. But even combined with near zero interest rates, they have not succeeded in jump-starting the economy.

There is no easy way for reflationary policies to overcome the deep structural contradictions that have built up since the bubble economy of the 1980s. The banks' mountain of unrecoverable loans (which probably totals over $1,000bn) and the black hole of overvalued shares and property concealed under the fictitious figures currently entered in bank and company accounts, remain an apparently insuperable obstacle to any economic revival. Short of the liquidation of a series of banks and major industrial conglomerates, in other words allowing a slump to take its course, it is hard to see how any recovery can develop.

Defying the inflation taboo of the last period, a number of US strategists have now began to advocate the unthinkable for Japan - a policy of deliberate long-term inflation. If zero interest rates have not stimulated any upturn in spending, either by companies or consumers, then (their argument goes) there must be a prolonged period of price rises which will effectively produce a negative real interest rate (i.e. the nominal interest rate minus the rate of inflation). If savings are thus threatened by prolonged inflation, companies and consumers will be persuaded to spend their money on goods and services. Moreover, negative real interest rates have the inestimable advantage for governments of eroding the real value of their national debt.

Support for such a policy, strictly to be applied to Japan and 'lesser breeds without the law', is gaining ground in Washington and EU capitals. Support for inflation, however, remains an abomination for the US and Europe. This is shown by the refusal of Greenspan, chair of the US Central Bank, to substantially cut US interest rates. The fears of the capitalists that spending packages will push budget deficits up to much higher levels underlines the dilemma they face in this period. Government debt has reached historically unprecedented levels, despite a period of neo-liberal policy. (The huge costs of mass unemployment and pensions for ageing populations is a big factor in this.) But in order to stave off total economic collapse, governments will be forced to resort to new spending packages. However, this will soon impose a crippling burden of debt on many states.

Nevertheless, as the Asian slump spreads to the West, the US and Europe may well face the very same kind of liquidity trap as Japan. In that situation, regardless of government policies, 'market forces' will sooner or later produce new inflationary effects. Whether these will be effective in reviving the economy is an entirely different question. At a certain point, the spectre of inflation, even hyper-inflation, would reappear. While it can be a stimulus in mild doses, inflation is a deadly cancer in its virulent form.

Capitalism will not be able to escape from its fundamental contradictions. Whatever the depth and duration of the coming world slump, however, the world economy will sooner or later, given the political weakness of the forces opposed to capitalism, move into a new period of cyclical growth. This will not allow the capitalists to repair the damage to the system's foundations - and the ruling class will face mounting mass opposition to its rotten system

Political crisis

The approaching economic crisis has already begun to reveal the rotten hollowness of the world's most powerful capitalist leaders. Clinton, leader of the world's lone superpower, is embroiled in the Lewinsky affair and is threatened with impeachment. This reflects a much deeper crisis of US capitalism's political machine, which is incapable of formulating, let alone implementing, a coherent economic and foreign policy. The political impotence of Obuchi's government in Japan reflects the crumbling of the LDP's social and political base.

In Europe most of the EU leaders are fanatically committed to EMU, which will be a major casualty of the coming slump, but can agree on little else. In Germany, Kohl faces the prospect of defeat in the coming elections. Capitalist leaders have yet to grasp the scale of the crisis facing them, let alone formulate a policy to ride it out. The real question is how did the bourgeois leaders get away with it in the last period? Governments of all complexions carried out neo-liberal policies which heaped super-profits on the rich while cutting the living standards of big sections of the working class and sections of the middle class. In several European countries, notably Italy, France, Belgium and Spain, this provoked massive waves of strikes and social protest. Yet governments of capitalist parties and also of pro-market 'socialist' parties were able to ride these out. Moreover, for a time bourgeois leaders were able to win support, or at least acquiescence, on the electoral level for the idea that the market is the only workable system and therefore the logic of market-forces and globalisation have to be accepted.

The electoral successes of pro-market governments arose from several factors. The prestige of the capitalist class - the appearance of social and economic power - was enormously enhanced by the collapse of Stalinism. Linked to that, the bourgeoisie was able to rely on the leaders of the traditional social democratic parties and trade unions for collaboration in carrying through pro-market policies.

Crucially, however, the capitalists' ability to gain wider electoral acceptance for free-market policies depended on the growth of the economy. This enabled them to spread a small sliver of their fabulous profits among a section of the middle class and skilled working class - who in most advanced capitalist countries form a wedge of floating voters whose choice of party determines the outcome of elections. Some even gained a small share of the booming financial and property markets, winning some acceptance for the idea that the further enrichment of the super-rich is a condition of increased prosperity for wider layers.

Deprived of their paupers' share of the fruits of growth, however, the acquiescence of the suburban 'middle class' will rapidly change to anger and opposition. There is already a deep reservoir of social discontent amongst this strata. They, too, have been hit by cuts in public services and are experiencing the insecurity of short-term job contracts. They cannot escape the general effects of the social alienation resulting from the dictatorship of the market - intense economic pressure on personal relations, rising crime, the commercial degradation of cultural life.

In the US, but also elsewhere, a large section of middle class and skilled workers have bought shares, or are now relying on pension schemes, annuities, life insurance, etc, which depend on the performance of shares. A major stock exchange crash would effectively wipe out their savings - provoking a tidal wave of anger against the profit system.

Historically, there has never been a mechanical link between economic crisis and mass political movements. The forms of struggle, and especially the timing, cannot be predicted in advance. But one thing is certain. A deep slump will shatter the illusions in capitalism which were built up in recent years (even though all the underlying features of a depression were already present). Consciousness will rapidly catch up with reality.

Capitalist leaders made no attempt to conceal their smug satisfaction when the crumbling Stalinist dictatorships were shaken by waves of mass protest after 1989. Thatcher, for instance, hypocritically championed 'people's power' in Eastern Europe, which Western leaders utilised as a cover for the restoration of capitalism. But as capitalism moves into a deep crisis, the system - like Stalinism in the 1980s - will also be shaken by a generalised social and political crisis. Capitalist regimes everywhere will face mass rebellion.

We have seen the outlines of such movements in recent years. In Belgium in 1996, the paedophile murder scandal provoked mass demonstrations against the rotten corruption of the state and main political parties. Workers and many sections of the middle class were drawn in. The 1995 strike wave in France evoked enormous sympathy from wide sections of society, including the middle strata and small business people. The pit closure crisis in Britain in 1992 also mobilised an extraordinary cross-section of society in two huge mass demonstrations. This is the music of the future.

It is the working class, however, which will provide the decisive forces in opposition to the effects of capitalist crisis. It remains the only force in society capable of fighting for a new social order. Undoubtedly, economic restructuring during the last 20 years has changed the structure of the working class. Some of the former 'heavy battalions' have been greatly diminished or even disappeared. Yet new contingents which have developed on the basis of new industries and services will, in the next period, begin to move into action, organise, and come to the fore as a decisive political force. Women workers, who now make up over half the workforce in some regions, will play a significant role in this process.

During the neo-liberal period the workers in many advanced capitalist countries suffered some serious set-backs. The leaders of the social democratic parties and trade unions were incapable of defending the gains of the post-war upswing. In fact, during the 1980s, most of them accepted the 'market' and 'globalisation' as justification for collaboration with capitalist governments in carrying through counter-reforms. The ideological counter-revolution launched by the capitalists internationally after 1989 played a big role in fragmenting and disorientating the active sections of the working class.

But the working class has not suffered the kind of shattering, historic defeat that was inflicted under fascist regimes in the 1930s. The proletariat has preserved its capacity to struggle, as recent European movements show. Recently there has also been an increase in strikes and other kinds of industrial protest in the US (the UPS strike, the GM shut-down) and Britain. This is only the beginning.

The main set-back of the 1980s and 1990s was a pushing back of working class consciousness. The capitalist class was only able to turn the clock back because of the political disarming of the working class. But a period of deep international crisis for the capitalist system will produce enormous struggles and a radicalisation of consciousness. What is required in addition is a programme to defend the interests of the working class and fight for an international socialist transformation. The starting point is a clear analysis of the present economic crisis and a perspective for its unfolding in the months ahead.

Neo-liberalism and Keynesianism

Neo-liberalism, or 'new-liberalism', is a return to the liberal or 'free market' policies which prevailed in the mid-nineteenth century during the first period of capitalism's world-wide industrial expansion, dominated by British capitalism. Its slogan was 'laissez-faire', or 'leave alone', and it favoured international free trade and non-interference of government in the national economy. It was based on the notion that the market (directed by 'an invisible hand') is self-regulating and that the pursuit of individual self-interest ultimately produces the best outcome for everyone.

The industrial bourgeoisie used laissez-faire policies to destroy the earlier mercantilist practices, under which vested interests such as landowners, the monarchy, merchant-bankers, etc, monopolised various fields of production and trade. However, late-developers like US, German and Japanese capitalism, followed protectionist policies (defending their developing industries with tariffs) until they were strong enough to compete openly on world markets.

Keynesianism takes its name from the British economist John Maynard Keynes, who after the great crash of 1929 advocated increased government expending on public works and social welfare in order to stimulate demand and 'pump-prime' or jump-start the stagnant economy. His policies were hardly implemented in the 1930s, except in the US New Deal, which was not very effective in reviving the US economy.

Keynesianism came into its own after the second world war on the basis of new social and economic relations which produced a prolonged economic upswing. Within the national economies Keynesianism supported increased state intervention through nationalisation of some basic industries, higher levels of welfare expenditure financed from progressive taxation, and government manipulation of spending, taxation and monetary policy to try to smooth out the boom-slump cycle, particularly to stimulate demand during a downturn.

Internationally, Keynesianism supported a politically managed money system (the so-called Bretton Woods system), with fixed exchange rates based on the dominant role of the US dollar, which was pegged to gold at a fixed price. However, subject to approval by the (US-dominated) IMF, exchange rates could be adjusted in a crisis to protect national economies. Trade was gradually liberalised through tariff reductions under the auspices of the GATT (General Agreement of Tariffs and Trade), but international capital flows and financial markets were subject to government regulation.

The acceleration of world inflation in the late 1960s, which marked the exhaustion of the post-war upswing, led to a breakdown of the Bretton Woods system, to floating exchange rates, and the growth of capital flows outside the control of national governments. Faced with declining levels of profit, big business and finance capital stepped up the pressure to roll back state intervention nationally and internationally and to open up the free movement of capital. Back to neo-liberalism.

First published in the October 1998 edition of *Socialism Today,*
theoretical and discussion journal of the
Socialist Party, the British section of the CWI.

Addenda

Congress Resolutions and Amendments which were defeated or remitted.

Section One - World Relations

Swedish amendment on the class character of China.
From Per-Åke Westerlund, Laurence Coates and Elin Gauffin.
Remitted for further discussion to the IS.
Explanation: While agreeing with the main points on China in the document, there is need for further clarification on the class character. The position of the document is that China is "moving irrevocably in a capitalist direction" (para 195[of Congress draft]). But contrary to the analysis of the former USSR-republics or ex-Yugoslavia, the document seems to describe an unfinished process, or even the beginning of a process: "the regime is clearly set on transforming China to capitalism" (para 208). Of course, Marxists should not be trapped into pure yes-or-no descriptions, but have an rounded out analysis of the ongoing processes. On the other hand, lagging behind could lead to wrong conclusions on our tasks and China's role internationally.
We believe that the process in China is completed on the same lines as in the former USSR and Belarus, as explained in the document, paragraphs 331-332. State ownership and contradictions remaining from Stalinism will exist after the restoration of capitalism has been completed. These are in short the main argument for changing some formulations in paragraphs 195, 208, 209.

Amendment: The process of capitalist restoration started with the land reform 1978. A turning point, which increased the speed of the process, was in 1989 with the events in Tiananmen Square and the workers' protests linked to it, followed by the fall of Stalinism in Eastern Europe.

During the process of globalisation in the 90s, China has become integrated into world capitalism. The ruling bureaucracy changed sides as their colleagues in Poland, Russia etc., did. The state monopoly of foreign trade has been abolished. China's economy has become the world's second biggest recipient of FDI. Exports equal 18% of GDP (or 4.5% in purchasing parity). Multinationals employ 17-18 million workers, 10% of the urban work force. China was for a long time a model country of the IMF and contributed with one billion US dollars to the first IMF-package for Thailand.

This process is not only economic, but social as well. "Everything that led to Koumintang's collapse in 1949 is back, but worse than then: corruption, poverty, inflation, banditry, inequality", was how communist veteran Liu Binyan, described the development. In Shanghai, the night clubs with prostitution of the 30s have reopened, run by the Chinese secret police, the old triads (mafia) or Taiwanese "businessmen". Mass unemployment is officially 18-20 million, probably only a fifth of the real figure.

Neither devaluation nor hesitation to implement the massive privatisation programmes can block the coming crisis. The world crisis of capitalism is going to hit China in no fundamentally different way than in other countries. All the signs of the Asian crisis are there: banks with bad loans, huge debts, deflation, mass unemployment. The bubble is going to burst. This has been underlined by the market nervousness following the crisis of the "itics", the investment arms of regional governments. The strong central power, which is a Stalinist remnant, is already in process of being undermined and the coming crisis will create new and stronger centrifugal pressures.

China's role in the region is described in the document. In Hong Kong, the unification with China has meant full backing for Hong Kong capitalism. Hunger striking trade unionists in Hong Kong correctly described government boss and multi billionaire Tung Chee-hwa: "He only helps capitalists, not us workers". To prop up the Hong Kong stock exchange, the Chinese government has bought shares for $15 billion. The Taiwan question further underlines China's capitalist-imperialist role in the region. From this follows the conclusion that the coming Chinese revolution is a social, socialist revolution, and that Marxists will not advocate critical support of China in regional conflicts or wars.

Section Two - Europe

Swedish amendment on EMU from the Swedish EC.

The EMU project has been the central strategic aim of Europe's governments throughout the 1990s. With the start of EMU on January 1st 1999 the struggle against this counter revolutionary project, a vital political question and task for the Marxists, will enter a new phase.

Our position can be summarised as follows:

The long term viability of the EMU project, and the idea of a capitalist united Europe, are ruled out.

EMU does not solve any of the fundamental problems facing capitalism, it raises class and international contradictions to new levels.

The CWI emphasises the decisive role of mass struggle in the defeat of EMU.

EMU flows not from a position of strength, but from the crisis of European capitalism: internationally in relation to its external rivals in America and Asia; and internally where it faces the strongest working class with the highest achievements. The world downturn can, especially in the event of a slump, result in the collapse of EMU before 2002. However, a collapse is not the only perspective, especially in the short term.

The bourgeoisie have invested enormously in this project. EMU is the means by which they hope to carry through a historically imperative counter revolutionary programme of cuts and attacks on Europe's post war reforms: dismantling of welfare; privatisations/ mergers of state-owned infrastructure; "Americanisation" of labour markets etc. The failure of national attempts to carry through his programme is a key factor holding the EMU powers together, despite the numerous risks and drawbacks of EMU.

EMU collapse will have catastrophic consequences for the ruling class: a massive loss of prestige and standing on the international arena, a further weakening of the European capitalists against their main rivals, and a massive loss of face at home. The entire establishment with isolated exceptions is pro-EMU. Every government will be completely compromised.

It will threaten not just EMU but also EU, risking break-up: a European "civil" trade war starting with competitive devaluations, and especially threatening the German-French axis which has been of strategic importance for capitalism since the Second World War.

An EMU fiasco will take its toll on banks and multinationals, which have invested in the project, as well as governments. It would lead to capital flight, relocation of multinationals and new crashes on financial markets.

For these reasons, it's clear the bourgeoisie will not abandon EMU lightly. They will resort to all possible means, manoeuvres, threats and concessions to save "their" project. This can include a dilution of the stability pact criteria or simply turning a blind eye to violations; IMF-style "EMU rescue packages" for member states threatening to quit, facing economic collapse, revolutionary upheavals etc. Some of the present eleven may split from the EMU but be forced to return later as a result of retaliatory measures. Even in the event of a complete break-up, new attempts will be made to patch things up and launch a "new" version of EMU. The dilemma facing the ruling classes is that they have no "plan B".

A break up of the present EU would mean a fundamental change in post war world politics. It would cripple one of the three blocs, which would tend to pull apart in the frantic search for new markets and international alliances. It would raise national tensions within Europe to crisis levels. EMU does not solve these problems, the contradictions merely assume another form, also with explosive consequences.

The EMU question underlines the central and decisive role of the working class and the CWI's struggle to build a new mass international, as the only force that can unite Europe and prevent, in a longer term perspective, a nightmare repetition of history

The Swedish amendment was put to the vote at Congress. The IS called for a vote against. Full delegate votes: For 5, Against 22, Abstentions 5. Consultative votes: For

3, Against 11, Abstentions 0. The amendment was lost.

Resolution from the Austrian Section on Globalisation

Explanation: This is not an amendment but a resolution which deals with a series of points raised in the documents on Europe and World Relations. If the World Congress adopts this resolution these two documents would have to be changed accordingly.

Amendment: Is Globalisation a fact?

As Marxists, it is our task to analyse processes. We have to separate facts from assertions, we have to be clear about the terms used and, as we aim to lead the working class, it is also our task to highlight the political background to processes. The bourgeoisie use the term "Globalisation" as an ideological weapon against the working class, but is it also a scientific term in the sense of scientific socialism? Although the documents for the World Congress comment in passing that "Globalisation has become a reality thanks to the development of the world market, world trade, monstrous financial markets and the speed, size and interconnections of the movements of goods and information cross the world" (Congress Resolution on Europe, paragraph 29), there is no critical disputing and further examination of the processes. The situation as a whole is very complicated and contradictory (internationalisation versus regionalism, withdrawal of the state versus extension of the repressive apparatus), these contradictions have to be taken into account in our documents.

The emphasis of the International regarding "Globalisation" has changed. Whereas a few years ago regionalisation and the dominance of the Advanced Capitalist Countries (ACCs) had been put forward and an article entitled 'Global Myths' was published in Socialism Today (December 1996/January 1997), it is now stated in the documents for the World Congress that "Globalisation has become a reality". It is true that the documents on World Relations and Europe are dealing with certain aspects regarding 'Globalisation' (the slowing-down of the process, the basing on the nation state etc.,). However the 'Reality of Globalisation' theme dominates the document, compared to the mentioning of countervailing trends or factors, which would put the phenomenon 'Globalisation' into a more differentiated perspective. The political component ('Globalisation' as an ideological weapon of the bourgeoisie) is missing.

What is 'Globalisation'?

Although 'Globalisation' is an often used term there is no clear definition, a fact which gives room to different interpretations. The following points are mentioned:

The geographical spreading and the growing level of integration of world trade and new communication technologies make it possible to outsource services.

A strong growth of foreign direct investment (FDI) and therefore a strengthening of multinational companies, which have become more and more independent of a national base.

A global network of the finance markets: this encourages short-term investments, accelerates the flow of capital and makes it more difficult for national governments to intervene

A transformation of multinational companies into transnational companies without national identity, roots and links

An acceleration of monetary processes, but also processes in the real economy and a growing international integration ("domino-effect").

Comparing the above-mentioned points with what Lenin wrote in 'Imperialism, The Highest Stage of Capitalism', i.e. the last stage which production has come to, a stage which it cannot go beyond:

The concentration of production and capital and the formation of monopolies.

The fusion of finance capital with the industrial capital and, on the basis of this finance capital, the emergence of a finance oligarchy as the ruling layer of the bourgeoisie.

The export of capital compared to the export of goods.

The division of the world between the gangs of capitalists.

The end of the division of the world and imperialist wars as one main characteristic of imperialism.

Regarding world trade, FDI and the finance market there are "proofs" for and against 'Globalisation' – depending on the used statistics.

World trade

It is undoubtedly right, that there has been a growth of world trade in the last period but firstly this is not a new development and secondly the significance of exports and the narrowness of the flow of goods have to be taken into account.

On the one hand it is right that the share of export of the world-GNP has grown from 1% (1820) to over 8.7% (1913) and to 15% (1995). But on the other hand exports are only 15.9% (exports of goods) or 20% (exports of goods and services) of the GDP of the OECD which dominates the world trade. From 1960 to 1990 the share of export regarding the international output had doubled to 20% - but this also means, that in the "global supermarket" 80% are produced for the domestic markets.

Moreover, to a predominant extent world trade takes place between the 3 economic blocks (85% of world trade), within these blocks (Western Europe approximately 2/3, North America 1/3, Asia fi) and/ or within the multinational companies (1/4 of world trade) - the majority of people are excluded from world trade.

Trade has been liberated (by the end of the 1950s the tariffs had been reduced from 40 to 15%, up to the 1990s they were reduced to an average of 4%). But in fact this was mainly to open up the markets of the ex-colonial countries. The ACC knew how to protect themselves through special regulations. The lastest steps of the IMF and World Bank are also aimed at the creation of new markets for the imperialist countries.

Foreign Direct Investment

Foreign direct investment is, as the world-export of goods and services, seen as a main factor in the process of economic involvement. In fact, FDI rose from 1960 to 1992 from $67.7 billion dollars to $1,949 trillion, an annual 11% increase. Since the beginning of the 1980s the capital flow in the form of FDI rose per year by 27.8%, which is three times faster than exports rose (11.1%) and four times faster than the world GNP (9.8%).

On the other hand is the fact that FDI is only a small proportion of the overall investments - that means that the overwhelming part is invested on domestic markets. The US Economist Krugmann argues that the record capital outflow in 1993 only withdrew 3% investment from the domestic markets of the rich north. In Germany the FDI accounts for not more than 6% of the investments as a whole, the overwhelming part of investment is in the home market.

There is also an extreme concentration of FDI in the ACCs. In the early 1990s 75% of FDI was concentrated in the 3 blocks (with 14% of world population). 90% of FDI had its origin in only 10 countries, two thirds of which came from four countries (USA, Japan, Germany, GB).

Financial markets

The crisis of capitalism/ the "tendency of the rate of profit to fall" and the fact that it is increasingly difficult to materialise profits, has led to capital flight into the speculative sector of economy. Optimal preconditions for this were established through the liberalisation of the financial markets and new technologies. This led to an explosion of the financial trade which today has reached unimaginable dimensions.

Altogether we can say, that a number of processes, analysed by Lenin in 'Imperialism', have intensified. Much more important than the quantitative growth of cross border economic activities is the question whether there has been a qualitative change.

Nation states

The relationship between capital and the nation state is one of the contradictions of capitalism. A new quality would in fact exist if capital would detach itself from its national basis. Is this the case?

Has finance capital lost its national links and is there really a significant number of transnational companies existing, companies without national integration and anchoring and with a management to match? Since "productive capital" is increasingly speculative, since there is speculation, for example, with money from pension funds, it is doubtful how "stateless" the finance capital really is.

In relation to the transnational companies we have to state that only a very tiny minority of companies has successfully transformed themselves from being multinational to becoming transnational companies. The workforce and the markets are still mainly in the domestic country or region. World-wide only 5% of all workers work in multinational or transnational companies and their suppliers. And even nearly all major international publicly quoted companies do not have more then 10% of their shares owned by foreigners. In the management of multinational companies foreigners are rare.

The distance to the market, the infrastructure of the ACCs, and a stable political situation are important conditions for the capital to decide where to locate. However capitalism still needs the national state to assert its interests (the extension of the repression apparatus - the armament and increasing competence of the police, surveillance, the switching from conscription to professional armies - show a trend in the direction of a stronger orientation towards the nation state).

The regionalisation/ building of blocks raises the question if in the future the blocks could take over the role of the nation states, if a "European bourgeoisie" could develop? The increasing tensions between the European states, which will intensify with the end of economic downturn (that fact is dealt with in the document on Europe), point in another direction.

Therefore, the most important question is not why multinational companies threaten all the time to move production from one country to another, but why the overwhelming majority of them do not move but stay in their home-base.

New quality?

Does 'Globalisation' really mean the end of the possibility for political regulation and are the governments losing their power to act in relation to the economy?

There is no doubt that there is growing "internationalisation", a process which is inherent in capitalism and has therefore existed since its early beginnings. The question is what is the new quality. Why are terms like "internationalisation", "imperialism" and "neo-liberal politics" not sufficient anymore to characterise the character of the period? Where was the leap from quantity to quality? What is meant by talk of a "new phase"? Capitalism has run through several phases since its formation, but now with 'Globalisation' they (not the IS, but capitalist propagandists) try to suggest, that it is a post-imperialist phase.

Capitalism has become global again in so far that, since the collapse of Stalinism, it has spread over the whole world. At the same time capital has launched an ideological offensive. However economically it is in a crisis. While there is no such thing as a "global culture" or a "global democracy", the "global attacks on the working class" are present all the time.

Naturally, capitalism, which is not completely static, has changed, but the key things in relation to 'Globalisation' are the ideological, political and economical attacks against the working class in the name of 'Globalisation'.

'Globalisation' is used to switch the responsibility for the neo-liberal policy of the 1990s from the national governments to a far away, almost esoteric level ("the market is omnipotent"). As capitalism "became" the market economy or even social market economy, neo-liberalism, imperialism "became" 'Globalisation'. 'Globalisation' did not come out of the blue, but is the result of political decisions of the last period. In that sense it is wrong, when the document on Europe reads: "the process (of Globalisation) has been accelerated by political decisions" (para 27). The liberalisation of the financial markets and the reductions of trade-barriers were political decisions. Technological innovations, of course, were an instrument to help capital to be more flexible, but they were definitely not the source of this process.

Although we as Marxists have a more differentiated and scientific approach towards 'Globalisation', in the public discussions and in the consciousness of the working class 'Globalisation' stands for a process where a) governments and companies are totally relieved of their responsibility for social grievances and, b) where it is conveyed that every resistance is futile, because capital is flexible.

Fighting against illusions

In the documents there is a special emphasis on the aspect that "there are no national scopes". In the June 1996 issue of Socialism Today, No. 9, we find a different emphasis: "Most importantly the book (Globalisation in Question) challenges the idea that the national state is powerless before the national market and its representative institutions ...the assertion that national states - especially in the advanced countries – are capable of defining national economic and social priorities is welcome."

Because of the election victories of the European Social Democracy, but also as a reaction to the social movement of the recent years against neo-liberal politics, proposals for Keynesian measures are back on the agenda. There is a necessity to stand up against this because again there is an attempt to create illusions that through the correct (i.e. Keynesian) policies it is possible to build "capitalism with a human face". We always stood up against this illusion, but a total rejection of possibilities on a national scale (which, though unquestionably smaller still exist) would make every national fight against attacks or for improvements ad absurdum.

The size of possibilities on a national scale is not only dependant on economic conditions but also, to an important part, on the power relations between the classes. In the past we never argued one-sidedly with economic factors and have never reduced our demands because of these "objective facts", but we always stressed the political component.

In the trade unions there are contradictory ideas - looking paralysed at the 'Globalisation' and using it as an excuse not to fight and even put their hopes in a "new red Europe" (the realisation of the Social Union, a "offensive employment policy"). In the case of Austria - where because of its geographical nearness to eastern Europe and because of its extraordinary export orientation (OECD: 15.9% of GDP, Austria: 25.3% of GDP) the question of industry locating and moving is of outstanding importance. The trade unions, using 'Globalisation' as an excuse, have watered down their demands and activities leading to the situation that in 1999, the relative wage cost in manufacturing will be more then 10% below its level in 1995. One of many extortions done in the name of 'Globalisation' and against which we have to stand up - ultimately on an international scale.

To write, "today's world is more ungovernable" (Europe, paragraph 29) supports the excuses from trade unionists, politicians and bosses who argue that "they would like, but cannot act because of Globalisation". Practically, 'Globalisation' is often used as a threat - which is not put into practice - to achieve improvements for capitalists on a national scale.

The internationalisation of the economy and the globalisation of attacks on the working class create chances for us. It is more "logical" that resistance can ultimately only be successful on an international scale and that therefore it is necessary to organise internationally. Because the room for concessions becomes smaller for capitalism, even "reformist demands" reach the limits of the system very fast and the resistance becomes political faster.

It is not a formal question if using the term 'Globalisation' is "politically correct". Rather this term is seen by the public and the working class as linked to powerlessness and should therefore be rejected. 'Globalisation' is used by the bourgeoisie as an ideological weapon against the working class and must be dealt with as such! The fact is that capitalism is in a global crisis, that it tries to use global attacks on the working class to overcome this crisis and that global resistance against this is necessary.

The Austrian amendment was put to the vote at Congress. The IS called for a vote against. Full delegate votes: For 1, Against 31, Abstentions 1. Consultative votes: For 0, Against 14, Abstentions 0. The amendment was lost.

Section Three - The Former Workers' Parties

German EC Amendments.
[Proposed changes to paragraphs 37, 39 and 48 of Congress draft document].
All remitted for further discussion to the IS.

[Pragraph 37] The reasons that these [new Left formations] have developed in this way [a rightward direction] was because of developments in the international economic and political situation. The days where reformism, ideologically based on the ideas of state-controlled capitalism and the "social market economy", could achieve progress are long gone. The U-turn made by the Socialist-Communist government in France within a year of its 1981 election, symbolised that traditional reformism had reached an impasse. Capitalism is on the decline. The increase in profits was only possible through the intensified exploitation of the working class, the ex-colonial countries and through the looting of the inner market in the form of privatisation. That is the economic content of neo-liberalism. This process of deregulation, flexibilisation and privatisation started in the 80s. The fall of Stalinism helped the bourgeoisie and made possible the scale and tempo of this process, which we experienced during the 90s. The breakdown of Stalinism seemed to have shown the inferiority of the planned economy. The bourgeoisie could portray all elements of state economy, state regulation to protect the working class, and the public sector as inefficient and anachronistic. The leaders of the left, with a few exceptions, were unable to explain the real reasons behind the downfall of the Stalinist countries and capitulated, faced with the ideological offensive of the bourgeoisie. They lost their faith to build an alternative to capitalism. From the very beginning the leaders of new left formations were impressed by the alleged superiority of the "free market" and consequently neither had an alternative against concrete neo-liberal attacks nor against capitalism in general.

[Paragragph 39] The beginning of the present economic crisis means that the bourgeoisie can't go on like before with their neo-liberal economic policy and their propaganda. They will be forced to nationalise banks gone bankrupt, to reintroduce capital controls and elements of Keynesian demand-policy and other tools of state interventionism. We can see the beginning of this process in the countries which have already been hit hard by the recession. The obvious failure of the "free market" is the basis for the reawakening of left reformist ideas and programmes in the workers' movement and in connection with that, the emergence of new mass reformist currents and parties. Part of this process will be a new broad discussion on an alternative to capitalism and on socialist ideas. But socialist ideas won't come up in a clear, worked-out Marxist fashion, but in a more confused manner. During this process, being part of coming class struggles, we will get the opportunity to prove that only a revolutionary-internationalist programme can offer a way out of capitalist misery.

[Paragraph 48] The onset of a deep recession and crisis will lead to a development of consciousness amongst the working class. The existing alienation with the establishment will develop to an anti-capitalist consciousness and to greater openness for socialism. We can see the early stages of the re-emergence of reformist ideas amongst intellectuals and workers. This is one basis for the development of new workers' formations in the course of the next years. The other will be a further increase in the class struggle, both industrially and politically, which will lead to generalised movements of the proletariat. We cannot foresee exactly how new workers' parties will develop. They will not come out of the blue. In different countries it will develop differently and out of different sources. In many countries developments within the trade unions will be the decisive factor for the emergence of new political mass formations of the proletariat. This can develop first through left wing opposition currents within the old trade unions or through smaller more left wing unions. This could be seen in the development of the US Labor Party (US LP). Although it must be said that the US LP is not a new mass party and that it is not at all certain that it will develop into a mass party. In other cases it might be that a regroupment of existing left wing currents, maybe including split-offs from the (Ex-) CP's or even social democratic parties, can lay the basis for a new formation. This happened in Turkey where the ÖDP was formed by different left-wing currents and was able to attract some substantial forces. Again the ÖDP is not yet a mass party of the working class and it is not certain that the ÖDP will become a mass party. It is also possible that in some countries we will see the emergence of different kinds of local or regional formations, which only after a period maybe come together as national forces. In such cases we will have to implement extreme flexible tactics with different orientations in different regions. For the period up to the next world congress it is likely that the idea of new workers' parties can gain mass support in some countries and that in some countries the basis will develop for new formations. But it is not most likely that within the next three years we will see the full development of new mass parties. The issue can develop...

[Add in paragraph 74] After the last sentence ("One crucial task in this period is to assist in the process of rebuilding the idea of socialism as an alternative to capitalism"): "It is important for us today to explain the reasons for the emergence of Stalinism and the collapse of the Stalinist system."

Founding Conference of Democratic Socialist Movement,
CWI Section in Nigeria, July 1998

Glossary

ANC: African National Congress, South Africa

BNP (Sri Lanka): A past split from the Sri Lankan SLMP towards left reformism / centrism.

CDU: Christian Democratic Union, German bourgeois party

CSU: Bavarian Christian Social Union, sister partner of the German CDU

EU: European Union
EMU: European Monetary Union

FARC: Revolutionary Armed Forces of Colombia

FALANTIL: Armed wing of East Timorese Liberation Front

FSLN: Nicaraguan National Sandanista Liberation Front

IMF: International Monetary Fund
IEC: International Executive Committee, elected by the World Congress
IS: International Secretariat, elected from the IEC, organises between the IECs

KCTU: Korean Congress of Trade Unions

LCR: Revolutionary Communist League, France
LDP: Liberal Democratic Party, Japanese bourgeois party
LO: Workers' Struggle, France

MST: Landless Movement, Brazil

NAFTA: North American Free Trade Association

OECD: Organisation for Economic Co-operation and Development

PAN: National Action Party, Mexico
PASOK: Panhellenic Socialist Party, Greece
PCE: Spanish Communist Party
PDS: Party of Democratic Socialism, Germany
PRC: Party of Communist Refoundation, Italy
PRD: Democratic People's Party, Indonesia
PRI: Institutional Revolutionary Party, Mexico
PS: Socialist Party, France
PSOE: Spanish Socialist Party
PSCh: Chilean Socialist Party
PSTU: United Socialist Workers' Party, Brazil
PT: Workers' Party, Brazil

SFIO: Socialist Party, the French section of the Second International until 1970
SLFP: Sri Lanka Freedom Party, populist bourgeois nationalist party
SPD: Social Democratic Party, Germany

UN: United Nations
USFI: United Secretariat of the Fourth International

WTO: World Trade Organisation

ZANU(PF): Ruling party in Zimbabwe

Contacting the CWI

The Committee for a Workers' International has affiliated parties and organisations in more than 35 countries on all continents. The way to contact our comrades differs from country to country. Some you can contact directly. For others, it is easier to do it via the CWI offices in London... e-mail to the International Office of the CWI: inter@dircon.co.uk or contact us at PO Box 3688; London; E9 5QX; Britain. Telephone: + 44 181 533 0201. Fax: + 44 181 985 0757. Our website is on: http://www.clubi.ie/dojo/cwi/inde

If you want to know more about us in...Israel/Palestine, Mexico, Nigeria, Norway, Pakistan, Poland, Spain...then contact the CWI international offices above.

Argentina: Casilla de Correos 53; CP 1617; Los Polvorines; Buenos Aires
Australia: Militant Socialist Organisation; PO Box 1015; Collingwood; Victoria 3066. phone: + 61 3 9650 0160; e-mail: militant@mira.net
Austria: Sozialistische Offensive Vorwärts; Kaiserstrasse 14/11; 1070 Wien. phone: + 43 1 524 6310; fax: + 43 1 524 6311; e-mail: sov@gmx.net
Belgium: Militant Links; Pb 2, 9000 Gent 21 phone: + 32 9 232 1394; fax: + 32 9 232 1394; e-mail: militant@altern.org
Brazil: Caixa Postal 2009; CEP 01060-970; Sao Paulo S.P. phone: + 55 11 277 2384; fax: + 55 11 296 6237; e-mail: sr-cio@uol.com.br
Britain: Socialist Party; 3-13 Hepscott Road; London; E9 5HB. phone: + 44 181 533 3311; fax: + 44 181 986 9445; e-mail: campaigns@socialistparty.org
Canada: e-mail: simone@interlog.com
Cyprus: e-mail: adeadoro@zeus.cc.ucy.ac.cy
Chile: Celso C Campos; Casilla 50310; Correo Central; Santiago. phone: + 56 2 622 9004
CIS: 125167 Moscow a\Ya 37; Moscow. e-mail: pabgem@glas.apc.org
Czech Republic: e-mail: budoucnost@email.cz
France: ECIJ; 17, Rue Armand Carrel; 93100 Montreuil. phone: + 33 1 4851 9705; fax: + 33 1 4857 6862
Germany: Sozialistische Alternative; Hansaring 4; 50670 Köln. phone: + 49 221 13 45 04; fax: 00 49 221 13 72 80; e-mail: savbund@aol.com
Greece: Xekinima; Odos Maisonos 1; Vathis Platia; 104 38 Athens. phone/fax: + 30 1 524 7177; e-mail: xekinima@ath.forthnet.gr

India: Dudiyora Horaata; PO Box 1828; Bangalore 560018. e-mail: admin@horata.ilban.ernet.in
Ireland North: Socialist Party; 2nd Floor; 36 Victoria Square; Belfast BT1. phone: + 44 1232 232 962; fax: + 44 1232 311778; e-mail: socialist@belfastsp.freeserve.co.uk
Ireland South: Socialist Party; 141 Thomas St; Dublin 8. phone/fax: + 353 1 677 25 92; e-mail: dublinsp@clubi.ie
Italy: e-mail: dond001@it.net
Japan: CWI Japan; Urbain Higashi Mikuni 9-406; Higashi-Mikuni 2-10; Yadokawa –ku; Osaka-shi. phone/fax: + 81 6 396 6998; e-mail: nixsc@d1.dion.ne.jp
Netherlands: Offensief; PO Box 11561; 1001 GN Amsterdam. e-mail: offensief@offensief.demon.nl
Portugal: e-mail: cwi_portugal@hotmail.com
Scotland: CWI Scotland; 5th Floor; 73, Robertson Street; Glasgow G2 8QD. phone: + 44 141 221 7714; e-mail: ssv@mail.ndirect.co.uk
South Africa: Socialist Alternative; PO Box 596; Newton; 2113; Johannesburg. phone: + 27 11 342 2220; e-mail: mnoor@icon.co.za
Sri Lanka: United Socialist Party; 261/1 Kirula Road; Narahempito; Colombo 5. phone: + 94 1 508 821
Sweden: Offensiv; Box 374; S- 123 03 Farsta. phone: + 46 8 605 9400; fax: + 46 8 556 252 52; e-mail: offensiv@stockholm.mail.telia.com
USA: *New York*: Labor Militant; PO Box 5447; Long Island City; New York, 11105. phone: + 1 718 204 2506; fax: + 1 718 204 2548; e-mail: FranAlan@aol.com.
California: 3311 Mission Street; suite 135; San Francisco; California 94110. e-mail: progress@ix.netcom.com

Other Publications

Other publications from the CWI include:

Uprising in Albania by Lynn Walsh
£1.50 + 40p (postage & packing)
No to Maastricht: No to a Bosses Europe - Fight for a Socialist Europe
(in five languages) *£1.50 + 40p (postage & packing)*
South Korea: The Tiger Strikes by Ann Cook
£1.50 + 40p (postage & packing)
The Future for Socialism (CWI/CIO European School 1996 Reports)
£1.50 + 40p (postage & packing)
Che Guevara: Symbol of Struggle by Tony Saunois
£2.00 + 40p (postage & packing)
Indonesia: An Unfinished Revolution by Ann Cook
£1.50 + 40p (postage & packing)

All these pamphlets are available from
CWI Publications,
3/13 Hepscott Road, London, E9 5HB, Britain.
Telephone: ++44 0181 533 0201.
Fax: ++44 0181 985 0757
Special Offer: 5 pamphlets for £5.00 (postage free)